LEGAL PRACTICE COURSE

Solicitors and Money Laundering

Related titles by Law Society Publishing

Execution of Documents
Mark Anderson & Victor Warner
1 85328 980 9

Solicitors Accounts Manual – 9th edition
The Law Society
1 85328 907 8

Solicitors and Financial Services
Peter Camp
1 85328 805 5

Practice Management Handbook
Edited by Peter Scott
1 85328 915 9

Titles from Law Society Publishing can be ordered from all good bookshops or direct from our distributors, Marston Book Services (tel. 01235 465656 or email law.society@marston.co.uk). For further information or a catalogue, email our editorial and marketing office at publishing@lawsociety.org.uk.

SOLICITORS AND MONEY LAUNDERING

A Compliance Handbook

Peter J Camp LL.B Solicitor

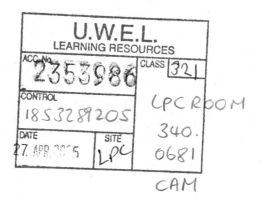

The Law Society

Peter Camp, the author of *Solicitors and Money Laundering*, quotes extensively from the Law Society's official guidance in the text of this book. For the avoidance of doubt, the views expressed in this publication should be taken as those of the author.

Readers should note that the Law Society's official *Money Laundering Guidance* was distributed to the profession in January 2004 and represents the Law Society's views on this subject.

ISBN 1–85328–920–5

Published in 2004 by the Law Society
113 Chancery Lane, London WC2A 1PL

Typeset by J&L Composition, Filey, North Yorkshire
Printed by Antony Rowe Ltd, Chippenham, Wilts

Contents

Preface

Significant changes have been made to the way in which solicitors are regulated as a result of the Money Laundering Regulations 2003 (which came into force on 1 March 2004). Further obligations have been imposed upon the profession as a result of the Proceeds of Crime Act 2002 and the Terrorism Act 2000. Solicitors can no longer ignore the need for detailed internal anti-money laundering procedures. The risk from inadvertent involvement in money laundering is substantial; in extreme cases, lack of an appropriate system or ignoring a suspicion of criminal activities can lead to a criminal conviction and imprisonment.

This topic is one that will, no doubt, continue to develop. At the time of writing the European Commission has recently issued a preliminary set of draft articles for a third Money Laundering Directive, designed to consolidate previous Money Laundering Directives. The UK Treasury has also instituted a consultation and is seeking assessments of the proposed draft articles before finalising any response.

This book aims to assist solicitors in identifying their obligations under the Proceeds of Crime Act and provides practical advice on setting up anti-money laundering systems within their offices so as to comply with the Money Laundering Regulations.

The first part of the book contains details of the substantive law as it applies to solicitors (Chapters 1–8) and details of regulations (Chapter 9). The second part (Chapters 10–12) contains practical guidance on the application of the law and regulations including guidance on reporting obligations, internal procedures and how to spot money laundering transactions in a solicitor's practice.

I gratefully acknowledge the assistance I have derived from the Law Society's published *Money Laundering Guidance*. This guidance is quoted extensively in the book and extracts from the guidance appear in the appendices. Particular thanks are also due to Alison Matthews of Irwin Mitchell and a member of the Law Society's Money Laundering Task Force. She has made many useful comments that have been incorporated into the text. However, the responsibility for the views expressed in the book remains mine and only where the context allows should these views be taken as being endorsed by the Law Society.

Peter Camp
July 2004

Table of cases

Table of statutes

Table of statutory instruments and European legislation

European Union

Table of Directives

PART 1

Substantive Law

CHAPTER 1

Money laundering and the solicitors' profession: an overview

1.1 INTRODUCTION

In recent years, successive governments have taken steps to increase intelligence information regarding serious criminal activities. To this end they have introduced legislation which requires the disclosure of knowledge or suspicion of criminal activities. This legislation is aimed at those whose services may be used by the perpetrators of crimes, typically banks and other financial institutions and professional businesses such as solicitors and accountants. Failure to disclose can be a serious crime in itself. Initially the requirements to disclose were limited to crimes involving terrorism and drug trafficking (see the Prevention of Terrorism (Temporary Provisions) Act 1989) and the Drug Trafficking Offences Act 1986). However, in 1994, requirements to disclose a wider range of criminal activities (i.e. activities relating to indictable offences) were introduced by an amendment to the Criminal Justice Act 1988 contained in the Criminal Justice Act 1993. More recently, more draconian measures requiring disclosure were introduced in the Proceeds of Crime Act 2002 (PoCA 2002).

In addition to the criminal law, regulation of businesses which potentially could be used by criminals was introduced with the Money Laundering Regulations 1993 (now the Money Laundering Regulations 2003, SI 2003/3075). Both sets of Regulations were introduced into UK law as a result of European Directives.

Where disclosure is necessary, the procedure is normally for disclosure to be made to the National Criminal Intelligence Service (NCIS). NCIS is an intelligence-gathering organisation. A large proportion of NCIS's staff is seconded from different national and international agencies, all of whom contribute to the fight against serious and organised crime. These include the Metropolitan Police Service, the Home Office, the Benefits Agency, the Medicines Control Agency, the Association of Police Authorities, the Police Services of the UK, the Post Office, the Prison Service, Her Majesty's Customs and Excise, the Financial Services Authority, the Ministry of Defence, British Transport Police, MI5 and GCHQ.

NCIS specialises in four business areas: the provision of strategic intelligence overviews for national targeting of organised criminality; the supply of operational intelligence on the most difficult and dangerous criminal organisations; the supply of specialist co-ordinating functions and facilities for UK law enforcement; and the publication of intelligence 'know-how' products for law enforcement.

The solicitors' profession is an ideal target for criminals. Criminal property must be converted into apparently legitimate assets if it is not to be at risk of seizure by the authorities. Use of a solicitor's services to buy or sell property (real estate or business property) using the proceeds of crime or merely 'laundering' criminal proceeds through a solicitor's client account will potentially involve the solicitor in criminal activities. It is not possible for solicitors to argue that they did not know that their client was using their services in this way. The legislation imposes severe penalties on those who do not report when they know or suspect that they are involved with criminal property.

1.2   WHAT IS MONEY LAUNDERING?

The traditional view that money laundering simply involved 'cleaning dirty cash' (i.e. converting criminally obtained cash into clean money) is no longer appropriate. (One view is that the term 'money laundering' derived from the activities of Chinese laundries in Chicago in the hey-day of American organised crime.) 'Money laundering' encompasses a far wider range of criminal activities and today can be undertaken by the perpetrator of the original crime as well as by third parties on behalf of the perpetrator or others. It is an attempt to hide the proceeds of crime (by integrating such proceeds into other legitimate property or by confusing the audit trail) in such a way that the authorities cannot trace the proceeds back to the original crime.

There are three generally accepted stages to the money laundering activities of the criminal community:

1.   **Placement**: where cash is converted into non-cash assets.
2.   **Layering**: where several transactions are undertaken for no other reason than to confuse the audit trail between the original crime and subsequent proceeds.
3.   **Integration**: the final destination of the criminal proceeds.

Solicitors could find themselves inadvertently involved in any of these stages.

1.2.1   Placement

A large proportion of criminal property starts life as cash (this is particularly the case where drug trafficking is involved). The first thing the holder of such cash will wish to do is to convert the cash into a non-cash asset. It is increasingly difficult to pay large sums of cash into a bank account or through any other financial institution. The money launderer will therefore need to approach this in a more subtle way. Frequently this will involve a number of local cash businesses, for example taxi firms or retail shops. These businesses will regularly bank large amounts of cash and such deposits, being in the usual way of business, will not attract their banks' suspicion. If the money launderer can persuade owners of these businesses to bank some of the criminal cash at the same time as their own takings, substantial amounts of criminal money can be deposited in the banking system without suspicion being aroused. A cheque can then be drawn in favour of the criminal (or more likely some third party on behalf of the criminal) for the appropriate amount less, of course, the commission for providing this service.

Solicitors' involvement in placement is rare to the extent that it is unlikely that many solicitors will agree to receive large amounts of cash deposits. Clearly, if a client attempts to put the firm into funds for a transaction or for substantial costs using cash, suspicion should be aroused and steps should be taken to ascertain the legitimacy of funds. Where this proves to be impossible solicitors should act on their suspicion. However, it is possible that solicitors may be involved on the periphery. If, when acting for a cash business, a solicitor becomes aware of suspicious circumstances which point to the possibility of placement, he or she must take appropriate steps to avoid the risk of criminal liability. Further, solicitors asked to act on, say, a company formation, must be satisfied as to the commercial reason for the formation. Companies are frequently formed with a view to setting up bogus businesses in order that criminal proceeds can be laundered through those businesses.

1.2.2 Layering

Once any cash has been converted into a non-cash asset (e.g. a deposit account at a bank) the next stage in the money laundering activity is to ensure that the criminal property cannot be traced back to the crime. This stage is equally important for the criminal whose criminal property did not start as cash (e.g. where the crime involved fraud or the acquisition of non-cash assets illegally). As a result of the PoCA 2002 provisions relating to confiscation and civil recovery of criminal proceeds (see **Chapter 8**) it is of particular importance to the criminal to ensure that any property he or she possesses cannot be traced back to the original crime. Civil recovery provisions mean that it is now necessary for the authorities only to discharge a civil onus of proof (i.e. on the balance of probabilities) in order to seek and obtain a recovery order. Criminal property is defined in the PoCA 2002 as constituting a person's benefit from criminal conduct or representing such a benefit in whole or part, directly or indirectly (PoCA 2002, s.340). Consequently it does not matter how remote property is from the original crime; if the audit trail allows the authorities to trace the property back to the original proceeds of the crime (on the balance of probabilities) a recovery order may be granted. Layering is the attempt to ensure that this cannot happen.

Solicitors may frequently be involved inadvertently in the layering transaction. A firm's client account is ideal for layering purposes. If money can be passed through a client account and out the other side by a 'clean' client account cheque, this can amount to one step in the layering process. Obviously solicitors must be suspicious where potential clients ask that money be accepted into client account for onward transmission where the solicitor is not involved in any legal or commercial transaction on behalf of that client. The Law Society has recently amended the Solicitors' Accounts Rules 1998 providing additional guidance on the use of client account for non-legal purposes. Note (ix) to Rule 24 of the Rules now states:

> In the case of *Wood and Burdett* (case number 8669/2002 filed on 13 January 2004), the Solicitors' Disciplinary Tribunal said that it is not a proper part of a solicitor's everyday business or practice to operate a banking facility for third parties, whether they are clients of the firm or not. Solicitors should not, therefore, provide banking facilities through client account. Further solicitors are likely to lose the exemption under the Financial Services and Markets Act 2000 if a deposit is taken in circumstances which do not form part of a solicitor's practice. It should be borne in mind that there are criminal sanctions against assisting money launderers.

Again, the criminal is more likely to use subtle means of passing money through client account, rather than an 'up front' request. Frequently solicitors are involved in abortive transactions and most of these will be legitimate. However, consider the following scenario. A solicitor is instructed by a new client. Appropriate money laundering verification procedures are followed (for details of these requirements, see **Chapter 9**). The client instructs the solicitor on a property transaction; the client is buying commercial property for consideration of in excess of £1million. The client explains that there is an urgency surrounding this transaction; the deal must be completed by a specified date or it is likely to collapse. The solicitor agrees with the firm acting for the vendor that, because of the deadline, the two firms will proceed on the basis of a simultaneous exchange of contracts and completion – not an uncommon procedure. A week before the planned completion date, the purchaser's solicitor is put in funds by way of a cheque or BACS payment. The funds cover the amount required to complete plus costs and disbursements including stamp duty. A day or two before the planned completion date the client telephones his solicitor and explains that there has been a hitch in the arrangements. For whatever reason given, the transaction cannot proceed to completion. Since no contracts have been exchanged there is no legal reason why the client cannot, at this stage, pull out of the deal. The client asks that the solicitor bills for the work done and returns the balance of the money held in client account. Is this a genuine abortive transaction or a successful layering exercise which has allowed the client to pass in excess of £1 million through the client account and out the other side?

Solicitors and their staff must be concerned about any deal which does not complete where substantial sums are placed in their client accounts before being returned to the client or a third party on behalf of the client. Solicitors must also question the commerciality of deals and after any appropriate investigation, act on any suspicion they may have. (For further examples of layering, see **Paragraph 1.3**.)

1.2.3 Integration

The final stage in the money laundering exercise is integration – the final destination for the criminal proceeds. After passing the funds through a number of layering transactions, the criminal should be fairly confident that funds are now unlikely to be traced back to the original crime. He or she is now ready to invest the funds in a legitimate investment which will give a legitimate return and, for all intents and purposes, allow the appearance of non-criminal wealth.

NCIS have indicated that they believe that much of the criminal funds invested in the UK end up in commercial property. The UK commercial property market is an ideal final destination for criminal funds sourced from both the UK and abroad. There is the potential for capital growth as well as rental income. Inevitably, if funds are invested in commercial property, a solicitor is involved in the conveyancing. This involvement can bring the solicitor within the scope of the criminal law.

However, commercial property is not the only asset used as the final desti-nation for criminal funds. Some funds will be invested in genuine business deals (company acquisitions, corporate finance, partnership finance, or joint ventures). Any asset purchase or funding deal could potentially involve a firm in the money laundering exercise.

1.3 HOW ARE SOLICITORS INVOLVED?

It should be clear from the above, that solicitors could be involved in any or all three stages in a typical money laundering exercise. The following para-graphs expand on the details of a solicitor's potential involvement indicating that there really is no common area of practice that is not at risk. A departmental checklist can be found in **Chapter 12**.

1.3.1 Advice

It is clear from the substantive law that a solicitor need not be in possession of cash or other criminal property in order to run the risk of involvement in money laundering. One of the more dangerous offences from a solicitor's point of view is that of 'arrangements' contained in PoCA 2002, s.328 (for full details and commentary on this section, see **Chapter 2**). This section provides that an offence is committed if a person:

> enters into or becomes concerned in an arrangement which he knows or suspects facilitates (by whatever means) the acquisition, retention, use or control of criminal property by or on behalf of another person.

Thus a solicitor who gives advice knowing or suspecting that the advice facilitates the acquisition of criminal property could be guilty of this offence which carries a maximum punishment of 14 years' imprisonment. Tax evasion is a crime. In February 1999, Jack Straw MP (the then Home Secretary) said, 'Tax evasion offences are criminal offences . . . The [money laundering] legislation . . . does not treat them in any special way . . .' If a solicitor gives advice to a client which assists in a client's legitimate tax avoidance this is acceptable (and, indeed, a normal activity for solicitors). If, however, the advice leads to tax evasion such advice could lead to a charge under PoCA 2002, s.328.

1.3.2   Use of client account

A major reason why money launderers might target a solicitor's practice is the solicitor's client account. For all intents and purposes a client account is like a bank account. Any use of client account for other than a legitimate underlying legal purpose should give rise to suspicion. Solicitors must be careful not to mistake what appears to be a legitimate use of client account with improper use leading to money laundering. As noted above, those intent on money laundering will use subtle means to avoid a solicitor's suspicion. A solicitor delivers a bill of costs to a client following the successful completion of a transaction. The client sends a cheque in payment of the costs. Sometime later, the same sum is received into the solicitor's client account by way of a BACS transfer. The payment comes from a third party who informs the firm that they have agreed to pay the client's costs associated with the transaction. One way or another, the solicitor will have to return the overpaid costs to the client or third party – money has been passed through client account and out again on a genuine client account cheque.

Particular care must be taken when a solicitor is asked to act as a stakeholder (i.e. holding money in client account on behalf of a third party until the happening of a specified event). This is an everyday occurrence in conveyancing transactions and where the property or other transaction appears genuine, no great risk will occur. However, if the instructions are such that the solicitor is only being asked to act as stakeholder without involvement in the underlying transaction, this should give rise to concern and appropriate enquiries should be made to check the legitimacy of the transaction. Solicitors' undertakings or guarantees are particularly useful to criminals. If they can persuade their victims to part with funds against the undertaking of a solicitor 'to hold the funds to the order of' the victim until the happening of a specified event, the victim is more likely to readily part with the funds.

Solicitors and their cashiers must at all times be vigilant to the possible misuse of client account. Unusual transactions and transactions involving the movement of funds through client account where, for whatever reason, there is no underlying legal transaction should be considered carefully and, if necessary, reported internally in accordance with the firm's procedures (for details of such procedures, see **Chapter 11**).

1.3.3 Purchase or sale of property/assets

Either as part of the layering exercise or as the final destination for criminal proceeds, property purchase or sale can form part of a money laundering exercise. If a client is involved in providing false information to a bank or building society as part of a mortgage transaction, the loan becomes criminal property (the proceeds of mortgage fraud). The property purchased with the mortgage funds becomes criminal property. When the property is sold, the proceeds of sale become criminal property. If the proceeds of sale are used to purchase another asset, that other asset becomes criminal property. If the asset is used as security to borrow money, that money becomes criminal property. The definition of criminal property is wide enough to catch all these items (for full details of the definition, see **Chapter 2**). A solicitor's involvement in any of these activities could risk involvement in money laundering if the solicitor knows or suspects that criminal property is involved.

Conveyancing and property lawyers are clearly at risk. However, the risk is not limited to real property transactions. Transactions involving shares, other securities and investments could equally give rise to risk of money laundering.

1.3.4 Hiding behind corporate or other vehicles or devices

Criminals involved in the laundering of criminal proceeds will frequently wish to avoid the use of their own names (particularly in the light of the identification procedures set out in the Money Laundering Regulations (see **Chapter 9**)). Consequently they are likely to seek to hide behind a corporate identity or seek to distance themselves from the transaction through the use of trusts or powers of attorney. Solicitors instructed to create companies or draft trust deeds or powers of attorney are clearly at risk of involvement in money laundering where such vehicles are being used for criminal purposes. Equally, solicitors instructed to act as directors, trustees or donees under a power of attorney where there is no commercial or other reason for the appointment may find themselves acting as a front for criminals.

1.3.5 Drafting documentation

A major need for any successful money launderer is the ability to move funds from one account to another or across one frontier to another jurisdiction. To do so through the legitimate banking system, an apparently genuine reason for the transfer of the funds will have to be found; a reason which will satisfy the suspicions of the bankers involved. If the launderer is able to produce genuine documentation prepared by a reputable firm of solicitors his or her task will be made much easier.

Loan documentation, drafted by solicitors, can be used as a reason for the transfer of funds – funds paid to discharge the loan or funds received to discharge a loan.

1.3.6 Confidentiality and privilege

Money launderers will frequently make use of a solicitor's services in the mistaken belief that any information given in the course of a solicitor's retainer is confidential and sometimes subject to the concept of privilege. They believe that a solicitor is prohibited from disclosing information received in the course of practising as a solicitor. Consequently any suspicion (or knowledge) of a criminal purpose will, they believe, not be passed on to the authorities.

It is undoubtedly true that such an obligation applies in both a solicitor's duty in law and in professional conduct. Lord Denning MR stated in *Parry-Jones* v. *The Law Society* [1969] 1 Ch 1:

> as between solicitor and client there are two privileges. The first relates to legal proceedings – commonly called 'legal professional privilege'. . . . The second privilege arises out of the confidence subsisting between solicitor and client. . . . The law implies a term into the contract whereby a professional man is to keep his client's affairs secret.

The money laundering legislation has made serious inroads into the duties of confidentiality and privilege. First, the definition of legal professional privilege for criminal proceedings has been codified by the Police and Criminal Evidence Act 1984 (PACE). Section 10 of that Act provides:

(1)   . . . items subject to legal privilege means:

    (a) communications between a professional legal adviser and his client or any person representing his client in connection with the giving of legal advice to the client;

    (b) communications between a professional legal adviser and his client or any person representing his client or between such an adviser and any other person made in connection with or in contemplation of legal proceedings and for the purposes of such proceedings; and

  (c)   items enclosed with or referred to in such communications and made:

      (i)   in connection with the giving of legal advice; or

      (ii) in connection with or in contemplation of legal proceedings and for the purposes of such proceedings they are in possession of a person who is entitled to possess them.

  (2)   Items held with the intention of furthering a criminal purpose are not items subject to legal privilege.

PACE, s.10(2) provides that items are not to be considered as privileged where they are held 'with the intention of furthering a criminal purpose'. The House of Lords in *R* v. *Central Criminal Court* ex p. *Francis* v. *Francis* [1989] 1 AC 346, held that the 'intention' in PACE, s.10(2) did not have to be the solicitor's intention. Provided someone had the intention to further a criminal purpose, items held would not be privileged.

Secondly, the PoCA 2002 requires solicitors to disclose their knowledge or suspicions of a client's involvement in money laundering in certain circumstances (either by way of a defence or by way of an obligation). PoCA 2002 provides that such disclosures made by a solicitor in accordance with the requirements are 'not to be taken to breach any restriction on the disclosure of information (however imposed)' (see s.338 and **Chapter 2**).

As a result of these changes some commentators have suggested that a solicitor's duty in confidentiality has ceased to apply in many professional relationships (see Morris-Cotterill, 'Fraud Guide', [1992] *Gazette*, 14 February).

Privilege, as it applies to money laundering scenarios, is a complex topic. It is covered in **Chapter 5** of this book and Chapter 4 of the Law Society Guidance (See **Paragraph 1.4** for details of Guidance).

1.4   LAW SOCIETY GUIDANCE

A number of criminal offences contained in the PoCA 2002 (notably s.330 and 331 – see **Chapters 5 and 6**), the Terrorism Act 2000 (notably s.21A – see **Chapter 5**) and the Money Laundering Regulations 2003, SI 2003/3075 (reg. 3(3) – see **Chapter 9**) all provide that:

In deciding whether a person committed an offence . . . the court must consider whether he followed any relevant guidance which was at the time concerned:

(a)   issued by a supervisory authority or any other appropriate body;

(b)   approved by the Treasury; and

(c)   published in a manner it approved as appropriate in its opinion to bring the guidance to the attention of persons likely to be affected by it.

A supervisory body, for these purposes, includes the Law Society.

The Law Society has issued Guidance to the solicitors' profession (*Money Laundering Guidance: Professional Ethics*, Pilot Edition, January 2004). Extracts from the Guidance appear thoughout the text of this book and in **Appendix B1**. The Law Society's Guidance is described as a 'pilot' and has not been submitted to the Treasury for approval. The Society has acknowledged that much of the legislation is new and untested. It is seeking comments from members of the profession on the Guidance and in the light of experience and feedback from the profession it will then consider whether to seek Treasury approval for subsequent editions. Consequently, the courts are not technically required to take the Guidance into account. However, as stated in the Guidance, a court 'may still take it into consideration' in deciding whether an offence has been committed.

1.5 CONCLUSION

It should be clear from the above that solicitors are at risk from inadvertent involvement in money laundering. The risk arises from the type of transaction solicitors are frequently involved with and from the fact that a criminal charge can follow from a solicitor's suspicion – it is not necessary for a solicitor to know that his or her client is involved in criminal activities. The PoCA 2002 contains a number of obligations relating to a solicitor's possible involvement in money laundering activities. It is no longer possible for solicitors to 'turn a blind eye' to a client's potential criminal transaction. Any suspicion must be acted upon and the firm must ensure that adequate safeguards and systems are in place requiring all partners and members of staff to be aware of the dangers of inadvertent involvement and to understand the detailed requirements of the legislation.

CHAPTER 2

Criminal offences: arrangements (PoCA 2002, s.328)

2.1 INTRODUCTION

The Proceeds of Crime Act 2002 (PoCA 2002) received the Royal Assent in June 2002. The PoCA 2002 is a substantial Act and contains many provisions outside the scope of this book. Part 7 of the PoCA 2002 deals with money laundering offences. Part 8 contains the offence of prejudicing an investigation. These provisions replace previous money laundering offences contained in the Criminal Justice Act 1988 (as amended by the Criminal Justice Act 1993), and the Drug Trafficking Act 1994. Part 7 came into force on 24 February 2003. In addition, the Terrorism Act 2000 contains further money laundering offences relating to terrorist property (these offences are dealt with in **Chapters 3** and **5**).

There are five criminal offences dealt with in PoCA 2002, Part 7. These are:

- **Section 327**: concealing.
- **Section 328**: arrangements.
- **Section 329**: acquisition, use and possession.
- **Sections 330, 331 and 332**: failure to disclose.
- **Section 333**: tipping off.

Of these five offences, the offence contained in s.328 (arrangements) is, perhaps, of greatest risk for solicitors. This offence is dealt with in this Chapter – subsequent chapters deal with the other offences.

The offence in s.328 is not new. Similar offences were to be found in the amended Criminal Justice Act 1988 (applying to the laundering of the proceeds of indictable offences), and the Drug Trafficking Act 1994 (applying to the proceeds of drug trafficking). However, PoCA 2002 brings these offences into one statute and makes some subtle but important changes to the way this offence applies.

2.2 THE OFFENCE

Section 328 provides:

> A person commits an offence if he enters into or becomes concerned in an arrangement which he knows or suspects facilitates (by whatever means) the acquisition, retention, use or control of criminal property by or on behalf of another person.

The offence is a serious one with severe penalties available to the courts for those found guilty. Under PoCA 2002, s.334 the penalty on summary conviction is imprisonment for a term not exceeding six months or a fine not exceeding the statutory maximum or to both, or on conviction on indictment, to imprisonment for a term not exceeding 14 years or a fine or both.

There are a number of points that can be made concerning this section.

A person commits an offence if he enters into or becomes concerned in an arrangement . . .

A solicitor is likely to satisfy this requirement as a result of the retainer between a solicitor and client. The retainer will be an arrangement for these purposes. However, it should be noted that a formal retainer is not necessarily required – any informal understanding between a solicitor and client could amount to an arrangement for these purposes if the arrangement leads to assistance in money laundering.

In the case of *P* v. *P* [2003] EWHC Fam 2260, Dame Elizabeth Butler-Sloss, P. gave guidance on the operation of PoCA 2002 in relation to family litigation. Some points made by the President of the Family Division of the High Court are likely to be relevant to other matters. In her judgment Dame Elizabeth stated

> There is a range of ways in which the legal professional might be 'concerned in' an arrangement. It was not submitted to me, nor do I believe it could be the case, that the offence under section 328 can only be committed at the point of execution of the arrangement. None of the parties before me [which included the Law Society, Bar Counsel, NCIS and the Inland Revenue] disagreed with the submission of Mr Mitchell that the act of negotiating an arrangement would equally amount to being 'concerned in' the arrangement.

. . . which he knows or suspects . . .

The section introduces a double test of knowledge or suspicion. First it is necessary for the prosecution to show that the alleged offender knew or suspected that the arrangement would facilitate the acquisition, retention, use or control of criminal property. Secondly (as noted below) the definition of 'criminal property' for these purposes requires that the alleged offender knows or suspects that the property constitutes or represents the benefit (directly or indirectly) from criminal conduct.

Knowledge should not cause a problem when interpreting this section. If a solicitor knows that his or her arrangement with a client will facilitate money laundering then the solicitor risks a criminal conviction if no steps are taken to avoid liability. Difficulties can arise when a client admits to the commission of a crime (typically tax evasion). If the client agrees to disclose the tax evasion to the authorities, the solicitor may be able to continue with the arrangement but should still consider whether a report is necessary. If the client refuses to disclose the solicitor may withdraw from the matter and will not, therefore, be involved in the arrangement. In this situation, a solicitor may still have an obligation to report under PoCA 2002, s.330 (see **Chapter 5**) but the concept of privilege may provide a defence.

Suspicion is a more difficult concept. Some people are more suspicious than others. What will amount to suspicion for the purposes of this statute? In 1995, the Law Society issued a series of common questions and answers on the, then, legislation which also referred to 'suspicion' (see the Law Society's Professional Standards Bulletin No.14). In answer to the question, 'Some people are more suspicious than others – what does the legislation mean by suspicion?' the answer given was 'The Law Society believes that a more objective than subjective test will be applied.'

There was support for this answer in the legislation in force in 1995. For example, the Criminal Justice Act 1988 (as amended) contained a similar offence to 'arrangements' under PoCA 2002 and also required knowledge or suspicion. However, the amended Criminal Justice Act 1988, s.93A(4) provided a defence in the following terms:

> In proceedings against a person for an offence under this section, it is a defence to show:
>
> (a) that he did not know or suspect that the arrangement related to any person's proceeds of criminal conduct; or
> (b) that he did not know or suspect that by the arrangement the retention or control by or on behalf of [another] of any property was facilitated . . .

The Law Society argued that, given the need for the prosecution at any trial to prove its case beyond reasonable doubt, the defence was unnecessary unless the section was interpreted as only requiring the prosecution to prove 'suspicion' on an objective basis. The section then allowed the alleged offender to use a subjective test of suspicion by way of defence.

The PoCA 2002 does not include anything equivalent to the amended Criminal Justice Act 1988, s.93A(4). This has led to some commentators taking the view that the courts will apply an objective test of suspicion under the new legislation. The counter argument is that where the legislation requires an objective test it now expressly states that this is the case. For example, PoCA 2002, s.330 (for full details of this section, see **Chapter 5**) refers expressly to the situation where a 'person knows or suspects or has reasonable grounds for knowing or suspecting . . .'

Whatever test the courts eventually decide upon, it is clearly of practical importance for solicitors to do more than simply sit back and wait for suspicion to arise. Solicitors must be more proactive and must encourage their staff to be so. Any unusual transaction must be considered suspicious until enquiry has allayed that suspicion. Transactions that should give rise to concern and therefore should be investigated include:

- **Unusual settlement transactions**
  Consider the circumstances where, on an asset purchase, less funds are required on completion than expected by reference to the contractual provisions. Clients may excuse this by indicating that they have paid a direct deposit to the vendor. This typically indicates a possible mortgage or loan fraud. The property (i.e. the asset being purchased) is being over-valued for security purposes. The genuine price paid is the lesser amount.

- **Unusual instructions**
  The key to avoiding criminal liability is to know the client and know the typical transactions expected to be undertaken in the firm. Accepting instructions in a matter which is outside the normal type of work undertaken by the firm should give rise to a risk assessment – enquiries should be made to ensure that this is a legitimate transaction and one that the firm has competence to undertake.

  For example, a small traditional firm specialising in private client work should be suspicious if a new client requires the firm to act on a complex commercial transaction involving significant values. If the remuneration offered seems too good to be true, it probably is! Criminals wishing to launder money might take the (often erroneous) view that a small firm has less sophisticated money laundering procedures in place. Equally, larger commercial firms should be suspicious where commercial clients instruct them on private client matters beyond the scope of their normal work. Even if they have staff who are competent (or who could gain competence) the question should always be asked: 'Why are we being instructed?'

- **Secretive client**
  The Money Laundering Regulations 2003, SI 2003/3075 (see **Chapter 9**) require solicitors to obtain evidence of identity for most new clients. A client who is unwilling or unable to produce such evidence should give rise to concern. To continue to act without such evidence may put the firm in breach of the regulations and the lack of such evidence without good reason may give rise to suspicion that any arrangement might facilitate the acquisition, retention, use or control of criminal property. It is good practice to apply the identification procedures to all new and existing clients even if this is not strictly required by the regulations. By doing so, a solicitor is going somewhere towards allaying suspicion. Without such evidence, the authorities' case for showing suspicion is made easier.

Equally, it is necessary to consider identification of corporate and trust clients – in most cases going beyond the simple task of satisfying the firm that the company or trust fund exists. It is too easy for launderers to hide behind such vehicles so the identification procedures should be applied to those controlling the appropriate vehicle (i.e. the directors/shareholders of a company or the trustees/beneficiaries of the trust fund). Details of the requirements relating to client identification and recommended procedures are contained in **Chapter 9** and **Chapter 11**.

- **Cash transactions**

In a solicitor's practice, large cash transactions are usually rare and as such should give rise to concern. These might involve sale or purchase transactions involving cash or large sums of cash used to discharge the solicitor's costs. Of course, the use of cash in any transaction is not unlawful. Of itself, a client proposing to use cash does not give rise to an illegal act. However it must put the solicitor on notice that the transaction might be one involving 'placement' (see **Chapter 1**) and as such the solicitor should not proceed unless he or she is satisfied as to the legitimacy of the transaction.

In some ethnic communities, cash is still the preferred currency for business transactions. Solicitors acting for members of such communities may be satisfied that a cash transaction is the norm. However, in most circumstances the use of large sums of cash should give rise to a sensible concern.

Many firms impose a cash limit (i.e. a maximum sum that can be accepted in cash). Frequently this is set at £500 but some firms have set a limit as low as £250.

Where cash is legitimately used, solicitors should refer to guidance in the Solicitors' Accounts Rules 1998 (SAR). The Law Society's 'Guidelines: Accounting Procedures and Systems' are contained in Appendix 3 SAR. These state (Guideline 3) that 'the firm should have procedures for identifying client money and controlled trust money, including cash, when received in the firm, and for prompt recording the receipt of the money . . .'

In earlier guidance (see '*Complying with the Solicitors' Accounts Rules: A Practical Guide*' published by the Law Society, 1996) the following was stated:

Receipt of Cash

When cash is received from a client, particularly a large amount, consideration should always be given to the Money Laundering Regulations.

Any cash receipts should be counted in the presence of the client by the relevant fee earner and another member of staff. Care should be taken to check for any forged bank notes.

A receipt should be issued to the client and the client's signature should be obtained. A copy of the receipt should be retained on a central file. A posting slip should then be completed in the same manner as for cheques but should specify that the sum was received in cash. The cash, together with the posting slip, should immediately be passed to the accounts department for banking that day.

Withdrawal of cash
The following points should be considered when withdrawing client's money in cash:

- A posting slip should be completed in duplicate by the fee earner. The original should be passed to the accounts department and the copy retained on the client's file. The posting slip should indicate why cash is required.
- The fee earner should seek the client's written authority to make a withdrawal by cash and a copy of that authority should be passed to the accounts department and retained on a central file.
- The cash should be counted by the fee earner in the presence of the client/recipient and another member of the firm.
- A signed receipt should be obtained and a copy passed to the accounts department for retention on a central file.
- Particular attention should be paid to security when withdrawing cash from the bank.
- It is a breach of the Accounts Rules to have client petty cash, as all client's money should be held in a client account at a bank or building society. Petty cash will usually be required only in respect of office expenditure, though it may be used to pay disbursements on behalf of a client, e.g. oath fees.

- **Suspect territories**
  The definition of criminal property includes, in certain cases, property derived from overseas transactions (see below). Consequently solicitors should be satisfied as to the source of any funding used as part of transactions and in particular should be aware of the dangers of receiving funds from overseas suspect territories.

  Some countries worldwide have lower levels of regulation than others. Particular care must be taken when any party to the transaction is based in or moves money from or to such countries. The Financial Action Taskforce was formed in 1989. It is an intergovernmental body with members from 32 countries and the European Commission. It publishes and updates a list of non-co-operative countries and territories ('NCCTs'). This list can be accessed by logging on to the following website: **www.oecd.org/fatf**

. . . facilitates (by whatever means) the acquisition, retention, use or control . . .

The arrangement (where a solicitor 'enters into or becomes concerned in an arrangement') must be such that the solicitor knows or suspects that it facilitates the acquisition, retention, use or control of criminal property. This is a very wide concept. Previous legislation (e.g. the Criminal Justice Act 1988 as amended) simply referred to the act of facilitating the retention or control of criminal property. PoCA 2002 extends this to now include 'acquisition and use'.

All of the examples given in **Chapter 1** could be said to be facilitating the acquisition, retention, use or control of criminal property. The use of the words 'by whatever means' ensure that the act of facilitation could be undertaken by a solicitor by placing money in client account; by transferring funds; by acting on the purchase/sale of property; or, as noted previously, simply by giving advice.

. . . criminal property . . .

Section 340(3) defines criminal property. Property is criminal if:

   (a)   it constitutes a person's benefit from criminal conduct or it represents such a benefit (in whole or part and whether directly or indirectly), and

   (b)   the alleged offender knows or suspects that it constitutes or represents such a benefit.

Section 340(2) defines criminal conduct as that which:

   (a)   constitutes an offence in any part of the United Kingdom, or

   (b)   would constitute an offence in any part of the United Kingdom if it occurred there.

The first point to note from this definition is that criminal property can be the benefit (however small) of a crime or it can (directly or indirectly) represent the benefit of a crime. The property does not have to be the original criminal proceeds. As a result of this definition, if cash is stolen, it is criminal property. If the stolen cash is used to buy an asset, the asset will be criminal property. If the asset is used as security to obtain a loan, the loan will become criminal property.

Section 340(5) provides that a person benefits from conduct if he obtains property as a result of or in connection with the conduct. Property includes (s.340(9)) money; all forms of property real, personal, heritable or moveable; or things in action and other intangible or incorporeal property. Further, property is obtained by a person if he obtains an interest in it, which is defined in relation to land as any legal estate or equitable interest or power and in relation to other property as including references to a right (including a right to possession) (s.340(10)).

Where a person receives a pecuniary advantage as a result of conduct he is taken to have received a sum of money equal to the value of the pecuniary advantage for the purposes of these provisions (s.340(6)).

The benefit must have derived from criminal conduct. The previous legislation limited this to benefit from indictable offences (i.e. serious criminal offences), drug trafficking and terrorism offences. The PoCA 2002 does not replicate this restriction. Any criminal act which gives rise to a benefit can form the basis of a money laundering offence.

Further, the criminal conduct need not have occurred in the UK. As can be noted from the definition in s.340(1), the conduct will be criminal if it would have constituted a crime if it had occurred in the UK. There is no requirement in the statute that the conduct must constitute a crime in the jurisdiction in which it occurred.

This has led to the so-called 'Spanish bullfighter' problem. The argument is made that any legitimate income earned by a bullfighter in Spain would amount to criminal property in the UK. Bullfighting in Spain is legal, but it is a criminal activity in the UK. Anyone who, with knowledge or suspicion, facilitated the retention, control etc. of this income could be guilty of an offence.

Equally, however, overseas criminal property (i.e. the benefit of overseas crime) cannot form the basis of a money laundering offence if the conduct undertaken overseas is not a crime in the UK. An obvious example would be a sum of money sourced from an overseas jurisdiction where money was removed from the jurisdiction in breach of that jurisdiction's exchange control regulations. Since the UK does not currently have exchange control regulations, the activity of removing the funds from the overseas jurisdiction would not constitute a crime if it had occurred in the UK. It may, however, be that a client who is willing to breach overseas exchange control regulations might be prepared to breach other obligations. Solicitors should carefully consider all the surrounding facts before determining that a client in breach of overseas exchange control regulations does not give rise to concern.

One problem associated with this definition relates to the proceeds of tax evasion. As noted above, UK tax evasion is a criminal offence and as such can give rise to money laundering. What about the proceeds of overseas tax evasion? Can such proceeds form the basis of a money laundering charge if such proceeds are brought into the UK?

There appears to be a divergence of views on this. Some commentators take the view that the proceeds of overseas tax evasion should be treated in exactly the same way as the proceeds of UK tax evasion. However, others take the view that the offence concerned should be defined by reference to the overseas tax authority. In this case the activity will not be a UK crime if it had occurred in the UK. For example, it is undoubtedly a crime in the US to evade US taxation. If the definition of the crime includes the specific victim (i.e. the US tax authorities) the evasion of US tax would not be a crime in the UK if it had occurred in the US.

Solicitors should, however, err on the side of caution. Until such time as the courts give a definitive interpretation of overseas criminal conduct for these purposes it would seem sensible to act upon any knowledge or suspicion of such overseas activities and follow the appropriate procedures to avoid personal liability.

Finally, in relation to the definition of criminal property, it should be noted that PoCA 2002 makes it clear (in s.340(4)) that it is immaterial for the purposes of the definition:

(a) who carried out the conduct;
(b) who benefited from it;
(c) whether the conduct occurred before or after the passing of this Act.

. . . by or on behalf of another person.

To be guilty under PoCA 2002, s.328, the accused must facilitate the acquisition, retention, use or control of criminal property 'by or on behalf of another person'. This offence is not aimed at the original perpetrator of the crime but at some other person who assists in the laundering of the criminal property of the perpetrator or other person.

However, in the context of a solicitor's practice, this does not mean that a solicitor can only be guilty of an offence where the act of facilitation is done for or on behalf of the solicitor's client. In most cases, the risk of committing this offence will arise from a client retainer in circumstances where the client is acting suspiciously. Since knowledge or suspicion is a necessary element of the crime, it follows that such knowledge or suspicion is most likely to arise in relation to the client's conduct from information received in the course of acting for a client.

In some cases, a solicitor may be acting for an innocent client but nonetheless, his or her actions could facilitate the acquisition, retention use or control of criminal property by the person on the other side of the transaction. Completing the transaction in these circumstances could give rise to liability under PoCA 2002, s.328. Take, for example, a solicitor acting for a lender of money (a bank or building society) who is not acting for the borrower. The lender's solicitor acquires certain information in the course of acting that gives rise to a suspicion that the borrower has given false information as part of the borrower's loan application. To continue to completion without taking appropriate steps could be facilitating the acquisition of criminal property by the borrower. The false information relied upon by the lender could bring about a loan or mortgage fraud; the loan itself could therefore be criminal property.

This particular point is worth making to clients and members of staff who might find a solicitor's money laundering procedures to be burdensome and unhelpful. Clients should be notified that the procedures are not simply designed to ensure that a solicitor is not involved with money laundering. A good system is designed to ensure that innocent clients are not inadvertently dragged into a money laundering investigation as a result of other parties to the transaction who might have criminal intent.

2.3 DEFENCES

Section 328(2) provides for a defence where the accused makes an authorised disclosure in accordance with the provisions of PoCA 2002, s.338. Since the defence under s.338 applies equally to the offence of concealing (s.237 – see **Chapter 3**) and to the offence of acquisition, use and possession (s.329 – see **Chapter 3**), details of the defence are to be found in **Chapter 4**.

Disclosure in accordance with s.338 is by far the most important and relevant defence for solicitors. However, for the sake of completeness, there are two further defences specified in the section.

First it is a defence that the accused intended to make a disclosure under s.338 but had a reasonable excuse for not doing so (s.328(2)(*b*)). Although there is currently no judicial definition of what would amount to a 'reasonable excuse', solicitors should note that neither the duty of confidentiality nor legal professional privilege provide a reasonable excuse for these purposes. Section 338(4) states that 'an authorised disclosure is not to be taken to breach any restriction on the disclosure of information (however imposed.)'

Secondly it is a defence that the act (i.e. the prohibited act of facilitation) 'is done in carrying out a function [the accused] has relating to the enforcement of any provision of [the PoCA 2002] or of any other enactment relating to criminal conduct or benefit from criminal conduct.'

CHAPTER 3

Criminal offences: other money laundering offences

3.1 INTRODUCTION

Although the offence involving arrangements is likely to have the greatest impact on solicitors, there are two other money laundering offences contained in the Proceeds of Crime Act 2002 (PoCA 2002), both of which involve criminal property (as defined). Section 327 of PoCA 2002 creates the offence of 'concealing etc.' and PoCA 2002, s.329 creates the offence of 'acquisition, use and possession'. Both these offences could give rise to difficulties unless solicitors take appropriate action to avoid risks. Both offences carry the same penalty on conviction as that applicable to 'arrangements', i.e. on summary conviction, imprisonment for a term not exceeding six months or a fine not exceeding the statutory maximum or both, or on conviction on indictment, imprisonment for a term not exceeding 14 years or a fine or both.

In addition to these two offences, a further money laundering offence is contained in the Terrorism Act 2000, s.18. Details of this offence are included at the end of this chapter.

3.2 CONCEALING ETC: THE OFFENCE

Section 327 of the PoCA 2002 makes it an offence to:

- conceal criminal property;
- disguise criminal property;
- convert criminal property;
- transfer criminal property;
- remove criminal property from England and Wales or from Scotland or from Northern Ireland.

The PoCA 2002 also makes it clear (s.327(3)) that for these purposes concealing or disguising criminal property includes concealing or disguising its nature, source, location, disposition, movement or ownership or any rights with respect to it.

Solicitors are likely to be less at risk from this offence – as noted, the offence of 'arrangements' is more likely to be relevant. The offence does not specifically refer to the need for the acts to be carried out with knowledge or suspicion. However, since the requirement of the offence is to conceal etc. criminal property and the term criminal property is defined, an element of suspicion does arise as part of this offence. As has been noted (see **Chapter 2**) the definition requires that the alleged offender knows or suspects that property constitutes or represents a benefit from criminal conduct.

As a result of this, it is not inconceivable that a solicitor could find himself or herself involved in this offence. A solicitor who holds money in a client account and who transfers such funds or arranges for the removal of such funds from England and Wales could be guilty of an offence if he or she simply suspects that the money constitutes or represents a benefit from criminal conduct.

An important point to note is that the offence (unlike the offence in s.338) is not limited to committing the prohibited act for or on behalf of another. Obviously a solicitor could be charged with concealing etc. criminal property on behalf of a client. However, the perpetrator of the original criminal act can also be guilty if the perpetrator conceals etc. his or her own criminal property. This has an important result. The offence of concealing etc., therefore, amounts to money laundering and in certain specified circumstances (notably under PoCA 2002, s.330) a solicitor is required to disclose knowledge or suspicion of any person engaged in money laundering (for details of this requirement, see **Chapter 5**). This might require a solicitor to report a client where the solicitor knows or suspects that a client is removing his own criminal property from the jurisdiction (e.g. where the solicitor is aware that the client has evaded UK taxation and is buying a property abroad). This could be so, even if the solicitor is not involved in any arrangement relating to that criminal property.

3.3   CONCEALING ETC: DEFENCES

Like the offence of arrangements the most important defence in s.327 is one of disclosure. Provided a solicitor makes an authorised disclosure under s.338 (and, if necessary, has appropriate consent to continue acting) no offence will be committed under s.327. Details of this important defence are contained in **Chapter 4**.

Also, in common with the offence of arrangements, two further defences are available.

First it is a defence that the accused intended to make a disclosure under s.338 but had a reasonable excuse for not doing so (s.327(2)(b)). As noted above, neither the duty of confidentiality nor legal professional privilege provide a reasonable excuse for these purposes. Section 338(4) states that 'an authorised disclosure is not to be taken to breach any restriction on the disclosure of information (however imposed)'.

Secondly it is a defence that the act (i.e. the prohibited act of concealment etc.) 'is done in carrying out a function [the accused] has relating to the enforcement of any provision of [the PoCA 2002] or of any other enactment relating to criminal conduct or benefit from criminal conduct.'

3.4   ACQUISITION, USE AND POSSESSION: THE OFFENCE

Section 329(1) makes it an offence to:

- acquire criminal property;
- use criminal property;
- have possession of criminal property.

Clearly this offence could apply to solicitors – particularly in relation to the holding of client money where such money is criminal property. The offence is not, however, limited to money.

As with the offence of concealing (s.327) criminal property for the purposes of s.329 is defined in the same way as for the offence of arrangements (s.328 – see **Chapter 2**). An element of knowledge or suspicion is necessary.

Also, the offence can apply to the perpetrator of a crime. A thief who steals property is guilty under the Theft Act 1968. Having acquired the stolen property and having possession of the stolen property means that the thief can also be charged and convicted under the PoCA 2002. For the same reasons as noted above (PoCA 2002, s.330 and see **Chapter 5**) a solicitor may be required to report knowledge or suspicion that a client is engaged in money laundering (the definition of money laundering includes the offence under s.329) simply because the solicitor knows or suspects that the client has committed a crime and is therefore in possession of criminal property.

One problem with this offence arises from the wide definition of criminal property for these purposes (see **Chapter 2**). Since criminal property includes property which represents a benefit from criminal conduct, it is quite possible that property which is legitimately obtained by a person could be treated as criminal property simply because an audit trail is capable of tracing the property back to a crime. Further, a solicitor may be concerned about the payment of costs from a client whom he knows has no legitimate source of income. Potentially the solicitor in these circumstances could be guilty of an offence on the basis of his possession and suspicion that the money is criminal property.

Fortunately, the legislators have foreseen this problem and a defence of 'adequate consideration' is available (see **Paragragh 3.5**).

3.5 ACQUISITION, USE AND POSSESSION: DEFENCES

A defence is available where a person makes an authorised disclosure under PoCA 2002, s.338. This is dealt with in **Chapter 4**.

Also, in common with the offence of arrangements (s.328) and concealing (s.327), two further defences are available.

First it is a defence that the accused intended to make a disclosure under s.338 but had a reasonable excuse for not doing so (s.329(2)(*b*)). As noted above, neither the duty of confidentiality nor legal professional privilege provide a reasonable excuse for these purposes. Section 338(4) states that 'an authorised disclosure is not to be taken to breach any restriction on the disclosure of information (however imposed).'

Secondly it is a defence that the act (i.e. the prohibited act of acquisition, use or possession) 'is done in carrying out a function [the accused] has relating to the enforcement of any provision of [the PoCA 2002] or of any other enactment relating to criminal conduct or benefit from criminal conduct.'

There is, however, the further defence of 'adequate consideration'. Section 329(2)(*c*) provides that a person does not commit an offence under s.329(1) if 'he acquired or used or had possession of the property for adequate consideration'. Subsection (3) gives further guidance on this defence.

First, consideration is to be taken as inadequate for the purposes of acquisition of property if the value of the consideration is significantly less than the value of the property. Secondly, a person uses or has possession of property for inadequate consideration if the value of the consideration is significantly less that the value of the use or possession. Finally, the provision by a person of goods or services which he knows or suspects may help another to carry out criminal conduct is not consideration.

As a result of these provisions solicitors should treat the defence of adequate consideration with care. Take the following scenario by way of example. A solicitor is acting for a client on a house purchase. The solicitor is aware that the client is on benefits and has no legitimate source of income. When it comes to the payment of the solicitor's fees, the client makes the payment in cash. The solicitor suspects that the cash may be the proceeds of crime but takes the view that the provision by him of the conveyancing services amounts to adequate consideration. This defence is likely to be flawed. First, it is highly probable that the solicitor was suspicious about the house purchase transaction. If that was the case then completing the house purchase is likely to be an offence under s.328 (arrangements). Secondly, the defence of adequate consideration could not apply to the costs if the solicitor suspects that the services have helped the client to carry out criminal conduct.

However, in other circumstances, the defence may be of benefit. The Crown Prosecution Service guidance for prosecutors (referred to in paragraph 2.30 of the Law Society's Guidance) states that the defence will apply where professional advisers receive money for or on account of costs provided the charges are reasonable and there is no suspicion that the client is using their services to carry out criminal conduct.

3.6 TERRORISM ACT 2000, S.18

A further money laundering offence appears in the Terrorism Act 2000. Section 18 of that Act provides:

(1) A person commits an offence if he enters into or becomes concerned in an arrangement which facilitates the retention or control by or on behalf of another person of terrorist property –

    (a) by concealment,
    (b) by removal from the jurisdiction,
    (c) by transfer to nominees, or
    (d) in any other way.

(2) It is a defence for a person charged with an offence under subsection (1) to prove that he did not know and had no reasonable cause to suspect that the arrangement related to terrorist property.

The offence is similar to those covered under the PoCA 2002. It covers arrangements made to facilitate the retention or control of terrorist property and provides that such facilitation can be by concealment etc. or in any other way. Like the offence under PoCA 2002, s.328 (arrangements) it is not necessary for the accused to have possession of the terrorist property – for example, advising a client in circumstances where the advice assists in the retention of terrorist property will be sufficient.

The crime itself does not specify a requirement for knowledge or suspicion. However, subsection (2) provides for a defence if the person charged can show that he had no knowledge and no reasonable cause to suspect that the arrangement related to terrorist property. Two points are worthy of note regarding this defence. First, the reference to 'no reasonable cause to suspect' suggests that an objective test will be used to determine suspicion. If the individual did not suspect (subjectively) no defence will be available if a reasonable person would have suspected. Secondly, the onus of proving no knowledge or reasonable cause for suspicion rests upon the defence – not the prosecution. Once the prosecution prove that an arrangement exists which falls within subsection (1) a conviction will follow unless the defence can discharge their onus of proof.

It is obviously necessary for the legislation to cover activities relating to terrorist property in addition to those offences involving criminal property. If property used by terrorists is the proceeds of crime, then the offences in PoCA 2002 can obviously be relevant. However, it is also possible that quite legitimate funds are made available for terrorist purposes. It is this possibility which gives rise to the money laundering offence under the Terrorism Act 2000.

The Act defines terrorist property for the purposes of s.18. Section 14 of the Act states:

(1)   In this Act 'terrorist property' means:

    (a)   money or other property which is likely to be used for the purposes of terrorism (including any resources of a proscribed organisation),

    (b)   proceeds of the commission of acts of terrorism, and

    (c)   proceeds of acts carried out for the purposes of terrorism.

(2)   In subsection (1):

    (a)   a reference to proceeds of an act includes a reference to any property which wholly or partly, and directly or indirectly, represents the proceeds of the act (including payments or other rewards in connection with its commission), and

    (b)   the reference to an organisation's resources includes a reference to any money or other property which is applied or made available, or is to be applied or made available, for use by the organisation.

The penalty on conviction under the Terrorism Act 2000, s.18 is, on indictment: imprisonment for a term not exceeding 14 years, a fine or both; or on summary conviction: imprisonment for a term not exceeding six months, a fine not exceeding the statutory maximum or both. Further offences under the Terrorism Act 2000 are considered in **Chapter 5**.

CHAPTER 4

Authorised disclosures

4.1 INTRODUCTION

The three money laundering offences created by the Proceeds of Crime Act 2002 (PoCA 2002), (s.327 concealing; s.328 arrangements; and s.329 acquisition, use and possession) all have a common defence available. Each section provides for this defence using the same wording:

. . . a person does not commit such an offence if:

(a) he makes an authorised disclosure under section 338 and (if the disclosure is made before he does the act mentioned in subsection (1) *[the prohibited act]*) he has the appropriate consent.

For solicitors, the authorised disclosure defence is probably the most important and widely used defence. The PoCA 2002 has introduced some complex rules, and failure to comply with these rules will often render the defence ineffective.

In most cases, it will be necessary for solicitors to make an authorised disclosure before undertaking the act prohibited by the relevant section. In these cases, it is important that the concept of appropriate consent is considered carefully.

4.2 AUTHORISED DISCLOSURES (POCA 2002, S.338)

4.2.1 Definition

Section 338(1)(*a*) of PoCA 2002 defines an authorised disclosure as a disclosure made to:

- a constable;
- a customs officer;
- a nominated officer.

In each case the disclosure, made by the alleged offender, should relate to the knowledge or suspicion that the property is criminal property.

4.2.2 Disclosure to NCIS

In practical terms, the reference in s.338(1)(*a*) to a constable or a customs officer means that the disclosure is made to the National Criminal Intelligence Service (NCIS). For practical details associated with disclosures to NCIS, see **Chapter 10**.

4.2.3 Disclosure to a nominated person

Disclosure to a nominated officer is disclosure to a firm's Money Laundering Reporting Officer (MLRO). In practice, many firms' internal money laundering procedures will identify a person (frequently a partner) who has been appointed as MLRO. The PoCA 2002 and the Money Laundering Regulations 2003 (see **Chapter 9**) rename this person a 'nominated officer'.

Section 338(5) states that a disclosure to a nominated officer is a disclosure which is made to a person nominated by the alleged offender's employer to receive authorised disclosures. Further, the disclosure must be made in the course of the alleged offender's employment and in accordance with the procedure established by the employer for the purpose.

Consequently, in order that members of a firm can benefit from this defence, it is important that all firms adopt appropriate procedures for internal disclosure of knowledge or suspicion of money laundering and that these procedures include the appointment of a person to the role of nominated officer. Firms undertaking relevant business (see **Chapter 9** for a full definition) and therefore subject to the Money Laundering Regulations 2003 must appoint a nominated officer. Firms not subject to the regulations should still consider making such an appointment to enable members of the firm to make internal disclosures and thereby to benefit from the authorised disclosure defence.

It is not strictly necessary for the nominated officer to be a partner or principal in a firm of solicitors. However, in practice, the individual should be a senior member of the firm's management. Severe penalties (including imprisonment for up to five years) can be imposed upon the nominated officer for a failure to comply with his or her obligations under PoCA 2002. Further, under the Money Laundering Regulations 2003 (see **Chapter 9**) a nominated officer must consider, in the light of any relevant information available in the firm, whether a disclosure gives rise to knowledge or suspicion of money laundering. The individual should, therefore, be in a sufficiently senior position to gain access to all relevant information held by the firm concerning clients or others suspected of money laundering.

Although, in the context of a nominated officer, PoCA 2002 refers to a person's employer and a person's employment, s.340(12) provides that:

references to a person's employer include any body, association or organisation (including a voluntary organisation) in connection with whose activities the person exercises a function (whether or not for gain or reward).

The subsection goes on to state that references to employment must be construed accordingly.

Consequently, a sole practitioner or partner in a firm of solicitors will be able to treat the firm as an employer for these purposes and will be treated as being in employment when making authorised disclosures.

4.2.4 Form of disclosure

Section 338(1)(*b*) states that the disclosure (whether made to NCIS or to a nominated officer) is to be made in the form and manner prescribed by order under PoCA 2002, s.339. This section allows the Secretary of State, by order, to prescribe the form and manner of any disclosure under s.338 and to require that additional information be provided if it is necessary for the purposes of any decision taken to start a money laundering investigation.

At the time of writing (June 2004) no order has yet been made regarding the form and content of disclosures under s.338. It is expected that in due course the Secretary of State, under the provisions of s.339, will make an order.

In the meantime, a form of disclosure for use by solicitors when making authorised disclosures to NCIS can be found on the website of NCIS at **www.ncis.gov.uk** (see also **Chapter 10** and **Appendix C4**).

For internal disclosure purposes, firms should publish their own precedent for use by members of the firm. A suggested form of an internal disclosure is given in **Appendix C3**.

4.2.5 Time of disclosure

Section 338(2) and (3) provide for two alternative conditions regarding the timing of the disclosure.

Under subsection (2), the disclosure, to satisfy the requirements of the section, can be made 'before the alleged offender does the prohibited act'. The prohibited act for these purposes would be the act of concealment, etc. under s.327; the act of entering or becoming concerned in an arrangement which facilitates under s.328; or the act of acquisition, use or possession under s.329.

This is, by far, the most practical way to approach the defence. As soon as knowledge or suspicion arises a disclosure should be made to the nominated officer. Most firms of solicitors will not wish to encourage their staff and partners to disclose knowledge or suspicion of money laundering directly to NCIS. Internal disclosure allows the firm to maintain control over what is happening in the firm. It allows for policy decisions to be taken centrally by one person (the nominated officer) or, in bigger firms, a panel of senior members of the firm. It therefore makes sense to have internal procedures requiring this defence to be applied by making an internal disclosure as soon as knowledge or suspicion arises and before any prohibited act is undertaken.

As an alternative, PoCA 2002 provides for a defence where the disclosure is made after the prohibited act.

Section 338(3) provides that a disclosure made after the alleged offender does the prohibited act may provide a defence if two further conditions apply. These are that:

- there was a good reason for the failure to make the disclosure before the prohibited act was undertaken; and
- the disclosure was made on the alleged offender's own initiative and as soon as it was practicable for it to be made.

This is clearly not as satisfactory as the first option. If the disclosure is made before the prohibited act, no further condition relating to the disclosure must be met – the defence is available. In order to obtain the benefit of the defence using the second alternative timing requirement, a solicitor will have to show good reason for failing to make the disclosure earlier and that the disclosure was made on his initiative. It is not yet clear how the courts will interpret the phrase 'good reason'.

Firms, in their internal procedures, should treat this second alternative very much as a back-stop procedure, available if necessary but not the norm.

4.2.6　Confidentiality

Many solicitors are concerned about their duty in confidentiality when making a disclosure. When a solicitor makes a disclosure to a third person (i.e. in this context, NCIS) which concerns the affairs of a client, the question of confidentiality naturally arises. A solicitor's duty in confidentiality extends to all matters communicated to a solicitor by the client or on behalf of the client, except in certain limited exceptional cases. In addition, any information contained in a disclosure may be privileged information. Communications made between a lawyer and a client are privileged if they are confidential and made for the purpose of seeking legal advice from a lawyer or providing legal advice to a client. Further, where litigation has started or is reasonably in prospect, communications made between a lawyer and client; a lawyer and an agent; or a lawyer and a third party are privileged if they are made for the sole or dominant purpose of the litigation.

The duty of confidentiality does not apply to information acquired by a solicitor where he or she is being used by a client to facilitate the commission of a crime (see section 16.02 of *The Guide to the Professional Conduct of*

Solicitors (1999)). Further, section 10(2) of the Police and Criminal Evidence Act 1984 (PACE) states that items are not privileged where they are held 'with the intention of furthering a criminal purpose'. The House of Lords has held that the reference to the word 'intention' in section 10(2) of PACE does not have to be that of the client or the solicitor. It is sufficient that a third party intends the solicitor/client communication to be made with a view to furthering a criminal purpose (see *R. v. Central Criminal Court ex parte Francis & Francis* [1989] AC 346).

Clearly, if a solicitor is required to disclose information by way of a defence to NCIS, the solicitor must ensure that such disclosure does not give rise to a breach of the duty in confidentiality or an improper disclosure of privileged information.

Section 338(4) PoCA 2002 provides: 'An authorised disclosure is not to be taken to breach any restriction on the disclosure of information (however imposed).'

This subsection clearly covers both confidential and privileged information. If a solicitor knows that a client has the intention to use his or her services to commit a money laundering offence under PoCA 2002, ss.327–329, any information acquired or communication made in relation to these services will not be confidential nor will it be privileged. Disclosure to NCIS will not be a problem.

However if a solicitor suspects a client may be using his or her services to commit a money laundering offence, the question of confidentiality or privilege depends upon the outcome of any investigation. If the solicitor's suspicions are confirmed, the information or communication is neither confidential nor privileged. If the suspicions turn out to be unfounded, the information or communication will remain confidential and privileged. However, providing the disclosure of such information or communication is made as an authorised disclosure within PoCA 2002, s.338, subsection (4) will ensure that the solicitor commits no breach of any disclosure obligations when a report is made to NCIS.

4.3   APPROPRIATE CONSENT (PoCA 2002, S.335)

As noted above, ss.327, 328 and 329 provide for a defence where an authorised disclosure is made by the accused and 'if the disclosure is made before he does the [prohibited act] he has the appropriate consent.' Also, as noted above, solicitors are encouraged to make any authorised disclosure before the prohibited act rather than relying upon the disclosure being made after the act and having to show that there was a good reason for a failure to make the disclosure earlier.

For this reason, it is vital to understand the meaning of appropriate consent and the rules attached to the definition in PoCA 2002, s.335.

To illustrate this point, consider the following scenario. A solicitor is acting for the vendor on a property transaction. Contracts have been exchanged and a date for completion has been agreed. The solicitor has no concerns about his client but, in the course of the transaction, becomes suspicious about the funds used by the purchaser (for whom he is not acting). Completing the sale is likely to amount to an arrangement which facilitates the acquisition, use or control of criminal property (if the funds do turn out to be criminal property) – PoCA 2002, s.328. Receiving the funds into client account will potentially be the offence of acquisition, use or possession of criminal property – PoCA 2002, s.329. Receipt of such funds may also amount to the offence of concealing – PoCA 2002, s.327.

In each case, the defence of an authorised disclosure is available. If the solicitor discloses his suspicions after completion (i.e. after the prohibited act) the defence will only be available if there was a good reason for his failure to make the disclosure before completion and the disclosure was made on his own initiative as soon as it was practicable for him to make it. It is unlikely that the simple contractual requirement to complete by a particular date will be a good reason for failing to make the disclosure before that date although, at the time of writing, there is no judicial interpretation of this term. Consequently the limited circumstances where the defence might apply in this situation include where the solicitor only became suspicious after the completion. If the conditions are not met, the disclosure does not fall within the definition of an authorised disclosure.

If, however, the solicitor's suspicion arose before the completion date it would be sensible for the disclosure to be made before completion (i.e. before the prohibited act). In this case, the defence would be available since the disclosure would amount to an authorised disclosure. Having made such disclosure, the solicitor could not then proceed to complete the matter without considering the further requirements of the PoCA 2002. The defence of authorised disclosure will only continue to apply if the prohibited act (i.e. completion) is undertaken with appropriate consent. (Note that in this scenario it may also be necessary to consider the offences of failure to disclose under PoCA 2002, ss.330 et seq – see **Chapter 5**.)

Section 335(1) PoCA 2002 defines appropriate consent as:

- The consent of the nominated officer to do a prohibited act if the authorised disclosure is made to the nominated officer.
- The consent of a constable to do a prohibited act if an authorised disclosure is made to a constable.
- The consent of a customs officer to do a prohibited act if an authorised disclosure is made to a customs officer.

Appropriate consent can therefore be given by a nominated officer (i.e. the firm's MLRO) or by the appropriate authorities (usually NCIS). Since most firms' policies will require members of the firm to report any knowledge or suspicion internally and before the prohibited act, it is vital that any policy includes a requirement that following an internal disclosure no further work should be undertaken on the file without the nominated officer's consent.

4.3.1 Appropriate consent by nominated officer

Where disclosure has been made internally to the firm's nominated officer, the officer can only give appropriate consent in accordance with the strict rules set out in PoCA 2002, s.336. This section provides that the nominated officer must not give consent unless the conditions set out in the section are satisfied. There are three conditions, any of which being satisfied will allow the nominated officer to give consent.

Condition 1 (s.336(2))

For this condition to apply the nominated officer must disclose to NCIS (the Act states 'to a person authorised for the purposes of this Part by the Director General of the National Criminal Intelligence Service') that the property is criminal property. Thereafter, before the nominated officer can give appropriate consent, NCIS must consent to the firm continuing to act in such a way that leads to the prohibited act being undertaken.

NCIS has issued a statement by way of guidance in relation to disclosures by the legal profession. A copy of this statement can be found in **Appendix B3**. This guidance makes it quite clear that NCIS will not accept requests for consent to take instructions in order to learn what a case is about. However, where there are suspicions that a stage to be taken by the solicitor in the transaction would involve the solicitor or client in an arrangement which is prohibited by PoCA 2002, s.328 or in concealing (s.327) or acquisition, use or possession (s.329) then a disclosure should be made. As noted above, until such time as the form of disclosure to NCIS is prescribed by order, a template is available from the NCIS website at **www.ncis.gov.uk**.

NCIS also operates a fast track scheme where the arrangement is time sensitive. If, for example, completion of a transaction is imminent, disclosure by the nominated officer to NCIS and the consent of NCIS will be necessary before completion can take place. NCIS has indicated that the time sensitive nature of the arrangement should be explicitly stated and highlighted in the written report faxed to the NCIS Consent Desk.

Condition 2 (s.336(3))

As an alternative to condition 1 above, appropriate consent can be given by a nominated officer if condition 2 applies. The nominated officer must make a disclosure to NCIS that property is criminal property and if, before the end of seven working days starting with the first working day after disclosure has been made, no notice of refusal of consent to undertaking the prohibited act is received from NCIS, consent can be given. A working day for these purposes is defined (s.336(9)) as a day other than Saturday, Sunday, Christmas Day, Good Friday or a day which is a bank holiday under the Banking and Financial Dealings Act 1971.

Obviously in all cases (but particularly where a solicitor is relying upon this second condition) it is important that the solicitor's records show exactly what has happened. The Law Society's *Money Laundering Guidance* (para. 7.7) states:

> Solicitors must ensure that they keep a copy of the report which they have submitted, as well as careful notes of all contacts which they subsequently have with NCIS or law enforcement agencies. These records should be kept on a separate file by the nominated officer. It would be prudent for these records to be kept by the nominated officer for as long as the transaction and identity records are kept, and probably longer as it can sometimes take many years before an investigation comes to fruition.

Condition 3 (s.336(4))

Where disclosure has been made to NCIS by a nominated officer, NCIS will usually acknowledge receipt and either refuse appropriate consent or provide appropriate consent. If consent is given, then obviously the nominated officer can then proceed to give appropriate consent to the fee earner. If consent is refused by NCIS, condition 3 may be relevant in determining whether the nominated officer can give consent to the fee earner.

This condition applies where the nominated officer discloses to NCIS that property is criminal property and before the end of seven working days starting with the first working day after disclosure has been made, notice of refusal of consent to undertaking the prohibited act is received from NCIS. Obviously, where NCIS have refused consent, no further work should be undertaken on the file if such work is likely to amount to a prohibited act. However, s.336(4) allows the nominated officer to give appropriate consent to such work after the moratorium period has expired. For these purposes, s.336(8) defines the moratorium period as 'the period of 31 days starting with the day on which the nominated officer is given notice that consent to the doing of the act is refused'.

Note that, unlike the reference to seven working days in the legislation, the reference to 31 days in the definition of the moratorium period is not a reference to working days.

Take the following example by way of illustration of these points.

A solicitor is acting for a client on the disposal of certain assets. Contracts have been exchanged and the completion is fixed for Friday 10 September. On

Wednesday, 8 September, the solicitor receives certain information from his client that leads him to suspect that the funds being used by the purchaser (for whom the solicitor is not acting) derive from criminal conduct. Completion of the transaction on 10 September is likely to amount to an arrangement which facilitates the retention, use or control of these criminal funds (PoCA 2002, s.328). It would also mean that the solicitor would acquire and possess criminal property when the completion money was placed into his client account (PoCA 2002, s.329). Possibly there would also be a breach of PoCA 2002, s.327 (concealing). In all the circumstances, it would be advisable for the solicitor to report his suspicions. The timetable for reporting is as follows:

8 September	Solicitor reports his suspicions to the firm's nominated officer. Although the contractual completion date is only two days away, completion cannot go ahead without the appropriate consent of the nominated officer. If completion did proceed without the consent, the defence of disclosure would not be available.
8 September	The nominated officer cannot give consent to completion unless he has satisfied one of the conditions in PoCA 2002, s.336. Because of the time sensitive nature of this matter, it is likely that he will contact NCIS using the fast track procedure. He makes a faxed disclosure to NCIS.
9–17 September	Seven working days must be calculated starting with the first working day after the nominated officer makes the disclosure. Consequently the first working day is Thursday 9 September. Omitting Saturday 11 and Sunday 12 September, the seventh working day is Friday 17 September. If during this period, NCIS consents to the firm undertaking the prohibited act, the nominated officer can give appropriate consent to completion proceeding.
20 September	If before the end of the seven working days (i.e. by midnight on Friday 17 September) the nominated officer has not received consent nor has he received notice of refusal of consent from NCIS, he has received deemed consent and may now give appropriate consent to the matter completing.
17 September – 17 October	If, during the seven working day period, NCIS notifies its refusal to give consent (worst case scenario, the refusal is given on day seven) the moratorium period will apply. This period starts on the day refusal of consent is given and lasts for 31 days.

	During this period, the prohibited act (i.e. the act of completion) cannot be undertaken since the defence of disclosure will not apply.
18 October	The moratorium period has now expired. Despite the refusal of NCIS, the nominated officer can now give appropriate consent and completion can now take place (assuming the purchaser is still willing or able to complete!)

For the sake of completeness, the following points, dealt with elsewhere in this book, should also be considered:

- Communication with the client and other side regarding the fact that completion cannot take place on the contractual completion date. It is possible that such communication could amount to the offence of tipping off under PoCA 2002, s.333 – see **Chapter 7**.
- Civil liability. If the client has suffered loss as a result of the delay in completion, there may be civil liability consequences – see **Appendix B1**.
- Disclosure on behalf of the client. In this scenario, if the client is innocent (i.e. the suspicions related to the funds of the purchaser) the client will require a defence against a possible charge under PoCA 2002. The client will be concerned in an arrangement (i.e. completion) and in consequence will need the same defence as the solicitor. In this case a joint disclosure by the nominated officer on behalf of himself and the client should be considered – see **Paragraph 4.4**.

4.3.2 Offence committed by nominated officer if improper consent is given

Where a member of the firm has made disclosure of criminal property to a nominated officer by way of a defence, the prohibited act cannot be undertaken without the appropriate consent of the nominated officer. As noted above, there are three alternative conditions that the nominated officer must satisfy before giving consent. If a nominated officer gives consent without satisfying any of these conditions, an offence is committed. Section 336(5) provides that:

A person who is a nominated officer commits an offence if:

(a) he gives consent to a prohibited act in circumstances where none of the conditions in subsections (2), (3) and (4) is satisfied, and

(b) he knows or suspects that the act is a prohibited act.

The penalty for such an offence is imprisonment for up to six months and/or a fine not exceeding the statutory maximum for summary conviction; imprisonment for up to five years and/or a fine for conviction on indictment (s.336(6)).

The nominated officer only commits an offence if the two requirements noted in s.336(5) apply. Not only must the nominated officer be shown to have given consent without any of the three conditions being satisfied but also he must be shown to have known or suspected that the act is a prohibited act.

Where a fee earner reports knowledge or suspicion that property is criminal property and the Money Laundering Regulations 2003 apply (see **Chapter 9**), a nominated officer should investigate the circumstance of the report. Regulation 7 of the regulations which states: 'Where a disclosure is made to a nominated officer, he must consider it in the light of any relevant information which is available to [the firm] and determine whether it gives rise to such knowledge or suspicion . . .'

Whether or not the regulations apply, it would be good practice for the nominated officer to follow this procedure. If, in the light of this internal consideration, the nominated officer comes to the conclusion that there are no grounds for knowledge or suspicion, he may give appropriate consent to the fee earner continuing to work on the file. For example, this might apply where the fee earner is a junior member of staff or a recently joined employee. A particular aspect of a transaction may arouse his suspicion and consequently a report might be made to the nominated officer. On considering the report along with other information held in the firm (including past dealings with the client) the nominated officer may come to the conclusion that there are no grounds for knowledge or suspicion and appropriate consent can be given without the need to satisfy any of the three conditions in PoCA 2002, s.336 and without the risk of committing a criminal offence under PoCA 2002, s.336(5). It goes without saying that particular care must be taken in these circumstances. Nominated officers should err on the side of caution and should only give appropriate consent outside the conditions of s.336 if, having considered all of the information, they have reached a view that no offence is being committed. In these circumstances it is vital for the nominated officer to record full and proper file notes.

4.3.3　Appropriate consent from the authorities

Section 335(1) PoCA 2002 defines appropriate consent as:

(a)　the consent of the nominated officer to do a prohibited act if the authorised disclosure is made to the nominated officer;

(b)　the consent of a constable to do a prohibited act if an authorised disclosure is made to a constable; or

(c)　the consent of a customs officer to do a prohibited act if an authorised disclosure is made to a customs officer.

As noted above, most firms will encourage all partners and other members of staff to make their disclosure of knowledge or suspicion internally to the firm's nominated officer. In such cases appropriate consent must be obtained from the nominated officer.

However, a valid defence is available if the disclosure is made to a constable or customs officer (although, in practice, this will be a disclosure to NCIS). There are two circumstances where consent from the authorities will allow the prohibited act to be undertaken.

- **Consent from NCIS.** If a disclosure is made to NCIS, their consent to do the prohibited act will amount to appropriate consent under s.335(1)(*b*) or (*c*).
- **Assumed consent from NCIS.** Section 335(2) provides that a person must be treated as having the appropriate consent if he makes an authorised disclosure to a constable or customs officer and either the condition in subsection (3) or subsection (4) is satisfied.

Condition 1: s.335(3)

If, before the end of seven working days starting with the first working day after disclosure has been made, no notice of refusal of consent to undertaking the prohibited act is received from NCIS, consent can be assumed. A working day for these purposes is defined (s.336(9)) as a day other than Saturday, Sunday, Christmas Day, Good Friday or a day which is a bank holiday under the Banking and Financial Dealings Act 1971.

Condition 2: s.335(4)

If, before the end of seven working days starting with the first working day after disclosure has been made, notice of refusal of consent to undertaking the prohibited act is received from NCIS, no further work should be undertaken on the file if such work is likely to amount to a prohibited act. However, consent can be assumed after the moratorium period has expired. For these purposes, s.335(6) defines the moratorium period as the period of 31 days starting with the day on which the person receives notice that consent to the doing of the act is refused.

These two conditions are very similar to the conditions applicable to the nominated officer when giving appropriate consent. Consequently, the timetable noted above could equally be relevant where a fee earner discloses not to the nominated officer but to NCIS direct.

4.4 AUTHORISED DISCLOSURES BY OR ON BEHALF OF OTHERS

In certain circumstances it is not just the solicitor who might need a defence to the money laundering offences contained in PoCA 2002, ss.327–329. In any particular transaction it will be the solicitor and the client who will be concerned in an arrangement. In some matters a barrister may also be involved in the arrangement. Consequently, solicitors should consider carefully who might need a defence and what steps can be taken in order to provide that defence.

If a client is an innocent party (and particularly if it is the information provided by the client which has given rise to any suspicion) the solicitor should consider joining in the client when disclosure is made to NCIS. One factor in determining whether the client should be joined in is whether it is possible for the solicitor to disclose details without being in breach of the tipping off offence (PoCA 2002, s.333) or the offence of prejudicing an investigation (PoCA 2002, s.342) – for both sections see **Chapter 7**).

NCIS, in its guidance relating to disclosures by the legal profession, makes the following points regarding disclosure by or on behalf of third parties:

5. In the event that a solicitor makes a disclosure before instructing counsel there would be no requirement for counsel to make a further disclosure if the facts upon which he would otherwise have disclosed remain as they were when the solicitor made the original disclosure.
6. Legal advisors must not assume that the other side in any matter has reported a suspicion to the NCIS and such enquiries should not be made of the NCIS.
7. Where the client of the legal advisor has joined in the disclosure that has been made the client would from the point of time when a disclosure is made to NCIS, not be regarded as having committed an offence under sections 327–329. Where a legal advisor makes a disclosure without the knowledge of their client then plainly and necessarily such protection for the client would not apply.

From clause 7 of the guidance, it is clear that if a client has joined in disclosure where the solicitor perhaps knows or suspects that another has or is intending to use criminal property, the protection of the defence will only apply from the point of time when disclosure was made. Disclosure made by a client does not operate retrospectively and does not provide a defence against activities undertaken before the disclosure.

Any joint disclosure must be to NCIS in order for the client to benefit from it. Although a solicitor may obtain a defence by disclosing knowledge or suspicion to the firm's nominated officer, such a disclosure will not operate as a defence for the client. The nominated officer is the person nominated by the alleged offender's employer and the disclosure must be made during the course of employment and according to the employer's established procedure.

CHAPTER 5

Failure to disclose: regulated sector

5.1 INTRODUCTION

The money laundering offences contained in the Proceeds of Crime Act 2002 (PoCA 2002) and the Terrorism Act 2000 (see **Chapters 2** and **3**) all require the alleged offender to take some action in relation to criminal or terrorist property. Section 327 of the PoCA 2002 requires an act of concealment etc; PoCA 2002, s.328 requires a person to enter into or become concerned in an arrangement which facilitates; s.329 requires the acquisition, use or control; Terrorism Act 2000, s.18 requires an act of assistance.

Without undertaking any of these acts, a solicitor is unlikely to be convicted under these provisions. A solicitor who, for example, interviews a new potential client and, in the course of the interview becomes suspicious of the funds the client intends to use as part of the transaction, may decline to accept the instructions. Simply having suspicion regarding a client's funds would not be sufficient to justify a charge under PoCA 2002 ss.327–329, or Terrorism Act 2000, s.18. Since no offence under these provisions has been committed (or is about to be committed) no disclosure of the suspicions to NCIS or internally by way of defence is necessary.

However, in certain circumstances, a failure to disclose knowledge or suspicion, or reasonable grounds for knowledge or suspicion, of money laundering is an offence even if no act in relation to the criminal or terrorist property is undertaken.

There are four offences of failure to disclose:

* Failure to disclose: regulated sector (PoCA 2002, s.330)
* Failure to disclose: regulated sector (Terrorism Act 2000, s.21A)
* Failure to disclose: nominated officers in the regulated sector (PoCA 2002, s.331)
* Failure to disclose: other nominated officers (PoCA 2000, s.332)

The first two offences are dealt with in detail in this chapter. The remaining two offences are covered in **Chapter 6**.

5.2 FAILURE TO DISCLOSE: REGULATED SECTOR (PoCA 2002, S.330).

5.2.1 The offence

Section 330 of the PoCA 2002 provides:

(1) A person commits an offence if each of the following three conditions is satisfied.

(2) The first condition is that he –

    (a) knows or suspects, or

    (b) has reasonable grounds for knowing or suspecting,

that another person is engaged in money laundering.

(3) The second condition is that the information or other matter –

    (a) on which his knowledge or suspicion is based, or

    (b) which gives reasonable grounds for such knowledge or suspicion,

came to him in the course of a business in the regulated sector.

(4) The third condition is that he does not make the required disclosure as soon as is practicable after the information or other matter comes to him.

There are a number of points that can be made concerning this section and in particular the three conditions that must be satisfied before the offence is committed.

First Condition

> . . . knows or suspects, or has reasonable grounds for knowing or suspecting . . .

Like many of the offences contained in PoCA 2002, this offence can be committed with knowledge or suspicion. However, unlike the other offences, the test of knowledge or suspicion is a subjective and objective test. An alleged offender can be found guilty under s.330 if he or she knows or suspects that another is engaged in money laundering. However, even if subjectively the offender had no actual knowledge or suspicion of matters upon which the charge is based, if the offender has reasonable grounds for knowledge or suspicion of these matters, that will be sufficient for the purposes of this section; the fact that the offender should have known or suspected is all that is required. Consequently an oversight by a solicitor or incompetence on the part of a solicitor might be sufficient to give rise to liability.

Solicitors must therefore be more proactive in considering whether a particular transaction gives rise to knowledge or suspicion of money laundering. Instead of simply reacting to information which might be suspicious, solicitors should ask themselves: Are there any suspicious circumstances arising from this particular transaction?

... that another person ...

The reference to another person means that as with the offence under PoCA 2002, s.328 (arrangements), this offence can be committed where the solicitor's knowledge or suspicion relates to the conduct of a client or some third party. It may be that concerns have arisen regarding the other side's client and that the solicitor's own client is above any suspicion – consideration must still be given to the requirements to report that other person.

... is engaged in money laundering.

Section 340(11) of the PoCA 2002 provides a definition for the term money laundering. It states:

Money laundering is an act which –

(a) constitutes an offence under section 327, 328 or 329,
(b) constitutes an attempt, conspiracy or incitement to commit an offence specified in paragraph (a),
(c) constitutes aiding, abetting, counselling or procuring the commission of an offence specified in paragraph (a), or
(d) would constitute an offence specified in paragraph (a), (b), or (c) if done in the United Kingdom.

Money laundering is, therefore, widely defined. Since it includes the offences of concealing etc. (PoCA 2002, s.327) and acquisition, use and possession (PoCA 2002, s.329) it follows that the perpetrator of the crime can be 'engaged in money laundering' (see **Chapter 3**).

The offence under PoCA 2002, s.330 obliges a solicitor to report knowledge or suspicion even if the solicitor is not involved in an arrangement which is likely to facilitate the acquisition, retention, use or control of criminal property. Unlike the defence requiring an authorised disclosure, this is a disclosure by way of obligation. It is the failure to disclose which is a criminal offence.

Note that the offence under s.330 can also be committed if a solicitor knows or suspects (or has reasonable grounds for knowing or suspecting) that another is engaged in an attempt, conspiracy or incitement to commit a money laundering offence or where another is engaged in aiding, abetting, counselling or procuring such an offence. However, solicitors must be careful to ensure that they do not report in circumstances where to do so would be inappropriate. A required report (termed a protected disclosure – see below) will not breach a solicitor's duty in confidentiality or be in breach of a solicitor's obligations arising from legal professional privilege. To benefit from this provision, the solicitor must know or suspect that another is engaged in money laundering or an attempt etc. The use of the word engaged suggests that some action must be taking place. Knowledge or suspicion that another person is likely in the future to undertake an act of money laundering or attempt etc. such an act is unlikely to give rise to an obligation to report; indeed such a report might be in breach of a solicitor's obligations in confidentiality and privilege.

Second condition

> ... the information or other matter –
>
> (a) on which his knowledge or suspicion is based, or
> (b) which gives reasonable grounds for such knowledge or suspicion,
>
> came to him in the course of business . . ..

Information received, other than in the course of business, does not give rise to an obligation to report. If a solicitor overhears a conversation in a public house suggesting that the speaker is engaged in criminal activities, this will not give rise to compulsory reporting, providing the solicitor is drinking in his private capacity. The fact that the information must be received in the course of business does not restrict the operation of this offence to information received on the office premises. However, the circumstances in which the information is received must suggest that the solicitor is operating in a business capacity at the time of receipt.

> ... in the regulated sector.

The regulated sector is defined in PoCA 2002, Part 1, Sched. 9. The definition was amended by the Proceeds of Crime Act 2002 (Business in the Regulated Sector and Supervisory Authorities) Order 2003, SI 2003/3074. This order (and thus the amended definition of the regulated sector) came into force on 1 March 2004. The following activities are activities which solicitors frequently undertake and will be (as a result of the order) within the regulated sector.

Schedule 9 Part 1 of the PoCA 2002 (as amended) provides:

> 1 (1) A business is in the regulated sector to the extent that it engages in any of the following activities in the United Kingdom –
>
> (a) a regulated activity specified in sub-paragraph (2) . . .'

Sub-paragraph (2) lists 10 activities, many of which could be relevant to a solicitor's practice. Sub-paragraph (3) states that: 'Paragraph 1(1)(*a*) . . . must be read with section 22 of the Financial Services and Markets Act 2000 and any relevant order under that section . . .'

Section 22 of the Financial Services and Markets Act 2000 provides:

> (1) An activity is a regulated activity for the purposes of this Act if it is an activity of a specified kind which is carried on by way of business and –
>
> (a) relates to an investment of a specified kind . . ..
>
> (5) 'Specified' means specified in an order made by the Treasury.

The most relevant order made by the Treasury is the Financial Services and Markets Act 2000 (Regulated Activities) Order 2001, SI 2001/544. This order (the RAO) lists both the activities of a specified kind and the investments of a specified kind.

The most common specified investments from a solicitor's point of view are:

- Shares in the share capital of any company (art.76 RAO).
- Instruments creating or acknowledging indebtedness, including debentures, loan stock, bonds and certificates of deposit (art.77 RAO).
- Government securities, including British Government Stocks (gilts) (art.78 RAO).
- Units in collective investment schemes, including unit trusts and shares in open-ended investment companies (art.81 RAO).
- Insurance contracts, including endowment policies, pension policies, annuities and insurance bonds.

Consequently, activities in a solicitor's corporate department (acquisitions, corporate finance) are likely to involve shares, debentures or corporate bonds. Activities in private client work (estate and trust administration) could involve the full range of specified investments. Settlements in matrimonial work could involve some or all of the specified investments.

Of the 10 activities listed in PoCA 2002, Sched.9, Part 1, para.1(2) the following involving specified investments are likely to be most relevant to solicitors:

- **Dealing in investments as agent**. Dealing is defined as buying, selling, subscribing or underwriting certain specified investments. A solicitor would be dealing where investments were being bought or sold as agent for a client.
- **Arranging deals in investments**. This would catch those circumstances where a solicitor made arrangements for a client to buy, sell, subscribe or underwrite certain specified investments.
- **Managing investments**. Solicitors who are sole trustees or personal representatives or trustees or personal representatives jointly only with others from their own firm will be managing if the trust fund or estate includes certain specified investments.
- **Safeguarding and administration**. Solicitors who hold documents of title to specified investments in safe custody and who are involved in administration activities relating to those investments will be undertaking this activity. Typically estate and trust work will give rise to this activity.
- **Advising on investments**. Giving advice on the merits of buying, selling, subscribing for or underwriting certain specified investments will be caught by this activity.

Section 19 of the Financial Services and Markets Act 2000 provides:

(1)   No person may carry on a regulated activity in the United Kingdom, or purport to do so, unless he is –

(a) an authorised person; or
(b) an exempt person.

Most solicitors are not authorised persons (i.e. they have not sought nor obtained authorisation from the Financial Services Authority). They are, however, able to undertake many activities which fall within the definition of regulated activities without authorisation as a result of the exemption for professionals provided in Part XX of the Financial Services and Markets Act 2000.

It must be understood that the definition of the regulated sector in PoCA 2002, s.330 (Duty to report: regulated sector), does not require the regulated activity to be undertaken with authorisation from the Financial Services Authority. An exempt regulated activity will fall within the regulated sector.

For further details of the way the Financial Services and Markets Act 2000 applies to solicitors, see *Solicitors and Financial Services: A Compliance Handbook* (3rd Edition, 2002) by Peter Camp, published by Law Society Publishing.

The other relevant activities that will bring a solicitor within the regulated sector as a result of PoCA 2002, Sched. 9, Part 1, para.1(1) (as amended) are as follows:

(f) estate agency work . . ..

Solicitors who provide estate agency services will, in respect of those services, fall within the regulated sector.

(h) the activities of a person appointed to act as an insolvency practitioner within the meaning of section 388 of the Insolvency Act 1986 . . .

Solicitors who are appointed as insolvency practitioners will be within the regulated sector. Solicitors who act for external insolvency practitioners or who act in insolvency matters without an appointment as an insolvency practitioner will not be caught under this head. However, depending upon the type of work, they may be caught under paragraph (l) below.

(i) the provision by way of business of advice about the tax affairs of another person by a body corporate or unincorporate, or in the case of a sole practitioner, by an individual . . .

Solicitors giving tax advice will be within the regulated sector. It appears that any tax advice is capable of triggering the definition of business in the regulated sector. For example, whilst activities relating to will drafting would not bring a solicitor into the regulated sector, if such activities were combined with inheritance tax planning advice this would be considered as business in the regulated sector.

(l)   the provision by way of business of legal services by a body corporate or unincorporate or, in the case of a sole practitioner, by an individual and which involves the participation in a financial or real property transaction (whether by assisting in the planning or execution of any transaction or otherwise by acting for, or on behalf of, a client in any transaction) . . ..

This paragraph is clearly aimed at extending the regulated sector to many activities undertaken by solicitors. The reference to financial or real property transactions has the effect of bringing all conveyancing transactions within the scope of the regulated sector.

The *Money Laundering Guidance* issued by the Law Society indicates that the interpretation of a participation in a financial transaction is less clear. The *Money Laundering Guidance* seeks clarity from the text of the 2nd European Money Laundering Directive (on which this definition is based). The Directive provides that the following should be included:

Independent legal professionals, when they participate, whether:

(1)   by assisting in the planning or execution of transactions for their client concerning the:

- buying and selling of real property or business entities;
- managing of client money, securities or other assets;
- opening or management of bank, savings or securities accounts;
- organisation of contributions necessary for the creation, operation or management of companies; or
- creation, operation or management of trusts, companies or similar structures; or

(2)   by acting on behalf of and for their client in any financial or real estate transaction.

The Law Society's *Money Laundering Guidance* indicates that managing client money is narrower than simply handling client money. Simply operating a client account is not intended to be caught within the regulated sector but holding money or receiving money on behalf of clients as part of a transaction, or holding or receiving money as attorney or trustee will be caught.

The Treasury has also confirmed that the following (by themselves) would not generally be viewed as participation in financial transactions:

- A payment on account of costs to a solicitor or payment of a solicitor's bill (because the solicitor is not participating in a financial transaction on behalf of the client).
- Legal advice (assuming such advice does not fall within one or more of the other categories defined as within the regulated sector).
- Participation in litigation (on the basis that litigation is not a transaction).
- Will writing (unless linked with, for example, tax advice).
- Publicly funded work.

(m) the provision by way of business of services in relation to the formation, operation or management of a company or a trust.

This paragraph clearly covers activities undertaken by solicitors relating to the formation of a company or the administration of a trust fund. There is some doubt over the reference to business services relating to the operation or management of a company. The Treasury has indicated that this phrase should not be interpreted to include any services which assist in the management or operation of a company.

In a letter (published on the NCIS website) written to the British Bankers' Association, the Treasury made the following points:

> Regulation (m) was intended to cover those who form, operate or manage companies (or trusts) when this activity is provided as a service by way of business. This addresses, among other things, the problem of 'front' or shell companies, which have been recognised as having been used in most complex money laundering operations . . .
>
> It has been argued that regulation (m) covers anyone providing any service by way of business to a company which happens to assist the management or operation of that company e.g. cleaners, advertising agencies or management consultants. Whereas the interpretation of the Regulations is ultimately a matter for the courts, such a wide interpretation of regulation (m) was not our intention and, we believe, is not warranted by the language of regulation (m).

Many services offered by solicitors to companies and trust funds will involve financial transactions. Some will be exempt regulated activities within the meaning of the Financial Services and Markets Act 2000. As such, these activities will be within the regulated sector regardless of regulation (m). Since the Treasury statement indicates that the interpretation is ultimately a matter for the courts, solicitors should, perhaps, err on the side of caution and assume activities relating to company clients and trust clients are likely to be within the regulated sector.

Third Condition

> . . . he does not make the required disclosure . . .

The required disclosure is disclosure of the information giving rise to knowledge or suspicion of another being engaged in money laundering. The disclosure must be to a nominated officer (i.e. the firm's MLRO) or to a person authorised for the purpose by the Director General of NCIS (PoCA 2002, s.330(5)(a)). Disclosure to NCIS in the usual way (see **Chapter 10**) will satisfy this requirement. Section 330(5)(b) provides that the form and manner of this disclosure can be prescribed by order under PoCA 2002, s.339. At the time of writing no such order has been made.

Any disclosure made will be treated as a protected disclosure under PoCA 2002, s.337. This section provides that such a disclosure is not to be taken to be a breach of any restriction on the disclosure of information (however imposed) if three conditions are satisfied. These three conditions are:

- The information or other matter disclosed came to the person making the disclosure in the course of his trade, profession, business or employment.
- The information caused the discloser to know or suspect or gave him reasonable grounds for knowing or suspecting that another was engaged in money laundering.
- The disclosure was made to a constable, a customs officer or a nominated officer as soon as is practicable after the information or other matter comes to the discloser.

Provided the three conditions are satisfied, a solicitor will not be in breach of any duty of confidentiality or obligations under the concept of legal professional privilege.

> . . . as soon as is practicable after the information or other matter comes to him.

Both the third condition and the benefit of protected disclosures require the disclosure to be made as soon as practicable after the information comes into the possession of the discloser. Consequently to avoid committing the crime and to benefit from the protection of s.337 (protected disclosures) solicitors must not delay in making their disclosures. The Law Society's *Money Laundering Guidance* states:

> It is not known how the courts will interpret 'as soon as practicable'. However delays in reporting which arise from taking legal advice or seeking guidance from the Law Society may be acceptable.

5.2.2 Law Society Guidance

Section 330(8) of the PoCA 2002 states:

> In deciding whether a person committed an offence under this section the court must consider whether he followed any relevant guidance which was at the time concerned:
> (a) issued by a supervisory authority or any other appropriate body;
> (b) approved by the Treasury; and
> (c) published in a manner it approved as appropriate in its opinion to bring the guidance to the attention of persons likely to be affected by it.

A supervisory body is defined in PoCA 2002, Sched. 9 and the term includes the Law Society.

The Law Society has issued guidance to the solicitors' profession (*Money Laundering Guidance: Professional Ethics*, Pilot, January 2004). Extracts from the guidance appear in the text of this book and in **Appendix B1**. The Law Society's *Money Laundering Guidance* is described as a pilot and has not been submitted to the Treasury for approval. Consequently s.330(8) will not apply technically. However, as stated in the *Money Laundering Guidance*, a court 'may still take it into consideration' in deciding whether an offence has been committed under s.330.

5.2.3   Illustrations I

The following scenarios suggest circumstances where a solicitor may be at risk regarding a duty to disclose.

Scenario 1

A solicitor is acting in a corporate transaction, buying shares on behalf of an individual client. In the course of acting, the solicitor becomes suspicious that funds in the possession of the client and to be used on the purchase derive from criminal activities. The solicitor decides that because of the suspicion, she cannot continue to act for the client. She terminates the retainer, avoiding the risk of tipping off or prejudicing an investigation (see **Chapter 7**). Since the retainer has come to an end, the solicitor will not be involved in an arrangement and will not facilitate the acquisition, retention, use or control of criminal property. In order to decide whether a report must nonetheless be made, the solicitor must consider:

- Does she know or suspect that another is engaged in money laundering? On the facts it appears that the client has in his possession criminal property. This would amount to engaging in money laundering as a result of the offence of acquisition, use or possession (PoCA 2002, s.329).
- Has the information on which her suspicion is based come into her possession as a result of business in the regulated sector? The solicitor is acting on the purchase of shares. This is likely to involve advice on the purchase of a specified investment and may consequently be an exempt regulated activity. Further, the transaction is likely to involve participation in a financial transaction. In either case, it would appear that the solicitor is acting within the regulated sector.

The conclusion is, subject to any defence which might be available (see below), that a protected disclosure should be made as soon as practicable.

Scenario 2

A solicitor is approached by a client for tax advice. She is asked to give advice relating to a legal tax avoidance scheme to be implemented in the UK. The advice given will not amount to an arrangement which facilitates the acquisition, retention, use or control of criminal property. However, in the course of taking instructions, the client discloses to the solicitor that he holds funds abroad derived from overseas trading which have not been disclosed to the appropriate tax authorities. The solicitor is not asked to give advice or provide any services relating to this fund. Should she, nonetheless, report her knowledge? She must consider:

- Does she know or suspect the client is engaged in money laundering? She possibly has in her possession funds which should have been disclosed to an overseas tax authority (and possibly to the UK tax authorities). Money laundering includes the offence of acquisition, use or possession or an act which would have constituted such an offence if done in the UK (PoCA 2002, s.340(11)). Further enquiries need to be made but if, following these enquiries, there appears to be knowledge or reasonable grounds for knowledge that the client is engaged in money laundering PoCA 2002, s.330 would appear to be relevant;
- Has the information on which her suspicion is based come into her possession as a result of business in the regulated sector? It appears that it has come into her possession as a result of tax advice and in consequence within the regulated sector.

The conclusion is again, subject to any defence which might be available (see below), that a protected disclosure should be made as soon as practicable.

5.2.4 Defences

There are three defences listed in PoCA 2002, s.330:

(a) reasonable excuse for not disclosing;
(b) privilege;
(c) lack of specified training.

Reasonable excuse

Section 330(6)(*a*) states:

> But a person does not commit an offence under this section if:
>
> (a) he has a reasonable excuse for not disclosing the information or other matter . . ..

Reasonable excuse for these purposes has yet to be defined by the courts. Solicitors should, therefore, treat this defence with care. The Law Society's *Money Laundering Guidance* suggests that solicitors always 'document the reason for not making the disclosure'.

Section 330(6)(*b*) provides a defence if the information came into the possession of the solicitor in privileged circumstances (see below). The Law Society's *Money Laundering Guidance* states:

> Crown Prosecution Service legal guidance for prosecutors indicates that if a solicitor forms a genuine but mistaken belief that legal professional privilege applies (for example the client misleads the solicitor and uses the advice for a criminal

purpose), the solicitor would be able to rely on the reasonable excuse defence, **www.cps.gov.uk**.

Privilege

Section 330(6)(*b*) states:

> But a person does not commit an offence under this section if . . .
>
> (b)   he is a professional legal adviser and the information or other matter came to him in privileged circumstances . . ..

Circumstances will give rise to privilege if communicated or given to the professional legal adviser in three cases (s.330(10)):

(a)   The information is communicated or given to the legal adviser by a client (or by the client's representative) in connection with the giving by the legal adviser of legal advice to the client.

(b)   The information is communicated or given to the legal adviser by a person (or by the person's representative) seeking legal advice from the adviser.

(c)   The information is communicated or given to the legal adviser by a person in connection with legal proceedings or contemplated legal proceedings.

However, PoCA 2002, s.330(11) makes it clear that subsection (10) does not apply to information or other matter which is communicated or given with the intention of furthering a criminal purpose.

These provisions can provide a valuable defence but it is clear that the dividing line between successfully claiming the defence and failing to do so is narrow. Solicitors must rely upon the defence with caution. Where necessary they should refer to the appropriate law on evidence and/or obtain specialist legal advice. A number of points can be made which should assist solicitors in determining whether the defence applies.

WHAT COMMUNICATIONS ARE PRIVILEGED?

Case law can be helpful in determining what amounts to privilege as a matter of law. The Law Society's *Money Laundering Guidance* in paragraphs 4.6–4.14 (see extract in **Appendix B1**) provides a useful overview of relevant cases.

PROTECTED DISCLOSURES – POCA 2002, S.337

Disclosures made as a result of an obligation to disclose under s.330 and made in accordance with s.337 will be protected (see **Paragraph 5.2**).

However, s.337 does not just apply to obligatory disclosures under s.330. A voluntary disclosure where a solicitor receives information giving rise to knowledge or suspicion of money laundering in the course of his trade, profession, business or employment will be protected from any claim for a breach of a duty of confidentiality or legal professional privilege regardless of whether the information came into the possession of the solicitor in the regulated sector or not. Consequently, solicitors making a disclosure in accordance with s.337 will be protected – erring on the side of caution is a safe option.

RELYING UPON THE PRIVILEGE DEFENCE

Despite the fact that a disclosure would be protected, a solicitor may choose not to make an obligatory disclosure under PoCA 2002, s.330 and rely upon the defence of privilege in s.330(6). To do so they would have to be satisfied as to two conditions:

- The information must have come to the solicitor in privileged circumstances. Not all communications made by a client are privileged, but only those communicated in connection with the giving or seeking of legal advice or in connection with or contemplation of legal proceedings.
- The information must not have been communicated or given with the intention of furthering a criminal purpose.

If the client or third party provides information which is unrelated to legal proceedings or the giving or receiving of legal advice, the first condition will not have been satisfied.

If the client provides the information with the intention of furthering a criminal purpose, the second condition will not have been satisfied. This leaves the possibility that a solicitor mistakenly believes the information received from a client is privileged but later it turns out that the client had, all along, intended to further a criminal purpose through communicating the information to the solicitor. When the Proceeds of Crime Bill was passing through the House of Lords an attempt was made to amend the privilege defence by including a defence where the information was privileged or there were reasonable grounds for believing it to be privileged. This amendment was not adopted but a statement by Lord Rooker (the Government spokesman in the House of Lords) and quoted in the Law Society's *Money Laundering Guidance* is helpful:

> The criminal law is quite clear: where a criminal offence is silent as to its mental element, the courts must read in the appropriate mental element.
> Therefore, in circumstances where a legal adviser did not know that information was not legally privileged, the courts would read in a requirement that he could not be convicted unless he did know.

The Law Society's *Money Laundering Guidance* goes on to state:

> The effect of this statement is that a solicitor therefore only commits an offence under section 330 for failure to disclose if he receives information in circumstances which he knows are not privileged.

As an alternative, the defence of reasonable excuse may be available in these circumstances (see **Paragraph 5.2.4**, and in particular the guidance from the Crown Prosecution Service). However the Law Society advises that a solicitor is not absolved from looking at all the circumstances; he should not close his eyes to the obvious and the genuineness of his belief will be judged by the care he exercised in those circumstances.

WHO IS A PROFESSIONAL LEGAL ADVISER?

Communications between lawyers and clients will be privileged at common law if the appropriate conditions apply. The circumstances in which the information is received is what is important, not the status of the person receiving the information. Consequently, at common law communications made to non-qualified members of a solicitor's staff are capable of being privileged and, in litigation, often communications made to and by experts can be protected as privileged.

Section 330(6) of the PoCA 2002 applies the defence of privilege to professional legal advisers. This would appear to rule out the defence where information was passed to a non-solicitor employee or, in litigation, to an expert. This anomaly was identified by the Law Society and brought to the attention of the Government. The Law Society's *Money Laundering Guidance* recognises that if this restricted definition of professional legal advisers applies 'it would mean that solicitors could not pass privileged information to their staff or experts in case they, in turn, felt they should disclose to NCIS'.

The Government's response was to provide a definition of the term professional legal adviser. This definition does not appear in PoCA 2002 but in the Money Laundering Regulations 2003 (for details of the regulations, see **Chapter 9**). Regulation 7(6) states: 'Professional legal adviser includes any person in whose hands information or other matter may come in privileged circumstances.'

Whilst it is not satisfactory to interpret primary legislation by using definitions in secondary legislation, the Money Laundering Regulations 2003 indicate a wider definition for this term which should, in appropriate cases, encompass a solicitor's non-qualified staff and experts.

Lack of specified training

The third defence appears in PoCA 2002, s.330(6) and (7) which provides a defence if a person:

(a) ... does not know or suspect that another is engaged in money laundering, and

(b) ... has not been provided by his employer with such training as is specified by the Secretary of State by order for the purposes of this section.

The offence in PoCA 2002, s.330 imposes a subjective and objective test of knowledge or suspicion (see **Paragraph 5.2**). This defence applies if the accused can show on a subjective or objective basis that he or she did not know or suspect another was engaged in money laundering.

In addition it is necessary to show that specified training had not been provided by the person's employer.

Employer for these purposes means someone who employs others, i.e. the defence will only apply to someone who is an employee, not a partner. Although the definition of employer and employment is extended by PoCA 2002, s.340(12) (see **Chapter 3**), this extended definition only applies to the terms where used for the purposes of a disclosure to a nominated officer.

The specified training requirements are contained in the Money Laundering Regulations 2003, SI 2003/3075. For details of these regulations, see **Chapter 9**. Regulation 3(1)(c) requires those carrying on relevant business to:

take appropriate measures so that relevant employees are –

(i) made aware of the provisions of these regulations, Part 7 of the Proceeds of Crime Act 2002 (money laundering) and sections 18 and 21A of the Terrorism Act 2000; and

(ii) given training in how to recognise and deal with transactions which may be related to money laundering.

Clearly it would be embarrassing for a firm (not to say unlawful under the regulations) not to provide employees with training and for an employee to use the defence in s.330(7). Firms must therefore ensure that employees are unable to use such a defence by providing the necessary level of training. For more details of the training obligations, see **Chapter 9**.

5.2.5   Illustrations II

The following illustrations indicate how a defence might apply to a possible charge under PoCA 2002, s.330.

Scenario 1

A solicitor is asked to provide tax advice to a client. The client admits that over the last three years he has not fully disclosed his income and capital gains to the Inland Revenue. The purpose of the solicitor's instructions is to advise on how to legitimise the situation. Does the solicitor have an obligation to disclose under PoCA 2002, s.330? He must consider:

- Does he know or suspect or have reasonable grounds for knowing or suspecting that the client is engaged in money laundering? On the basis that the client is likely to be in possession of criminal property, the answer would appear to be 'yes.'
- Did the information arise in the course of business in the regulated sector? Tax advice is within the regulated sector.

The initial conclusion therefore must be that a disclosure must be made. Do any of the defences apply? The obvious possibility is the defence of privilege under PoCA 2002, s.330(6). The following points can be made.

- The solicitor is a professional legal adviser.
- The information appears to have been provided in privileged circumstances, i.e. it was communicated by a client in connection with the giving by the solicitor of legal advice to the client.
- It does not appear that the information was communicated with the intention of furthering criminal conduct.

The conclusion is likely to be that the defence of privilege will apply and therefore there is no requirement to make the disclosure.

Note that if a disclosure was made (even though the information was privileged) the solicitor would not incur a liability for breach of his professional obligations in confidentiality or privilege on the basis that the disclosure would be a protected disclosure under PoCA 2002, s.337.

Scenario 2

A solicitor is acting for a client on a matrimonial dispute. In the course of giving advice relating to ancillary relief the solicitor discovers that the funds to be used in connection with a settlement may constitute the proceeds of tax evasion. Does the solicitor have a duty to report his knowledge or suspicion? He must consider:

- Does he know or suspect that another is engaged in money laundering? The answer would appear to be 'yes' since the funds are in the possession of an individual (his client or the other party to the proceedings) and his suspicion is that they are the proceeds of tax evasion.
- Did the information arise in the course of business in the regulated sector? This is more difficult. Advising on ancillary relief is unlikely to be a regulated activity under the Financial Services and Markets Act 2000. If, in the course of giving such advice, the solicitor has given advice about the tax affairs of his client, this will bring the matter within the regulated sector. Do the services involve participation in a financial or real property transaction? If real property is involved in the settlement, again this is likely to bring the matter into the regulated sector. Other financial settlement provisions could bring it within the meaning of a financial transaction. Probably the only safe course would be to assume that this is within the regulated sector.

- Would any defence arise? Since the information came into the possession of the solicitor in the course of giving legal advice or in connection with legal proceedings it would appear that it is privileged. Note, however, that privilege does not attach to a communication received from the other side. Consequently, the defence could only apply if the communication came from the client. Even if it turned out later that the client was intending to further a criminal purpose (by including the criminal proceeds in a financial settlement), the solicitor should either be able to rely upon Lord Rooker's statement in the House of Lords (no mental element – see above) or the reasonable excuse defence as per the Crown Prosecution Service's guidance (see **Paragraph 5.2.4**).

However, two further important points must be considered.

First, if the solicitor did report his knowledge or suspicion, this would be a protected disclosure and despite the fact that a defence might be available, no breach would occur of the solicitor's professional obligations relating to confidentiality or privilege.

Secondly, and more importantly, if the solicitor advises the client not to proceed and the solicitor chooses to withdraw from the retainer, the solicitor is unlikely to be involved in an arrangement. However, if the solicitor chooses to continue to act for the client, his future actions could themselves amount to a money laundering offence. The settlement could be an arrangement which facilitates the acquisition, use, retention or control of criminal property contrary to PoCA 2002, s.328. Advice suggesting the client should not disclose the details of the fund might amount to concealment contrary to PoCA 2002, s.327. Further, if any of the fund was to be paid into the solicitor's client account, this could amount to acquisition, use or possession contrary to PoCA 2002, s.329. Consequently, to avoid a money laundering offence, the solicitor should make an authorised disclosure (see **Chapter 4**) and only continue to act with appropriate consent. It is vital to recognise that the defence of privilege does not apply where there is a money laundering offence under PoCA 2002, ss.327–329.

For the sake of completeness, the earlier two illustrations are set out below with comments upon possible defences:

Scenario 1

A solicitor is acting in a corporate transaction – buying shares on behalf of an individual client. In the course of acting, the solicitor becomes suspicious that funds in the possession of the client and to be used on the purchase derive from criminal activities. The solicitor decides that, because of the suspicion, she cannot continue to act for the client. She terminates the retainer, avoiding the risk of tipping off or prejudicing an investigation (see **Chapter 7**). Since the retainer has come to an end, the solicitor will not be involved in an arrangement and will not facilitate the acquisition, retention, use or control of criminal property. In order to decide whether a report must, nonetheless be made, the solicitor must consider:

- Does she know or suspect that another is engaged in money laundering? On the facts it appears that the client has in his possession criminal property. This would amount to engaging in money laundering as a result of the offence of acquisition, use or possession (PoCA 2002, s.329).
- Has the information on which her suspicion is based come into his possession as a result of business in the regulated sector? The solicitor is acting on the

purchase of shares. This is likely to involve advice on the purchase of a specified investment and may consequently be an exempt regulated activity. Further, the transaction is likely to involve participation in a financial transaction. In either case, it would appear that the solicitor is acting within the regulated sector.

- Does the defence of privilege apply? Although the communication appears to be given by a client seeking legal advice, it also appears that the information is given with the intention of furthering a criminal purpose. The solicitor has decided not to act for the client and on that basis the assumption must be made that the solicitor believes that to continue to act would involve a criminal purpose.

The conclusion is that a protected disclosure must be made as soon as practicable. Failure to do so would risk prosecution under PoCA 2002, s.330.

Scenario 2

A solicitor is approached by a client for tax advice. She is asked to give advice relating to a legal tax avoidance scheme to be implemented in the UK. The advice given will not amount to an arrangement which facilitates the acquisition, retention, use or control of criminal property. However, in the course of taking instructions, the client discloses to the solicitor that he holds funds abroad derived from overseas trading which have not been disclosed to the appropriate tax authorities. The solicitor is not asked to give advice or provide any services relating to this fund. Should she, nonetheless, report her knowledge? She must consider:

- Does she know or suspect the client is engaged in money laundering? She possibly has in her possession funds which should have been disclosed to an overseas tax authority (and possibly to the UK tax authorities). Money laundering includes the offence of acquisition, use or possession or an act which would have constituted such an offence if done in the UK (PoCA 2002, s.340(11)). On the facts, there appears to be knowledge or reasonable grounds for knowledge that the client is engaged in money laundering. Further enquiries need to be made but if, following these enquiries, there appears to be knowledge or reasonable grounds for knowledge that the client is engaged in money laundering then PoCA 2002, s. 330 would appear to be a concern.
- Does any defence apply? It would appear that although the communication was made by a client to the solicitor, this communication was not made in connection with the giving of legal advice by the solicitor to the client. The solicitor is not required to give advice nor provide any legal services regarding this fund.

The conclusion is that a protected disclosure must be made as soon as practicable. Failure to do so would risk prosecution under PoCA 2002, s.330.

5.2.6 Penalty

Under section 334(2) a person guilty of an offence under PoCA 2002, s.330 is liable, on summary conviction, to imprisonment for a period of six months or to a fine not exceeding the statutory maximum or to both; on conviction on indictment, to imprisonment for a term not exceeding five years or to a fine or to both.

5.3 FAILURE TO DISCLOSE: REGULATED SECTOR (TERRORISM ACT 2000, S.21A)

5.3.1 The offence

Section 21A was inserted into the Terrorism Act 2000 by the Anti-terrorism, Crime and Security Act 2001. It states:

(1) A person commits an offence if each of the following three conditions is satisfied.

(2) The first condition is that he
    (a) knows or suspects, or
    (b) has reasonable grounds for knowing or suspecting,
    that another has committed an offence under any of sections 15 to 18.

(3) The second condition is that the information or other matter –
    (a) on which the knowledge or suspicion is based, or
    (b) which gives reasonable grounds for such knowledge or suspicion,
    came to him in the course of business in the regulated sector.

(4) The third condition is that he does not disclose the information or other matter to a constable or to a nominated officer as soon as practicable after it comes to him.

There are a number of points that can be made concerning this section and in particular the three conditions that must be satisfied before the offence is committed.

Condition 1

    . . . knows or suspects, or . . . has reasonable grounds for knowing or suspecting . . .

The offence can be committed where there is an objective or subjective test of knowledge or suspicion.

    . . . that another has committed an offence under any of sections 15 to 18
    [Terrorism Act 2000]

Section 15 creates an offence of fund raising for the purpose of terrorism. It is an offence to provide money or property or invite another to provide money or property intending it to be used or having reasonable cause to suspect that it will be used for terrorism. Further it is an offence to receive money or property intending it to be used or having reasonable cause to suspect that it will be used for terrorism.

Section 16 creates an offence of use or possession for the purpose of terrorism. It is an offence to use or possess money or property for the purpose of terrorism or intending it should be used for terrorism.

Section 17 creates an offence of funding arrangements. It is an offence for a person to enter into or to become concerned in an arrangement as a result of which money or other property is made available or is to be made available to another and there is knowledge or reasonable cause to suspect that it will or may be used for the purpose of terrorism.

Section 18 creates the offence of money laundering. Full details of this offence appear in **Chapter 3**.

Section 21A(11) provides that a person is to be taken to have committed an offence under sections 15–18 of the Terrorism Act 2000 if he has taken an action or has possession of money or property and he would have committed an offence if he had been in the UK at the time. Consequently, activities undertaken overseas can give rise to an obligation to report if such activities would have been an offence under the Terrorism Act 2000 if they had been undertaken in the UK.

Second Condition

> ... the information or other matter on which his knowledge or suspicion is based or which gives reasonable grounds for such knowledge or suspicion came to him in the course of business in the regulated sector.

The offence is limited to disclosing information which came into the possession of the solicitor in the course of business in the regulated sector. This term has been fully defined in **Paragraph 5.2.1**.

Third Condition

> ... he does not disclose the information or other matter to a constable or a nominated officer as soon as is practicable after it comes to him.'

The reference to a constable includes a reference to a person authorised for the purposes of this section by the Director General of NCIS (s.21A(14)). For practical purposes this means disclosure to NCIS. A nominated officer is defined in the same way as in PoCA 2002. Consequently, the nominated officer appointed by a firm for PoCA 2002 purposes will be the nominated officer for the purposes of Terrorism Act 2000 disclosures.

5.3.2 Law Society Guidance

Section 21A(6) Terrorism Act 2000 states:

> In deciding whether a person committed an offence under this section the court must consider whether he followed any relevant guidance which was at the time concerned:
>
> (a) issued by a supervisory authority or any other appropriate body;
> (b) approved by the Treasury; and
> (c) published in a manner it approved as appropriate in its opinion to bring the guidance to the attention of persons likely to be affected by it.

A supervisory body is defined in the Terrorism Act 2000, Sched. 3A and the term includes the Law Society.

The Law Society issued guidance to the solicitors' profession (*Money Laundering Guidance: Professional Ethics*, Pilot, January 2004). Extracts from the *Money Laundering Guidance* appear in the text of this book and in **Appendix B1**. The Law Society's *Money Laundering Guidance* is described as a pilot and has not been submitted to the Treasury for approval. Consequently, section 21A(6) will not apply technically. However, as stated in the *Money Laundering Guidance*, a court 'may still take it into consideration' in deciding whether an offence has been committed.

5.3.3 Defences

There are two defences listed in section 21A(5):

(a) Reasonable excuse for not disclosing.
(b) Privilege.

Reasonable excuse

Section 21A(5)(*a*) states:

> But a person does not commit an offence under this section if
>
> (c) he has a reasonable excuse for not disclosing the information or other matter . . ..

Reasonable excuse for these purposes has yet to be defined by the courts. Solicitors should, therefore, treat this defence with care. The Law Society's *Money Laundering Guidance* suggests that solicitors always 'document the reason for not making the disclosure'.

The commentary earlier in **Paragraph 5.2.4** (reasonable excuse defence in PoCA 2002, s.330) would appear to be relevant.

Privilege

Section 21A(5)(*b*) states:

> But a person does not commit an offence under this section if . . .
>
> (b) he is a professional legal adviser and the information or other matter came to him in privileged circumstances . . ..

Circumstances will give rise to privilege if communicated or given to the professional legal adviser in three cases (s.21A(8)).

(a) The information is communicated or given to the legal adviser by a client (or by the client's representative) in connection with the giving by the legal adviser of legal advice to the client.

(b) The information is communicated or given to the legal adviser by a person (or by the person's representative) seeking legal advice from the adviser.

(c) The information is communicated or given to the legal adviser by a person in connection with legal proceedings or contemplated legal proceedings.

However, section 21A(9) makes it clear that subsection (8) does not apply to information or other matter which is communicated or given with the intention of furthering a criminal purpose.

The wording of the privilege defence is the same as the defence to PoCA 2002, s.330. The detailed commentary on that defence earlier in **Paragraph 5.2.4** would appear to apply equally to the defence in the Terrorism Act 2000.

5.3.4 Penalty

Under section 21A(12) a person guilty of an offence under the Terrorism Act 2000, s.21A is liable, on summary conviction, to imprisonment for a period of six months or to a fine not exceeding the statutory maximum or to both; on conviction on indictment, to imprisonment for a term not exceeding five years or to a fine or to both.

CHAPTER 6

Failure to disclose: nominated officers

6.1 INTRODUCTION

As noted in **Chapter 5**, there are two other offences contained in the Proceeds of Crime Act 2002 (PoCA 2002) arising from a failure to disclose knowledge or suspicion of money laundering. Both these offences are aimed at nominated officers. These are:

- Failure to disclose: nominated officers in the regulated sector (PoCA 2002, s.331)
- Failure to disclose: other nominated officers (PoCA 2002, s.332).

These two offences are dealt with below.

6.2 FAILURE TO DISCLOSE: NOMINATED OFFICERS IN THE REGULATED SECTOR (POCA 2002, S.331)

6.2.1 The offence

Section 331 of the PoCA 2002 states:

(1) A person nominated to receive disclosures under section 330 commits an offence if the conditions in subsections (2) to (4) are satisfied.

(2) The first condition is that he
(a) knows or suspects, or
(b) has reasonable grounds for knowing or suspecting,
that another person is engaged in money laundering.

(3) The second condition is that the information or other matter
(a) on which his knowledge or suspicion is based, or
(b) which gives reasonable grounds for such knowledge or suspicion,
came to him in consequence of a disclosure made under section 330.

(4) The third condition is that he does not make the required disclosure as soon as is practicable after the information or other matter comes to him.

There are a number of points that can be made concerning this section and in particular the three conditions that must be satisfied before the offence is committed.

Subsection (1)

> A person nominated to receive disclosures . . .

This offence is aimed at those appointed as a nominated officer of a firm. Section 330(9) states that a disclosure to a nominated officer is a disclosure which is made to a person nominated by the alleged offender's employer to receive authorised disclosures under section 330 and is made in the course of the alleged offender's employment and in accordance with the procedure established by the employer for the purpose.

Although, in the context of a nominated officer, PoCA 2002 refers to a person's employer and a person's employment, section 340(12) provides that:

> references to a person's employer include any body, association or organisation (including a voluntary organisation) in connection with whose activities the person exercises a function (whether or not for gain or reward).

The subsection goes on to state that references to employment must be construed accordingly.

As noted in **Chapter 3** it is not strictly necessary for the nominated officer to be a partner or principal in a firm of solicitors. However, in practice, the individual should be a senior member of the firm's management. Because severe penalties can be imposed upon the nominated officer for a failure to comply with his obligations under PoCA 2002, care should be taken to ensure that the nominated officer is aware of his obligations (this is particularly the case when a non-partner or principal is appointed).

> . . . under section 330 . . .

Section 330 requires a disclosure of knowledge or suspicion or reasonable grounds for knowledge or suspicion of money laundering to a nominated officer or to NCIS. Details of this offence can be found in **Chapter 5.**

First Condition

> . . . (a) knows or suspects, or
> (b) has reasonable grounds for knowing or suspecting . . .

Like the offence contained in PoCA 2002, s.330, this offence can be committed where the nominated officer has knowledge or suspicion or reasonable grounds for knowledge or suspicion. A nominated officer can be found guilty under section 331 even if, subjectively, the nominated officer had no actual knowledge or suspicion of matters upon which the charge is based. If the nominated officer has reasonable grounds for knowledge or suspicion, that will be sufficient for the purposes of this section.

... that another is engaged in money laundering ...

The reference to another means that as with the offence under PoCA 2002, s.330, this offence can be committed where the nominated officer's knowledge or suspicion relates to the conduct of a client or some third party.

Further, the definition of money laundering in PoCA 2002, s.340(11) will apply to this offence. It states:

Money laundering is an act which –

(a) constitutes an offence under section 327,328 or 329,
(b) constitutes an attempt, conspiracy or incitement to commit an offence specified in paragraph (a),
(c) constitutes aiding, abetting, counselling or procuring the commission of an offence specified in paragraph (a), or
(d) would constitute an offence specified in paragraph (a), (b), or (c) if done in the United Kingdom.

For further commentary on this definition, see **Chapter 5**.

Second Condition

... the information or other matter

(a) on which his knowledge or suspicion is based, or
(b) which gives reasonable grounds for such knowledge or suspicion,

came to him in consequence of a disclosure made under section 330.

This condition is the key to the offence. The nominated officer only commits an offence if he or she fails to act on an internal disclosure made by another member of the firm under PoCA 2002, s.330.

It is vital that all firms adopt appropriate procedures for internal disclosure of knowledge or suspicion of money laundering and that from these procedures it is clear when a formal disclosure has been made to a nominated officer. Many firms will adopt procedures which allow informal discussions to be held between members of staff and more senior members of the management team where there is concern over an individual's responsibilities under PoCA 2002. Sometimes discussions are held with the nominated officer (perhaps on a no-name basis). Where applicable these procedures must be clearly identified as discussions and not as disclosures. Only by ensuring that procedures identify when a formal disclosure has been made can the nominated officer be sure when potential liability under section 331 arises.

One possibility is for firms to require all internal authorised or protected disclosures to be made formally, in writing and in an approved firm format. Under PoCA 2002, s.339 the Secretary of State may, by order, prescribe the form and manner in which a disclosure under section 330 (failure to report; regulated sector) or section 338 (authorised disclosures) must be made.

Although at the time of writing, no order has been made under section 339, it is clear from the wording that the prescribed form could apply to internal disclosures as well as to external disclosures. Until such time as an order is made, it is open to the senior management in the firm to determine the form of internal disclosures. A suggested format for such internal disclosures is contained in **Appendix C3**.

The disclosure by a member of the firm to a nominated officer in accordance with PoCA 2002, s.330 does not automatically require an external disclosure by the nominated officer. It is still necessary for the nominated officer to have knowledge or suspicion or reasonable grounds for knowledge or suspicion that another person is engaged in money laundering and for that information to have been received in consequence of a disclosure under section 330. It is possible that a nominated officer, on receiving the disclosure under section 330, considers its contents and comes to the conclusion that there are insufficient grounds to give rise to knowledge or suspicion (either subjectively or objectively).

Where a fee earner makes a disclosure under section 330 the nominated officer should consider the circumstances of the report. As noted previously, Regulation 7 of the Money Laundering Regulations 2003 (see **Chapter 9**) enforces this requirement when the Regulations apply. It states:

> Where a disclosure is made to a nominated officer, he must consider it in the light of any relevant information which is available to [the firm] and determine whether it gives rise to such knowledge or suspicion . . .

If, in the light of any internal consideration, the nominated officer comes to the conclusion, on both a subjective and objective basis, that there are no grounds for knowledge or suspicion, he or she will have no obligation to report to the authorities. This might apply where, for example, the fee earner is a junior member of staff or a recently joined employee. A particular aspect of a transaction may arouse his or her suspicions and consequently a disclosure under section 330 might be made to the nominated officer. On considering the report along with other information held in the firm (including past dealings with the client) the nominated officer may come to the conclusion that there are no grounds for knowledge or suspicion (either subjectively or objectively).

Finally, nominated officers should consider carefully the fact that for their obligations to have arisen under section 331 there must have been a disclosure under section 330. In other words, the disclosure under section 330 must have followed information received in the course of business in the regulated sector. The definition of the regulated sector can be found, together with commentary, in **Chapter 5**.

This is an important point. Section 332 of the PoCA 2002 (see below) imposes an obligation on nominated officers to disclose to the authorities any knowledge or suspicion of money laundering received by way of an internal disclosure outside the regulated sector. For such an obligation to arise, the test of knowledge or suspicion is a subjective test. The objective test only applies to disclosures made in the regulated sector.

Third Condition

> ... he does not make the required disclosure ...

The required disclosure is disclosure of the information giving rise to knowledge or suspicion of another being engaged in money laundering. The disclosure must be to a person authorised for the purpose by the Director General of NCIS (PoCA 2002, s.331(5)(*a*)). Disclosure to NCIS in the usual way (see **Chapter 10**) will satisfy this requirement. Section 331(5)(*b*) provides that the form and manner of this disclosure can be prescribed by order under PoCA 2002, s.339. At the time of writing no such order has been made.

Any disclosure made will be treated as a protected disclosure under PoCA 2002, s.337. (For the definition of a protected disclosure see **Chapter 5**.) Provided the conditions in the definition are satisfied, the nominated officer will not be in breach of any duty of confidentiality or obligations under the concept of legal professional privilege.

> ... as soon as is practicable after the information or other matter comes to him.

Both the third condition and the benefit of protected disclosures require the disclosure to be made as soon as practicable after the information comes into the possession of the nominated officer. Consequently, to avoid committing the crime and to benefit from the protection of section 337 (protected disclosures), nominated officers must not delay in making their disclosures.

6.2.2 Law Society Guidance

Section 331(7) of the PoCA 2002 states:

> In deciding whether a person committed an offence under this section the court must consider whether he followed any relevant guidance which was at the time concerned:
>
> (a) issued by a supervisory authority or any other appropriate body;
> (b) approved by the Treasury; and
> (c) published in a manner it approved as appropriate in its opinion to bring the guidance to the attention of persons likely to be affected by it.

A supervisory body is defined in PoCA 2002, Sched. 9, and the term includes the Law Society.

As noted in **Chapter 5**, the Law Society has issued guidance to the solicitors' profession (*Money Laundering Guidance: Professional Ethics*, Pilot,

January 2004). Extracts from the *Money Laundering Guidance* appear in the text of this book and in **Appendix B1**. The Law Society's *Money Laundering Guidance* is described as a pilot and has not been submitted to the Treasury for approval. Consequently, section 331(7) will not apply technically. However, as stated in the *Money Laundering Guidance*, a court 'may still take it into consideration' in deciding whether an offence has been committed under section 331.

6.2.3 Defences

There is only one defence in section 331(6). This states: '. . . a person does not commit an offence under this section if he has a reasonable excuse for not disclosing the information or other matter.'

As noted in **Chapter 5**, reasonable excuse for these purposes has yet to be defined by the courts. Solicitors should, therefore, treat this defence with care. The Law Society's *Money Laundering Guidance* suggests that solicitors always 'document the reason for not making the disclosure'. Note also, the circumstances where this defence might apply in relation to privileged information.

However, in relation to the defence available to a charge under PoCA 2002, s.331 what is notable is not the reasonable excuse defence but the lack of a privilege defence.

Take the following illustration from **Chapter 5**.

A solicitor is asked to provide tax advice to a client. The client admits that over the last three years he has not fully disclosed his income and capital gains to the Inland Revenue. The purpose of the solicitor's instructions is to advise on how to legitimise the situation. Does the solicitor have an obligation to disclose under PoCA 2002, s.330? He must consider:

- Does he know or suspect or have reasonable grounds for knowing or suspecting that the client is engaged in money laundering? On the basis that the client is likely to be in possession of criminal property, the answer would appear to be yes.
- Did the information arise in the course of business in the regulated sector? Tax advice is within the regulated sector.

The initial conclusion therefore must be that a disclosure must be made. Do any of the defences apply? The obvious possibility is the defence of privilege under PoCA 2002, s.330(6). The following points can be made.

- The solicitor is a professional legal adviser.
- The information appears to have been provided in privileged circumstances, i.e. it was communicated by a client in connection with the giving by the solicitor of legal advice to the client.
- It does not appear that the information was communicated with the intention of furthering criminal conduct.

The likely conclusion is that the defence of privilege will apply and therefore there is no requirement to make the disclosure.

However, the firm may have adopted a policy that members of the firm should always report any knowledge or suspicion of money laundering to the nominated officer. It is then for the nominated officer to determine whether or not a report should be made to NCIS. This is a sensible policy since it ensures that members of the firm are covered by making such internal reports and allows the nominated officer (who should be more familiar with the detail of the law) to make the final decision.

If the solicitor, in this scenario, reports his knowledge or suspicion to the nominated officer, even though the information came into the possession of the solicitor in privileged circumstances, the nominated officer is unlikely to have received the information in privileged circumstances. The information was not communicated to the nominated officer by the client in connection with the giving by the nominated officer of legal advice to the client. Even if it could be argued that the information was privileged, there is no available defence of privilege in PoCA 2002, s.331. Therefore, on the face of it, if the solicitor discloses his knowledge or suspicion to the nominated officer, even if the information came to the solicitor in privileged circumstances, the nominated officer is obliged to disclose to NCIS.

The Law Society's *Money Laundering Guidance* suggests in these circumstances the reasonable excuse defence might apply. The guidance states: 'It is the Law Society's view that in such circumstances a nominated officer has a reasonable excuse under section 331(6) for not disclosing.'

Some firms approach this problem in a different way. Many firms will have experienced litigators as partners or employees who will be well versed in the legal concept of privilege. An alternative approach is for a firm to identify an individual or small group of individuals (the privilege committee) who have the necessary expertise and to require, as part of the firm's money laundering policy, members of the firm initially to disclose details of any knowledge or suspicion of money laundering to the privilege committee. A decision can then be made as to whether the information is or is not privileged. If it is not privileged a formal disclosure can be made to the nominated officer, who in turn will then disclose to NCIS in accordance with PoCA 2002, s.331. If it is decided that the information is privileged, no formal internal disclosure is made and the issue of whether or not the nominated officer can rely upon the privileged circumstances in relation to his duty to disclose under section 331 becomes redundant.

A number of further points can be made regarding the possible use of this policy. First, an argument might be made that by disclosing information to the privilege committee, that committee is now in possession of information suggesting someone is engaged in money laundering. The information did not come into their possession in privileged circumstances for the same reason noted above in relation to the nominated officer. Does this information require them to now report to the nominated officer? If such a strict interpretation is placed upon the meaning of privileged circumstances, surely an equally strict interpretation should be placed upon the requirement that the information came to the privilege committee in the course of business in the regulated sector. It could be argued that the information did not come into their possession as a result of such business but in accordance with the firm's internal reporting procedures.

Secondly, if a firm chooses to adopt such a policy it should ensure that regardless of what decision is reached by the privilege committee appointed to consider the question of privilege, the fee earner who first brought his or her knowledge or suspicion to the attention of the committee must have the right to disclose his or her knowledge or suspicion to the nominated officer. Only in this way will the fee earner be covered in respect of any defence (if an authorised disclosure is required) or obligation (if a duty to disclose under PoCA 2002, s.330 arises).

6.2.4 Penalty

Under section 334(2) a person guilty of an offence under PoCA 2002, s.331 is liable, on summary conviction, to imprisonment for a period of six months or to a fine not exceeding the statutory maximum or to both; on conviction on indictment, to imprisonment for a term not exceeding five years or to a fine or to both.

6.3 FAILURE TO DISCLOSE: OTHER NOMINATED OFFICERS (POCA, S.332)

6.3.1 The offence

Section 332 of the PoCA 2002 states:

(1) A person nominated to receive disclosures under section 337 or section 338 commits an offence if the conditions in subsections (2) to (4) are satisfied.

(2) The first condition is that he knows or suspects that another person is engaged in money laundering.

(3) The second condition is that the information or other matter on which his knowledge or suspicion is based came to him in consequence of a disclosure made under section 337 or 338.

(4) The third condition is that he does not make the required disclosure as soon as is practicable after the information or other matter comes to him.

The wording of this section is very similar to the wording in PoCA 2002, s.331. It again is a criminal offence aimed at those appointed as nominated officers and the section obliges a nominated officer to make a required disclosure if the circumstances set out in the section apply. Since the wording of this section is similar to section 331, the commentary above on the application of section 331 can be applied with the following two points of contrast.

(1) Section 332 applies where the nominated officer receives disclosure under PoCA 2002, s.337 or s.338; section 331 applies where there is receipt of a disclosure under PoCA 2002, s.330.

This is an important contrast. Obviously, a disclosure under PoCA 2002, s.330 will only apply if the information on which the disclosure is based has been received in the course of business in the regulated sector. Section 332 will require a nominated officer to make a required disclosure where the original information was received in the regulated or non-regulated sector.

Section 332 refers to the nominated officer receiving a disclosure under PoCA 2002, s.337 or s.338. Section 337 covers protected disclosures and section 338 covers authorised disclosures. Protected disclosures cover a wide range of disclosures. Section 337 provides that such a disclosure is not to be taken to be a breach of any restriction on the disclosure of information (however imposed) if three conditions are satisfied. These three conditions are:

- The information or other matter disclosed came to the person making the disclosure in the course of his trade, profession, business or employment.
- The information caused the discloser to know or suspect or gave him reasonable grounds for knowing or suspecting that another was engaged in money laundering.
- The disclosure was made to a constable, a customs officer or a nominated officer as soon as is practicable after the information or other matter comes to the discloser.

Three circumstances will give rise to protected disclosures. Only the first in the list below would be relevant for the purposes of section 332. The other two would be disclosures in accordance with section 330 and thus the nominated officer's obligations would arise under section 331. In all circumstances the solicitor concerned will not be involved in an arrangement which would facilitate the acquisition, retention, use or control of criminal property.

- In the course of business in the non-regulated sector a solicitor knows or suspects that a person is engaged in money laundering and makes a disclosure to a nominated officer (even though there is no legal requirement for him to do so).
- In the course of business in the regulated sector a solicitor knows or suspects or has reasonable grounds for knowing or suspecting that a person is engaged in money laundering and makes a disclosure to a nominated officer.
- In the course of business in the regulated sector a solicitor knows or suspects or has reasonable grounds for knowing or suspecting that a person is engaged in money laundering and makes a disclosure to a nominated officer even though the defence of privilege applies.

Section 332 also applies where a disclosure is made to a nominated officer by way of a defence to a possible charge under PoCA 2002, ss.327–329 (the money laundering offences) – otherwise known as an authorised disclosure (see **Chapter 3**). Authorised disclosures will be made by way of defence regardless of whether the knowledge or suspicion of money laundering arose in the course of business in the regulated sector.

(2) Section 332 applies where the nominated officer knows or suspects that another person is engaged in money laundering; section 331 applies where the nominated officer knows or suspects or has reasonable grounds for knowing or suspecting that another is engaged in money laundering.

The objective test, when assessing whether the nominated officer knew or suspected another was engaged in money laundering only applies to section 331. For section 332, the nominated officer must know or suspect using a subjective test only.

6.3.2 Defences

Again, there is only one defence in section 332(6). This states '. . . a person does not commit an offence under this section if he has a reasonable excuse for not disclosing the information or other matter'.

The commentary on this defence as it applies to section 331 would appear to be relevant.

6.3.3 Penalty

Under section 334(2) a person guilty of an offence under PoCA 2002, s.332 is liable, on summary conviction, to imprisonment for a period of six months or to a fine not exceeding the statutory maximum or to both; on conviction on indictment, to imprisonment for a term not exceeding five years or to a fine or to both.

6.4 CONCLUSION

Given a combination of PoCA 2002, ss.331 and 332, it appears that a nominated officer will be required to disclose to NCIS any disclosure received from other members of the firm where such a disclosure gives rise to knowledge or suspicion on the part of the nominated officer of another engaging in money laundering (reasonable grounds for knowledge or suspicion will be sufficient if the obligation arises under s.331). This will be the case regardless of whether or not the member of the firm making the initial disclosure to the nominated officer is obliged to make the disclosure (as a result of PoCA 2002, s.330) or wishes to make the disclosure by way of a defence (PoCA 2002, s.338).

Consequently, it is vital that firms are able to clearly identify when a member of the firm has made a formal report to the nominated officer. It is, perhaps, safer for firms to encourage fee earners and others with concerns to discuss these concerns informally with more senior members of the firm rather than with the nominated officer. This should avoid inadvertently imposing an obligation upon the nominated officer to report to NCIS where there is a defence (e.g. privilege) or where no obligation to report arises (e.g. information arising in the non-regulated sector).

CHAPTER 7

Disclosures which prejudice an investigation

7.1 INTRODUCTION

There are two offences involving disclosures which are likely to prejudice an investigation. The first is contained in PoCA 2002, s.333 and is referred to by the designation tipping off. The second offence is contained in PoCA 2002, s.342 under the heading offences of prejudicing investigation. Both these offences are covered in this chapter.

The main distinction to be drawn between these two offences is the timing of the disclosure. Tipping off applies only where an authorised or protected disclosure has been made and a further disclosure is likely to prejudice an investigation. Section 342 does not require an authorised or protected disclosure to have been made.

7.2 TIPPING OFF (PoCA 2002, S.333)

7.2.1 The offence

Section 333(1) of the PoCA 2002 states:

> A person commits an offence if:
>
> (a) he knows or suspects that a disclosure falling within section 337 or 338 has been made, and
> (b) he makes a disclosure which is likely to prejudice any investigation which might be conducted following the disclosure referred to in paragraph (a).

For this offence to be committed, the solicitor must know or suspect that a disclosure has been made which is an authorised disclosure under PoCA 2002, s.338 or a protected disclosure under PoCA 2002, s.337. (For details of authorised disclosure, see **Chapter 3**; for details of protected disclosures, see **Chapter 5**.) It is sufficient, in both cases, that the disclosure has been made to a firm's nominated officer. It is not necessary for the initial disclosure to have been made externally to NCIS.

The second disclosure referred to in sub-paragraph (b) can be to the person referred to in the report (i.e. the person suspected of involvement in money laundering) or to any other person. Consequently, if the initial disclosure was made concerning a solicitor's client, the offence of tipping off can potentially be committed if the second disclosure (likely to prejudice an investigation) is made to:

(a) the client;
(b) any other adviser to the client (e.g. accountant, estate agent etc.);
(c) the person on the other side of the transaction;
(d) the other side's solicitor;
(e) the other side's other representative or agent.

If the initial disclosure was made concerning the other side's client, then the second disclosure (likely to prejudice an investigation) could also give rise to a criminal offence if it is made to any of those listed above including the solicitor's own innocent client.

The Law Society's *Money Laundering Guidance* states 'It is . . . not tipping off to include a paragraph about your obligations under the money launder-ing legislation in your firm's standard client care letter.' For an indication of possible terms of business, see **Chapter 11**.

It is not necessary that the solicitor knows that an initial disclosure has been made under PoCA 2002, ss.337 or 338. It is sufficient that the solicitor simply suspects that such a disclosure has been made.

Consequently, it is important that the firm's internal procedures include a requirement that once an authorised or protected disclosure has been made to the firm's nominated officer, no communication should be made by any fee earner concerning that transaction matter without the consent of the nomi-nated officer. In this way, firms can protect fee earners from inadvertently committing an offence under section 333 (tipping off).

Before making a protected or authorised disclosure to the firm's nomi-nated officer, fee earners should be permitted to make enquiries concerning a client or other party to the transaction in order to allay any possible causes for concern. Following these enquiries, the firm can then decide whether to act for a client or continue to act for an existing client. Since these enquiries will be made before any protected or authorised disclosure, the commun-ication made to a client or other person cannot give rise to an offence under section 333 (tipping off). However, care must be taken regarding these enquiries since it is still possible that such communications could give rise to an offence under PoCA 2002, s.342 (see **Paragraph 7.3.1**).

For the offence to be committed, it is necessary under subparagraph (2) for the accused to have made a second disclosure 'which is likely to preju-dice any investigation conducted following the [protected or authorised] disclosure . . .'. Two points need to be made regarding the wording of sub-paragraph (2).

First, the subparagraph does not require the accused to know or suspect that the second disclosure is likely to prejudice any investigation. This, it would appear, is simply a question of the prosecution showing that, as a matter of fact, the second disclosure was likely to prejudice any investigation. There is a defence (see **Paragraph 7.2.2**) that the accused did not know or suspect that the disclosure was likely to be prejudicial. However, since this appears in the statute as a defence, the onus of proof will rest with the accused. If the prosecution are able to show that, as a matter of fact, the second disclosure was prejudicial, it might be difficult for the accused to adduce evidence that, on a subjective basis, he or she did not know or suspect.

Secondly, what amounts to a likelihood of prejudicing an investigation will, ultimately, be for the courts to decide. However, it is clear from the wording of the paragraph that the investigation prejudiced by the second disclosure must have been conducted following the protected or authorised disclosure. If the second disclosure is prejudicial to some other investigation, section 333 (tipping off) will not apply (but perhaps, in these circumstances, there could be a prosecution under PoCA 2002, s.342 (see **Paragraph 7.3.1**)).

7.2.2 Defences

There are three defences listed in subsection (2). This states:

(2) But a person does not commit an offence under subsection (1) if –

(a) he did not know or suspect that the disclosure was likely to be prejudicial as mentioned in subsection (1);
(b) the disclosure is made in carrying out a function he has relating to the enforcement of any provision of this Act or of any other enactment relating to criminal conduct or benefit from criminal conduct;
(c) he is a professional legal adviser and the disclosure falls within subsection (3).

The wording of subsection (2) is replicated by way of a defence to a charge under PoCA 2002, s.342 (offences of prejudicing an investigation). Since the same defences can apply to both offences, these defences are dealt with in detail after the commentary on PoCA 2002, s.342 in **Paragraph 7.3.1**.

7.2.3 Penalty

Under section 334(2), a person guilty of an offence under PoCA 2002, s.333 is liable, on summary conviction, to imprisonment for a period of six months or to a fine not exceeding the statutory maximum or to both; on conviction on indictment, to imprisonment for a term not exceeding five years or to a fine or to both.

7.3 OFFENCES OF PREJUDICING INVESTIGATION (PoCA 2002, S.342)

7.3.1 The offence

Section 342 states:

(1) This section applies if a person knows or suspects that an appropriate officer (or in Scotland) a proper person is acting (or proposing to act) in connection with a confiscation investigation, a civil recovery investigation or a money laundering investigation which is being or is about to be conducted.

(2) The person commits an offence if –
   (a) he makes a disclosure which is likely to prejudice the investigation, or
   (b) he falsifies, conceals, destroys or otherwise disposes of, or causes or permits the falsification, concealment, destruction or disposal of, documents which are relevant to the investigation.

For the purposes of money laundering, this offence therefore applies where a solicitor (or member of staff) knows or suspects that an appropriate officer is acting or proposing to act in connection with a money laundering investigation and a disclosure is made which is likely to prejudice the investigation.

The offence can be committed at any stage of a transaction, whether or not a disclosure has been made. However, unlike the tipping off offence, there is no need for a protected or authorised disclosure to have been made. It is just necessary that there is knowledge or suspicion that a money laundering investigation is or is about to be undertaken. It is, however, likely to be relevant to solicitors, for example, where they have knowledge or suspicion of money laundering (either by the client or a third person) and they are considering making a report to NCIS. In this situation, if they choose to disclose to their client, or the other side, that they intend making a report to NCIS, this disclosure could give rise to an offence under PoCA 2002, s.342.

The reference in the section to an appropriate person is a reference to (PoCA 2002, s.378):

(a) an accredited financial investigator;
(b) a constable;
(c) a customs officer.

Further, for the purposes of section 342, in relation to a money laundering investigation, a person authorised for the purposes of money laundering investigations by the Director General of NCIS is also an appropriate officer.

A money laundering investigation is an investigation into whether a person has committed a money laundering offence (PoCA 2002, s.341(4)). A money laundering offence is defined in section 340(11) and is described fully in **Chapter 5**.

Like the offence of tipping off, the prohibited disclosure can be made to:

(a) the client;
(b) any other adviser to the client (e.g. accountant, estate agent etc.);
(c) the person on the other side of the transaction;
(d) the other side's solicitor;
(e) the other side's other representative or agent; or
(f) any other person.

The offence (again like the tipping off offence) does not require knowledge or suspicion that the disclosure is likely to prejudice the investigation. It is sufficient that, as a matter of fact, the disclosure is likely to prejudice the investigation (note the defence that the accused did not know or suspect that the disclosure was likely to prejudice an investigation – for a commentary upon this defence, see **Paragraph 7.4**).

7.3.2 Defences

This topic is dealt with in **Paragraph 7.4**.

7.3.3 Penalty

Under section 342(7) a person guilty of an offence under PoCA 2002, s.342 is liable, on summary conviction, to imprisonment for a period not exceeding six months or to a fine not exceeding the statutory maximum or to both; on conviction on indictment, to imprisonment for a term not exceeding five years or to a fine or to both.

7.4 DEFENCES APPLICABLE TO PoCA 2002, SS.333 AND 342

7.4.1 Introduction

As noted above, the three defences available to a charge under section 333 (tipping off) and section 342 (offences of prejudicing an investigation) are almost identical. The defence in section 333 is to be found in subsection (2); the defence in section 342 in subsection (3). These two subsections state (the wording from section 333(2) in round brackets with the alternative wording of section 342(4) in square brackets):

a person does not commit an offence under subsection (1) [2(a)] if-

(a) he (did) [does] not know or suspect that the disclosure was (is) likely to (be prejudicial as mentioned in subsection (1)) [prejudice the investigation];
(b) the disclosure is made in (carrying out a function he has relating to the enforcement of any provision of this Act) [the exercise of a function under this Act] or of any other enactment relating to criminal conduct or benefit

from criminal conduct [or in compliance with a requirement imposed under or by virtue of this Act] ;

(c) he is a professional legal adviser and the disclosure falls within subsection (3)[4].

Each defence will be dealt with in turn.

7.4.2 Section 333(2)(*a*) and section 342(3)(*a*)

... he (did) [does] not know or suspect that the disclosure was (is) likely to (be prejudicial as mentioned in subsection (1)) [prejudice the investigation] ...

As noted in the commentary on the two offences, there are no requirements in the offences themselves for the accused to know or suspect that their disclosure is likely to prejudice an investigation. The prosecution are likely to have to show that, as a matter of fact, the disclosure was likely to be prejudicial. However, by way of a defence, it is open for the accused to show, on a subjective basis, that he or she did not know or suspect that the disclosure would prejudice an investigation. The onus clearly shifts to the accused to prove the existence of evidence to support the defence. Given that the prosecution will already have adduced evidence that either the accused knew or suspected that a protected or authorised disclosure had been made or that the accused knew or suspected that a money laundering investigation was being or about to be conducted, it might be a difficult onus to discharge.

Undue reliance should not be placed upon this defence.

7.4.3 Section 333(2)(*b*) and section 342(3)(*b*)

... the disclosure is made in (carrying out a function he has relating to the enforcement of any provision of this Act) [the exercise of a function under this Act] or of any other enactment relating to criminal conduct or benefit from criminal conduct [or in compliance with a requirement imposed under or by virtue of this Act] ...

This defence is clearly aimed at law enforcement officers who, in carrying out their law enforcement activities, may make disclosures which technically could be prohibited by these sections. It is unlikely to be of any benefit to solicitors.

7.4.4 Section 333(2)(*c*) and section 342(3)(*c*)

... he is a professional legal adviser and the disclosure falls within subsection (3)[4].

This is clearly the most relevant of the defences applicable to solicitors. Sections 333(3) and 342(4) (the wording in both subsections is identical) state:

A disclosure falls within this subsection if it is a disclosure –

(a) to (or to a representative of) a client of the professional legal adviser in connection with the giving by the adviser of legal advice to the client, or

(b) to any person in connection with legal proceedings or contemplated legal proceedings.

However, the disclosure will not fall within the terms of this defence if it is made 'with the intention of furthering a criminal purpose'. (PoCA 2002, ss.333(4) and 342(5).)

The wording of this defence is similar to the defence of privilege contained in PoCA 2002, s.330 (see **Chapter 5**). However, it should be appreciated that the defence of privilege applies to information given *to* a professional legal adviser by a client or other person. This defence applies to information given *by* a professional legal adviser to a client or other person.

Keep in mind that the defence is only necessary if a disclosure has been made in the circumstances envisaged by either section 333 or section 342; in other words, a disclosure has been made which is likely to prejudice an investigation. Despite this fact, it might be possible for a solicitor to make such a disclosure to his or her client or to a third person if the defence applies.

This defence was considered in detail by Dame Elizabeth Butler-Sloss, P in her judgment in the case of *P* v. *P* [2003] EW HC Fam 2260. Her judgment sets out the facts of the case – extracts from the judgment are set out below:

> The husband and wife were married in April 1979. . . In January 2002, the wife filed her divorce petition. . . The wife made her application for financial relief, and a Financial Dispute Resolution appointment was listed for 18 July 2003 before a High Court Judge.
>
> The accountants' forensic reports were first made available in October 2002. The husband's accountant's reply to the wife's additional questions was supplied on 2 May 2003. It was not until . . . the 16 June that the wife's legal advisers became sufficiently concerned about the husband's financial position to consider that issues under PoCA 2002, Part 7 might arise. In particular, her legal team was concerned about the possibility of committing an offence under PoCA 2002, s.328. Based on the financial information, the wife and her legal team became suspicious that part of the matrimonial assets might be 'criminal property' within the meaning of the PoCA 2002. The wife's solicitors and counsel were worried that, in acting for the wife in litigation and/or settlement of a financial dispute, they might fall foul of the section 328 prohibition and might become concerned in an arrangement which might facilitate 'the acquisition, retention, use or control' of criminal property by the wife. Accordingly, they wrote to the NCIS making a disclosure . . .
>
> The solicitor's letter stated that an answer would be expected within seven days as to whether the solicitors 'should continue to take steps in the proceedings'. Further the letter sought advice as to whether in the light of the 'tipping off' rule, the letter could be disclosed to the husband's solicitors . . ..
>
> Crucially, the NCIS officer advised that the wife's solicitors were not permitted to tell either the other side, or their own client, that the disclosure report had been made, as it would contravene the tipping off provisions and/or the prohibition against prejudicing an investigation.

NCIS seem to have interpreted sections 333(4) and 342(5) very widely, taking the view that if a person intends to use the solicitor for a criminal purpose, even if this was unknown to the solicitor, the benefit of the defence in sections 333(3) and 342(4) would be lost.

In the light of the above facts, Dame Elizabeth Butler-Sloss had to consider the following issue (among other things): whether and in what circumstances a legal adviser, having made an authorised disclosure, is permitted to tell others of the fact that s/he has done so. In doing so, she had to consider the manner in which the 'legal professional adviser' exemption or defence applies. She quoted from the judgment of Lord Woolf CJ in *Governor and Company of the Bank of Scotland* v. *A Ltd* [2001] EWCA Civ 52; 1 WLR 754. This judgment concerned the exemption to the offence of tipping off contained in section 93D of the Criminal Justice Act 1988 – a provision in almost identical terms to PoCA 2002, s.333(2). Lord Woolf stated:

> During argument there was a discussion as to the extent of the defence provided by section 93D(4). Mr Crow helpfully drew our attention to the similarity between the language of section 93D(4) and the scope of legal professional privilege. Based on this assistance, we conclude that the subsection broadly protects a legal adviser when that adviser is engaged in activities which attract legal professional privilege.

Dame Elizabeth Butler-Sloss, in her judgment, went on to say:

> Sections 333 and 342 specifically recognise a legal adviser's duty in ordinary circumstances to make relevant disclosures, even where the result would be to tip off their client, where to do so would fall within the ambit of being in connection with the giving of legal advice or with legal proceedings actual or contemplated. A central element of advising and representing a client must be, in my view, the duty to keep one's client informed and not to withhold information from him/her. Since the function of the Act is to regulate the proceeds of criminal behaviour, it is clear that in every circumstance where a solicitor believes an authorised disclosure to the NCIS is necessary there will be at least a suspicion of criminal purpose. If, as the NCIS suggests, section 333(4) and 342(5) bite every time a party who is suspected of holding a criminal purpose is given notice that a disclosure has been or will be made to the NCIS (i.e. is 'tipped off'), then the legal professional exemptions in sections 333(3) and 342(4) would be rendered meaningless. Sections 333(4) and 342(5) must have some purpose and the interpretation suggested by the NCIS cannot in my view be correct. The exemption is lost if a disclosure to a client is made 'with the intention of furthering a criminal purpose'. . .
>
> But unless the requisite improper intention is there, the solicitor should be free to communicate such information to his/her client or opponent as is necessary and appropriate in connection with the giving of legal advice or acting in connection with actual or contemplated legal proceedings.

The Law Society has issued separate guidance on the impact of *P* v. *P*. This guidance is reproduced in **Appendix B2**. The guidance states:

This judgment arose in an ancilliary relief case and is particularly relevant to family proceedings. Solicitors must be extremely cautious, however, in seeking to extend its findings to general areas of practice. The Law Society considers that whilst it does give . . . general guidance on the interpretation of the statutory provisions dealing with tipping off (section 333) and prejudicing an investigation (section 342) solicitors must exercise the greatest caution . . .

Dame Elizabeth Butler-Sloss, in *P* v. *P*, did recognise the practical difficulties for the investigating authorities in her interpretation of the defence. She made it clear that there are no time constraints in the Act regarding disclosure to a client if the defence under sections 333(2) or 342(3) applies. Either a solicitor is able to make the disclosure or, if sections 333(3) or 342(4) apply, he is not entitled to do so. There is no middle ground. In the light of this, Dame Elizabeth did make a recommendation as to good practice. She said:

> I am, however, concerned that the purpose of the Act be respected, and that as a matter of good practice (as opposed to statutory obligation) the investigation authorities should be permitted time to do their job without frustration. In most cases I cannot see why a delay of, at most, seven working days before informing a client would generally cause particular difficulty to the solicitor's obligations to his client or opponent. Where appropriate consent is refused and a 31-day moratorium period is imposed, best practice would suggest that the legal adviser and the NCIS (or other relevant investigating body) try to agree on the degree of information which can be disclosed during the moratorium period without harming the investigation. In the absence of agreement, or in other urgent circumstances where even a short delay in disclosure would be unacceptable . . . the guidance of the court may be sought.

In the light of the above statement, NCIS has issued guidance in relation to disclosures by the legal profession. The full text of the guidance can be found in **Appendix B3**. However, the relevant paragraphs are set out below:

The NCIS preferred approach post-disclosure

14. Where the legal adviser has made a disclosure to the NCIS, the NCIS would prefer as a matter of practice the legal adviser not to make any reference to that fact during the 7 days following the disclosure or during the 31 days following a refusal of consent to the arrangement, unless not to do so would be in breach of a disclosure obligation imposed by the particular proceedings.
15. In the event that the legal adviser considers that a requirement of the legal proceedings is to require disclosure of the fact of the disclosure to the NCIS, but there has been no consent from NCIS within 7 days or the moratorium period is applicable, the legal adviser should firstly inform NCIS and try to seek agreement on the way ahead. In the absence of such agreement the legal adviser should consider making a without notice application to the Court for directions giving the NCIS an opportunity to make representations.

The appropriate procedures for making a without notice application to the court were set out by the Court of Appeal in *C* v. *S and others* [1999] 2 All ER 343 (a case which involved a potential breach of the tipping off provisions in section 93D(4) of the Criminal Justice Act 1988). In *The Bank of Scotland* v. *A Ltd* [2001] 1 WLR 752, the Court of Appeal suggested a similar procedure where the application could be made in private, without the client being a party to the application.

In conclusion, solicitors should be able to rely upon this defence where they are properly advising their client that they have made or will make an authorised or protected disclosure to NCIS because it is necessary and appropriate in connection with the giving of legal advice or acting in connection with actual or contemplated legal proceedings. If, however, the solicitor's intention is to make the disclosure in furtherance of criminal conduct, the defence is lost. As a matter of practice, however, solicitors should consider seeking the consent of NCIS to any disclosure and, if necessary, making a without notice application to the court for directions.

CHAPTER 8

Confiscation and Civil Recovery Orders

8.1 INTRODUCTION

This book has not been written to provide a comprehensive commentary on confiscation and recovery orders that can be made by the courts under their powers contained in the Proceeds of Crime Act 2002 (PoCA 2002), but to give guidance on a solicitor's obligations arising out of PoCA 2002, Part 7 (that part of the PoCA 2002 dealing with money laundering). However, as noted in **Chapter 1**, a major stage in the money laundering process is layering – the attempt to hide the proceeds of crime in such a way that it cannot be traced back to the original crime.

Those involved in money laundering may frequently attempt to use the services of solicitors to achieve their aim – the layering stage. This aim is increasingly important in the light of the confiscation and civil recovery procedures set out in PoCA 2002. If a criminal is able to launder successfully his or her criminal proceeds, it is unlikely that any recovery of those proceeds will be possible. If he or she is unsuccessful in the laundering process, those proceeds may be subject to confiscation or civil recovery.

8.2 CONFISCATION ORDERS (PoCA 2002, PART 2)

Under PoCA 2002, s.6 a Crown Court is required to proceed under the section if two conditions are satisfied:

(a) a defendant is convicted of an offence before the Crown Court or is committed to the Crown Court for sentencing or with a view to a confiscation order being considered; and
(b) the prosecutor asks the court to proceed under section 6 or the court believes it is appropriate to do so.

If these two conditions are satisfied, the court must decide whether the defendant has a criminal lifestyle and, if so, whether he has benefited from general criminal conduct. Alternatively, if the court decides that the defendant does not have a criminal lifestyle, it must still consider whether he has benefited from his particular criminal conduct.

A criminal lifestyle for these purposes is defined as arising from a conviction of an offence which constitutes conduct forming part of a course of criminal activity, committed over a period of at least six months and which is listed in PoCA 2002, Sched.2 (serious crimes including specified offences relating to drug trafficking, money laundering, terrorism, people trafficking, arms trafficking, counterfeiting and blackmail). Conduct will form part of a course of criminal activity if in the proceedings in which he was convicted he was convicted of three or more other offences from which he has benefited or in the period of six years ending with the day when the proceedings started, he was convicted on at least two separate occasions of offences from which he has benefited. The defendant must have obtained a benefit of not less than £5,000.

There is a distinction drawn between general criminal conduct arising from a criminal lifestyle and particular criminal conduct arising from the conduct upon which the specific conviction was based. This distinction is relevant to the assumptions the court can make and the amount recoverable under a confiscation order.

Once a court has decided that a defendant has benefited from either general or particular criminal conduct (the decision is taken by the court on a balance of probabilities – PoCA 2002, s.6(7)) it must decide upon the recoverable amount and make a confiscation order requiring the defendant to pay that amount. (There is a discretion where the court believes that any victim of the criminal conduct has started or intends to start proceedings against the defendant to recover in respect of any loss, injury or damage sustained.)

The amount of the recoverable sum is generally the amount equal to the defendant's benefit from the conduct concerned. If the defendant has a criminal lifestyle, the conduct concerned will be his or her general criminal conduct and the recoverable sum will be calculated by reference to all his or her criminal conduct, whether the conduct occurred before or after the passing of PoCA 2002 or whether the property was obtained before or after the passing of the PoCA 2002. If the defendant does not have a criminal lifestyle, the conduct concerned will be his or her particular criminal conduct which consists of the conduct constituting the offences for which he or she was convicted (at the same proceedings) and any other offences which the court will be taking into account in sentencing.

If the court decides that a defendant has a criminal lifestyle, it must make four assumptions in deciding whether the defendant has benefited from his or her general criminal conduct and in deciding the benefit from this conduct. The four assumptions are:

- Any property transferred to him at any time after the relevant day (generally the first day of the period of six years ending with the date when proceedings were started against him or her) was as a result of his or her general criminal conduct.

- Any property held by the defendant at any time after the date of conviction was obtained as a result of his or her general criminal conduct.
- Any expenditure incurred by the defendant after the relevant day was from property obtained by him or her as a result of his or her general criminal conduct.
- In any valuation of property obtained (or assumed to be obtained) by the defendant, he obtained it free of any other interests.

The court should only ignore these assumptions if either one or more of the assumptions is shown to be incorrect or there would be a serious risk of injustice if the assumption were made.

8.3   CIVIL RECOVERY ORDERS (PoCA 2002, PART 5)

In order to make a confiscation order, the criminal must have been convicted of a criminal offence (either in proceedings before the Crown Court or where there has been a committal to the Crown Court for sentencing or a committal with a view to a confiscation order being considered). In all cases, therefore, the court must have been satisfied that, beyond reasonable doubt, the individual had been involved in criminal conduct.

Civil Recovery Orders are new to the UK, and were introduced as a result of the PoCA 2002. They can be distinguished from confiscation orders on the basis that there is no need for a criminal conviction. These orders allow the recovery of property obtained through unlawful conduct and since the application is made in civil proceedings, the test of whether or not conduct is unlawful is on the balance of probabilities.

Section 240 of the PoCA 2002 provides that the general purpose of these provisions is to allow the enforcement authority (the Assets Recovery Agency) to recover in civil proceedings before the High Court property which is, or represents, property obtained through unlawful conduct. Further, PoCA 2002, Part 5 allows cash which is, or represents property obtained through unlawful conduct, to be forfeited in civil proceedings before a magistrates' court.

In both cases it is necessary for there to be unlawful conduct and this is defined in PoCA 2002, s.241 as conduct which is 'unlawful under the criminal law' or conduct which occurs outside the UK and is unlawful under the criminal law of that country and would be unlawful under the criminal law of the UK if it occurred in the UK.

It is for the court to decide on a balance of probabilities whether it is proved that unlawful conduct has occurred (s.241(3)).

8.3.1   Civil recovery in the High Court

Proceedings may be taken by the Assets Recovery Agency (the Agency) in the High Court against any person who holds recoverable property (PoCA 2002, s.243(1)). A claim form must be served on the respondent and any other person who holds associated property which the Agency wishes to be subject to a recovery order (PoCA 2002, s.243(2)).

Associated property means (PoCA 2002, s.245) property which is not itself recoverable property but includes:

- Any interest in recoverable property.
- Any other interest in the property in which recoverable property subsists.
- If the recoverable property is a tenancy in common, the tenancy of the other tenant.
- If the recoverable property is part of a larger property, but not a separate part, the remainder of that property.

An interim receiving order can be applied for (either before or after starting the proceedings for a recovery order). This will be an order for the detention, custody or preservation of property and the appointment of an interim receiver (PoCA 2002, s.246). The interim receiver is required to take such steps the court considers necessary to secure the detention, custody or preservation of the property and to establish whether or not the property to which the order applies is recoverable or associated property (PoCA 2002, s.247).

The interim receiving order must prohibit the person to whose property the order applies from dealing with the property, subject to the court making an exclusion to enable the person to meet reasonable living expenses or to carry on any trade, business, profession or occupation (PoCA 2002, s.252). Further, under PoCA 2002, s.253, whilst the order has effect the court may stay any action of legal process in respect of the property.

Where a court is satisfied that property is recoverable, under PoCA 2002, s.266, it must make a recovery order vesting the title to the property in the trustee for civil recovery (a person appointed by the court and nominated by the Agency). The functions of the trustee under PoCA 2002, s.267 are to secure the detention, custody or preservation of the property and, in the case of property which is not money, to realise the value of the property for the benefit of the Agency.

8.3.2   Recovery of cash in summary proceedings

For the purposes of these provisions, cash means:

- notes and coins in any money;
- postal orders;
- cheques of any kind, including travellers' cheques;

- bankers' drafts;
- bearer bonds and bearer shares.

On the application of the Commissioners of Customs and Excise or a constable, a magistrates' court may make an order for forfeiture of cash or any part of it if it is satisfied that the cash or part is recoverable property or is intended by any person for use in unlawful conduct (PoCA 2002, s.298) and the cash has been detained under PoCA 2002, s.295 (detention of seized cash – see below). Subject to any appeal, the cash forfeited is paid to the Consolidated Fund (PoCA 2002, s.300).

A customs officer or constable who is lawfully on any premises and who has reasonable grounds for suspecting that there is cash on the premises which is recoverable property or is intended by any person for use in unlawful conduct may search for cash there (PoCA 2002, s.289(1)). Equally, a customs officer or constable who has reasonable grounds for suspecting that a person is carrying cash which is recoverable property or is intended by any person for use in unlawful conduct may require the person to permit a search of any article in his or her possession or permit a search of his or her person and may detain the person for as long as necessary (s.289(2) and (3)). Such searches may only be exercised with the prior approval of a judicial officer (or if that is not practicable) a senior officer (a police officer of at least the rank of inspector or a customs officer of equivalent seniority).

Following the search the customs officer or constable may seize the cash (PoCA 2002, s.294) and whilst there are still reasonable grounds for suspicion that the cash is recoverable property or is intended by any person for use in unlawful conduct, may detain the cash for a period of 48 hours (PoCA 2002, s.295). This period may be extended by order made by a magistrates' court, initially for a period of three months and on a second application for extension for a further period of two years. The magistrates must be satisfied that the continued detention of the cash is justified while its derivation is being investigated or consideration is given to bringing proceedings against a person for an offence with which the cash is related or where proceedings have started but have not yet been concluded (PoCA 2002, s.295).

Thereafter, on the application of the Commissioners of Customs and Excise or a constable, a magistrates' court may make an order for forfeiture of cash or any part of it if it is satisfied that the cash or part is recoverable property or is intended by any person for use in unlawful conduct (PoCA 2002, s.298).

These provisions are subject to a condition that the cash is not less than the minimum amount. This amount is determined by order of the Secretary of State (PoCA 2002, s.303). The current minimum amount is £5,000 (The Proceeds of Crime Act 2002 (Recovery of Cash in Summary Proceedings: Minimum Amount) Order 2004, SI 2004/420).

8.4 PRODUCTION ORDERS (PoCA 2002, PART 8)

In order to carry out a confiscation, civil recovery or money laundering investigation the authorities may seek a production order requiring the production of material to an appropriate officer or requiring that the appropriate officer be given access to the material. Solicitors' clients might be the subject of an application for such an order and/or solicitors might find themselves the subject of an application.

Confiscation investigations, civil recovery investigations and money laundering investigations are defined in PoCA 2002, s.341. Confiscation investigations are investigations into whether a person has benefited from his or her criminal conduct, or investigations into the extent or whereabouts of his or her benefit from his criminal conduct. Civil recovery investigations are investigations into whether property is recoverable property or associated property; who holds the property; or its extent or whereabouts. A money laundering investigation is an investigation into whether a person has committed a money laundering offence.

An appropriate person must make the application. An appropriate person is defined as a constable or a customs officer, if the warrant is sought for the purposes of a confiscation investigation or a money laundering investigation or a named member of the staff of the Agency, if the warrant is sought for the purposes of a civil recovery investigation. The application is made to a judge entitled to exercise the jurisdiction of the Crown Court (where it is a confiscation or money laundering officer) or a judge of the High Court (if it is a civil recovery investigation).

The production order, if made, will specify the period within which the order must be complied with and this period will be a period of seven days from the date of the order unless the judge is satisfied that a shorter or longer period is appropriate.

Section 346 PoCA 2002 sets out the requirements for making a production order. The judge must be satisfied:

- That there are reasonable grounds for suspecting a person has benefited from criminal conduct (confiscation investigation) or property is recoverable or associated property (civil recovery investigation) or that a money laundering offence has been committed (money laundering investigation).
- That there are reasonable grounds for believing that the person specified is in possession or control of the specified material.
- That there are reasonable grounds for believing that the specified material is likely to be of substantial value to the investigation;
- That there are reasonable grounds for believing that it is in the public interest for the material to be produced or for access to the material to be granted.

If an order is made requiring an appropriate officer to be given access to material on any premises, an order can also be made granting entry in relation to the premises (PoCA 2002, s.347).

One important restriction on the granting of a production order and of particular relevance to solicitors and their clients is contained in section 348(1). This states 'A production order does not require a person to produce, or give access, to privileged material.'

Subsection (2) defines privileged material as 'any material which the person would be entitled to refuse to produce on the grounds of legal professional privilege in proceedings in the High Court'.

However, solicitors must bear in mind the decision of the House of Lords in *R v. Central Criminal Court ex p. Francis* v. *Francis* [1989] 1 AC 346. Items are not to be considered as privileged where they are held with the intention of furthering a criminal purpose. The House of Lords held that the intention did not have to be the solicitor's intention. Provided someone had the intention to further a criminal purpose, items held would not be privileged.

CHAPTER 9

Money Laundering Regulations 2003

9.1 INTRODUCTION

The Money Laundering Regulations 2003, SI 2003/3075 came into force on 1 March 2004 and implement the Second European Money Laundering Directive. The full text of the Regulations can be found in **Appendix A3**. When they apply, they impose a requirement that solicitors establish procedures relating to:

(a) training;
(b) client identification;
(c) record keeping; and
(d) reporting procedures;

The regulations are part of the criminal law. Failure to comply is a criminal offence.

Whilst the Proceeds of Crime Act 2002 (PoCA 2002) and the Terrorism Act 2000 apply to all firms of solicitors (there are few, if any, areas of a solicitor's practice which escape the risk of involvement in money laundering), the Money Laundering Regulations only apply to that part of a solicitor's practice which falls within the definition of 'relevant business'. Consequently, in theory, parts of a solicitor's practice may well fall outside the requirements of the Regulations. However, the Law Society's *Money Laundering Guidance* recommends solicitors to err on the side of caution. It states:

> . . . the scope of the ML Regulations 2003 is as yet untested in the courts, and there is some uncertainty as to their application in some cases. This lack of clarity means it would be wise to comply with the ML Regulations 2003 on a broad, rather than a narrow basis as a form of risk management within your firm. Solicitors may also wish to apply the requirements of the ML Regulations 2003 across the whole scope of their activities in order to protect against committing an offence under the statutory criminal law. This law applies even if the particular activities are not 'relevant business' and, therefore, are not covered by the ML Regulations 2003.

Firms of solicitors which are authorised to conduct mainstream regulated activities by the Financial Services Authority (FSA) are subject to the FSA

Money Laundering Sourcebook. Only a small minority of firms are so autho-rised and this book does not cover details of the FSA *Money Laundering Sourcebook*. Guidance notes have been issued by the Joint Money Laundering Steering Group.

9.2 RELEVANT BUSINESS

The Money Laundering Regulations 2003 only apply to that part of a solic-itor's practice which falls within the definition of 'relevant business'. Relevant business is defined in regulation 2(2) as meaning:

(a) the regulated activity of –
  (i) accepting deposits;
  (ii) effecting or carrying out contracts of long-term insurance when carried on by a person who has received official authorisation pursuant to Article 4 or 51 of the Life Assurance Consolidation Directive;
  (iii) dealing in investments as principal or as agent;
  (iv) arranging deals in investments;
  (v) managing investments;
  (vi) safeguarding and administering investments;
  (vii) sending dematerialised instructions;
  (viii) establishing (and taking other steps in relation to) collective investment schemes;
  (ix) advising on investments; or
  (x) issuing electronic money;
(b) the activities of the National Savings Bank;
(c) any activity carried on for the purpose of raising money authorised to be raised under the National Loans Act 1968 under the auspices of the Director of Savings;
(d) the business of operating a bureau de change, transmitting money (or any rep-resentation of monetary value) by any means or cashing cheques which are made payable to customers;
(e) any of the activities in points 1 to 12 or 14 of Annex 1 to the Banking Consolidation Directive (which activities are, for convenience, set out in Schedule 1 to these Regulations) when carried on by way of business, ignoring an activity falling within any of sub-paragraphs (a) to (d);
(f) estate agency work;
(g) operating a casino by way of business;
(h) the activities of a person appointed to act as an insolvency practitioner within the meaning of section 388 of the Insolvency Act 1986 or Article 3 of the Insolvency (Northern Ireland) Order 1989;
(i) the provision by way of business of advice about the tax affairs of another person by a body corporate or unincorporate or, in the case of a sole practitioner, by an individual;
(j) the provision by way of business of accountancy services by a body corporate or unincorporate or, in the case of a sole practitioner, by an individual;
(k) the provision by way of business of audit services by a person who is eligi-ble for appointment as a company auditor under section 25 of the

Companies Act 1989 or Article 28 of the Companies (Northern Ireland) Order 1990;

(l) the provision by way of business of legal services by a body corporate or unincorporate or, in the case of a sole practitioner, by an individual and which involves participation in a financial or real property transaction (whether by assisting in the planning or execution of any such transaction or otherwise by acting for, or on behalf of, a client in any such transaction);

(m) the provision by way of business of services in relation to the formation, operation or management of a company or a trust; or

(n) the activity of dealing in goods of any description by way of business (including dealing as an auctioneer) whenever a transaction involves accepting a total cash payment of 15,000 euro or more.

The wording of regulation 2(2) is nearly identical to the wording in PoCA 2002, Sched.9 (the definition of the regulated sector) and solicitors should accept that if they are acting within the regulated sector, they will be subject to the Money Laundering Regulations 2003.

The definition of the regulated sector is covered in **Chapter 5.** For the sake of completeness, set out below are the most common activities within a solicitor's practice which will fall within the definition of relevant business.

(a) regulated activities

Section 22 of the Financial Services and Markets Act 2000 provides:

(1) An activity is a regulated activity for the purposes of this Act if it is an activity of a specified kind which is carried on by way of business and –

(a) relates to an investment of a specified kind . . ..

(5) 'Specified' means specified in an order made by the Treasury.

The most relevant order made by the Treasury is the Financial Services and Markets Act 2000 (Regulated Activities) Order 2001, SI 2001/544 (RAO). This Order lists both the activities of a specified kind and the investments of a specified kind.

The most common specified investments from a solicitor's point of view are:

- Shares in the share capital of any company (art.76 RAO).
- Instruments creating or acknowledging indebtedness, including debentures, loan stock, bonds and certificates of deposit (art.77).
- Government securities, including British Government Stocks (gilts) (art.78).
- Units in collective investment schemes, including unit trusts and shares in open-ended investment companies (art.81).
- Insurance contracts, including endowment policies, pension policies, annuities and insurance bonds.

Consequently, activities in a solicitor's corporate department (acquisitions, corporate finance) are likely to involve shares, debentures or corporate bonds. Activities in private client work (estate and trust administration) could involve the full range of specified investments. Settlements in matrimonial work could involve some or all of the specified investments.

Of the 10 activities listed in regulation 2(2)(a), the following involving specified investments are likely to be most relevant to solicitors:

- Dealing in investments as agent. Dealing is defined as buying, selling, subscribing or underwriting certain specified investments. A solicitor would be dealing where investments were being bought or sold as agent for a client.
- Arranging deals in investments. This would catch those circumstances where a solicitor made arrangements for a client to buy, sell, subscribe or underwrite certain specified investments.
- Discretionary management of investments. Solicitors who are sole trustees or personal representatives or trustees or personal representatives jointly only with others from their own firm will be managing if the trust fund or estate includes certain specified investments.
- Safeguarding and administration. Solicitors who hold documents of title to specified investments in safe custody and who, at the same time, are involved in administration activities relating to those investments will be undertaking this activity. Typically estate and trust work will give rise to this activity.
- Advising on investments. Giving advice on the merits of buying, selling, subscribing for or underwriting certain specified investments will be caught by this activity.

Section 19 of the Financial Services and Markets Act 2000 provides:

(1) No person may carry on a regulated activity in the United Kingdom, or purport to do so, unless he is –

(a) an authorised person; or
(b) an exempt person.

Most solicitors are not authorised persons (i.e. they have not sought nor obtained authorisation from the FSA). They are, however, able to undertake many activities which fall within the definition of regulated activities without authorisation as a result of the exemption for professionals provided in Part XX of the Financial Services and Markets Act 2000.

It must be understood that the definition of relevant business in the Money Laundering Regulations 2003, does not require the regulated activity to be undertaken with authorisation from the FSA. An exempt regulated activity will fall within the definition of relevant business.

The other relevant activities that will bring a solicitor within the meaning of relevant business are as follows.

(f)   estate agency work . . ..

Solicitors who provide estate agency services will, in respect of those services, be carrying on relevant business.

(h)   the activities of a person appointed to act as an insolvency practitioner within the meaning of section 388 of the Insolvency Act 1986 . . .

Solicitors who are appointed as insolvency practitioners will be carrying on relevant business. Solicitors who act for external insolvency practitioners or who act in insolvency matters without an appointment as an insolvency practitioner will not be caught under this head. However, depending upon the type of work, they may be caught under paragraph (l) below.

(i)   the provision by way of business of advice about the tax affairs of another person by a body corporate or unincorporate, or in the case of a sole practitioner, by an individual . . .

Solicitors giving tax advice will be undertaking relevant business. It appears that any tax advice will be relevant business. For example, whilst activities relating to will drafting would not be relevant business, if such activities were combined with inheritance tax planning advice, this would be likely to be sufficient for these purposes.

(l)   the provision by way of business of legal services by a body corporate or unincorporate or, in the case of a sole practitioner, by an individual and which involves the participation in a financial or real property transaction (whether by assisting in the planning or execution of any transaction or otherwise by acting for, or on behalf of, a client in any transaction) . . ..

This paragraph is clearly aimed at extending relevant business to many activities undertaken by solicitors. The reference to 'financial or real property transactions' has the effect of bringing all conveyancing transactions within the scope of relevant business.

The *Money Laundering Guidance* issued by the Law Society indicates that the interpretation of participation in a financial transaction is less clear. The *Money Laundering Guidance* seeks clarity from the text of the Second European Money Laundering Directive (on which this definition is based). The Directive provides that the following should be included:

Independent legal professionals, when they participate, whether:

(1)   by assisting in the planning or execution of transactions for their client concerning the:

- buying and selling of real property or business entities;
- managing of client money, securities or other assets;
- opening or management of bank, savings or securities accounts;
- organisation of contributions necessary for the creation, operation or management of companies; or
- creation, operation or management of trusts, companies or similar structures; or

(2) by acting on behalf of and for their client in any financial or real estate transaction.

The Law Society's *Money Laundering Guidance* indicates that managing client money is narrower than simply handling client money. Simply operating a client account is not intended to be caught within the meaning of relevant business but holding money or receiving money on behalf of clients as part of a transaction will be caught.

The Treasury has also confirmed that the following (by themselves) would not generally be viewed as participation in financial transactions:

- A payment on account of costs to a solicitor or payment of a solicitor's bill (because the solicitor is not participating in a financial transaction on behalf of the client).
- Legal advice (assuming such advice does not fall within one or more of the other categories defined as within the regulated sector).
- Participation in litigation (on the basis that litigation is not a transaction).
- Will writing (unless linked with, for example, tax advice).
- Publicly funded work.

(m) the provision by way of business of services in relation to the formation, operation or management of a company or a trust.

This paragraph clearly covers activities undertaken by solicitors relating to the formation of a company or the administration of a trust fund. There is some doubt over the reference to business services relating to the 'operation or management of a company'. The Treasury has indicated that this phrase should not be interpreted to include any services which assist in the management or operation of a company.

In a letter (published on the NCIS website) written to the British Bankers' Association, the Treasury made the following points:

Regulation (m) was intended to cover those who form, operate or manage companies (or trusts) when this activity is provided as a service by way of business. This addresses, among other things, the problem of 'front' or shell companies, which have been recognised as having been used in most complex money laundering operations . . .

It has been argued that regulation (m) covers anyone providing any service by way of business to a company which happens to assist the management or operation of that company e.g. cleaners, advertising agencies or management consultants. Whereas the interpretation of the Regulations is ultimately a matter for the courts, such a wide interpretation of regulation (m) was not our intention and, we believe, is not warranted by the language of regulation (m).

Many services offered by solicitors to companies and trust funds will involve financial transactions. Some will be exempt regulated activities within the meaning of the Financial Services and Markets Act 2002. As such, these activities will be relevant business regardless of regulation (m). Since the Treasury statement indicates that the interpretation is ultimately a matter for the courts, solicitors should, perhaps, err on the side of caution and assume activities relating to company clients and trust clients are likely to be relevant business.

9.3 SYSTEMS AND TRAINING ETC. TO PREVENT MONEY LAUNDERING

Regulation 3(1) of the Money Laundering Regulations 2003 states:

Every person must in the course of relevant business carried on by him in the United Kingdom –

(a) comply with the requirements of regulations 4 (identification procedures), 6 (record-keeping procedures) and 7 (internal reporting procedures);

(b) establish such other procedures of internal control and communication as may be appropriate for the purposes of forestalling and preventing money laundering; and

(c) take appropriate measures so that relevant employees are –

(i) made aware of the provisions of these Regulations, Part 7 of the Proceeds of Crime Act 2002 (money laundering) and sections 18 and 21A of the Terrorism Act 2000; and

(ii) given training in how to recognise and deal with transactions which may be related to money laundering.

The requirements of regulations 4 (identification procedures), 6 (record-keeping procedures) and 7 (internal reporting procedures) are dealt with in **Paragraph 9.4** et seq.

The other procedures required by regulation 3(1)(*b*) might include those procedures identified earlier in this book, relating to the money laundering substantive law. For example, ensuring that a nominated officer is appointed; the establishment of procedures of internal control and communication; systems for disciplining those who ignore the procedures; and considering whether it is appropriate to appoint a privilege committee to determine whether the defence of privilege might apply in given circumstances. Further information can be found in Chapter 6 of the Law Society's *Money Laundering Guidance*.

Regulation 3(1)(c) requires firms to take appropriate measures to ensure relevant employees are trained in relation to the substantive law and in how to recognise and deal with transactions which may be related to money laundering.

There is no specification of what amounts to training for these purposes. Certainly, it does not require firms to provide face-to-face training with a tutor. The training obligations can be complied with by handouts, manuals, video and computer and web-based training. It is, however, important that firms design their training for all relevant staff and that the training is at an appropriate level for individual members of staff.

Fee earners (particularly those involved in higher risk areas of practice) will require full training on the substantive law, the firm's procedures and on recognition of transactions which may be related to money laundering. This training should be updated at frequent intervals.

Members of the accounts staff should also receive training since they will be handling client and other money. Secretaries and receptionists should receive training if they are likely to be in contact with clients. For example, if a fee earner makes an authorised disclosure to the firm's nominated officer as a result of suspicious circumstances and the firm's nominated officer then discloses to NCIS, the seven-working day period will start to run during which limited work only on the relevant file can be undertaken (for details, see **Chapter 4**). During that seven-day period, it might not be possible to explain to the client why nothing is being done on the file. The risk of tipping off may exist and even if the legal professional adviser defence applies, the preferred NCIS approach is not to disclose matters to the client during this period (see **Chapter 7**). Consequently, a fee earner may ask his or her secretary to field calls from the client or other party – the client might even turn up at reception to ascertain what is going on. In both cases the secretary and/or receptionist needs to be aware of the risks in communicating with the client or other side.

New members of staff should receive induction training relating to the firm's procedures. Even if new members of staff have received money laundering training at their previous employers, each firm will have their own internal procedures and it is vital for all members of staff to be aware of these procedures.

The obligation to comply with the procedures laid down in the Money Laundering Regulations 2003 is imposed upon the partners, in a partnership or the sole practitioner in a sole practice or an officer in an incorporated practice. It is, therefore, important that the firm maintains a record of compliance with the training obligations. An attendance sheet should be kept of all face-to-face training. Where other methods of training are used, appropriate records should also be kept.

Although the regulations came into force on 1 March 2004, the Treasury has made it clear that these obligations should be interpreted with common sense. It recognises that all relevant employees would not be fully trained by 1 March 2004. However, if necessary, firms should be able to demonstrate that they have implemented an on-going training programme satisfying the minimum requirements of regulation 3(1).

9.4   IDENTIFICATION PROCEDURES

9.4.1   The required procedures: regulation 4

Regulation 4 imposes obligations relating to identification of clients and others. It states:

(1)   In this regulation and in regulations 5 to 7 –
    (a)   'A' means a person who carries on relevant business in the United Kingdom; and
    (b)   'B' means an applicant for business.

(2)   This regulation applies if –
    (a)   A and B form, or agree to form, a business relationship;
    (b)   in respect of any one-off transaction –
        (i)   A knows or suspects that the transaction involves money laundering; or
        (ii)   payment of 15,000 euro or more is to be made by or to B; or
    (c)   in respect of two or more one-off transactions, it appears to A (whether at the outset or subsequently) that the transactions are linked and involve, in total, the payment of 15,000 euro or more by or to B.

(3)   A must maintain identification procedures which –
    (a)   require that as soon as is reasonably practicable after contact is first made between A and B –
        (i)   B must produce satisfactory evidence of his identity; or
        (ii)   such measures specified in the procedures must be taken in order to produce satisfactory evidence of B's identity;
    (b)   take into account the greater potential for money laundering which arises when B is not physically present when being identified;
    (c)   require that where satisfactory evidence of identity is not obtained, the business relationship or one-off transaction must not proceed any further; and
    (d)   require that where B acts or appears to act for another person, reasonable measures must be taken for the purpose of establishing the identity of that person.

This is probably the most onerous of the obligations applicable to solicitors who undertake relevant business. It requires firms to have in place procedures which ensure that satisfactory evidence of client identification is obtained for certain clients where relevant business is undertaken.

A number of points can be made regarding the wording of this regulation.

'A' means a person who carries on relevant business in the United Kingdom; and 'B' means an applicant for business.

Relevant business has been defined above. A will be the firm of solicitors. B will be the client – an applicant for business. This term is defined in regulation 2(1) as 'a person seeking to form a business relationship, or carry out a one-off transaction, with another person acting in the course of relevant business carried on by that other person in the United Kingdom'. Business relationship and one-off transaction are defined below.

This regulation applies if – (a) A and B form, or agree to form, a business relationship . . .

Identification procedures will be necessary if the solicitor and client form (or agree to form) a business relationship. This term is defined in regulation 2(1) as meaning:

any arrangement the purpose of which is to facilitate the carrying out of transactions on a frequent, habitual or regular basis where the total amount of any payments to be made by any person to any other in the course of the arrangement is not known or capable of being ascertained at the outset.

This term suggests an on-going relationship between the solicitor and the client where the total amount paid or to be paid cannot be ascertained. Examples might include trust administration or acting on an on-going retainer for a company or individual conducting all legal work as and when it arises.

This regulation applies if – (b) in respect of any one-off transaction –

(i)   A knows or suspects that the transaction involves money laundering; or (ii) payment of 15,000 euro or more is to be made by or to B . . .

If the relationship between the solicitor and client is not a business relationship (e.g. the amount involved in the transaction can be ascertained at the beginning of the transaction) it will be a one-off transaction. This is defined in regulation 2(1) as meaning 'any transaction other than one carried out in the course of an existing business relationship'.

However, where there is a one-off transaction, the requirement to obtain identification only applies if the solicitor knows or suspects the transaction involves money laundering or the amount involved is €15,000 or more. The current rate of exchange (as of July 2004) gives a value in sterling of £10,015. Under the old Regulations (the Money Laundering Regulations 1993) there was a similar definition. However, the rate of exchange for euros was set once a year. Under the 2003 regulations no such annual exchange rate is provided for. It is likely that the courts will apply the rate applicable when the transaction is entered into.

> This regulation applies if – (c) in respect of two or more one-off transactions, it appears to A (whether at the outset or subsequently) that the transactions are linked and involve, in total, the payment of 15,000 euro or more by or to B.

Firms cannot avoid the identification procedures by acting for a client on one or more matters where, individually, the matters involve sums less than €15,000 but collectively the sum involved is €15,000 or more if the matters are linked. The Regulations do not give a definition of linked for these purposes. The Law Society's *Money Laundering Guidance* states:

> Identification procedures must be undertaken for linked transactions that together equal or exceed the €15,000 exemption limit. Whether transactions are linked depends upon any obvious connection rather than an arbitrary time limit. However, for lower risk work concerning transactions between which there is no obvious link, a three month period may be a useful yardstick.

> A must maintain identification procedures which – (a) require that as soon as is reasonably practicable after contact is first made between A and B . . ..

If the Regulations require identification evidence to be obtained, it must be obtained as soon as is reasonably practicable after the first contact between the solicitor and the client. The Regulations do not define what is reasonably practicable. However, the 1993 Regulations contained a similar requirement – requiring evidence of identity to be obtained as soon as is reasonably practicable after contact is first made. These regulations provided supplementary provisions relating to this phrase – there is no reason why these supplementary provisions should not be used as guidance in the interpretation of the phrase in the 2003 Regulations. The relevant 1993 regulation provided (reg. 11(2)):

> In determining . . . the time span in which satisfactory evidence of a person's identity has to be obtained, in relation to any particular business relationship or one-off transaction, all the circumstances shall be taken into account including, in particular –
>
> (a) the nature of the business relationship or one-off transaction concerned;
> (b) the geographical locations of the parties;
> (c) whether it is practical to obtain the evidence before commitments are entered into between the parties or before money passes;
> (d) in relation to [one-off transactions], the earliest stage at which there are reasonable grounds for believing that the total amount payable by an applicant for business is ecu 15,000 or more.

Many firms will link the identification procedure to their new file opening procedures. In some cases firms will adopt policies which will not allow a file to be formally opened (no file number or reference is allocated to the client) until satisfactory identity procedures have been carried out. In all cases, it makes sense to adopt a policy which requires completion of the identification procedures before significant sums are accepted into client account.

> B must produce satisfactory evidence of his identity; or such measures specified in the procedures must be taken in order to produce satisfactory evidence of B's identity;

This is the key to the required procedures. If the identification procedures apply to a client, the client must either produce satisfactory evidence of identity or the firm's procedures should specify what actions can be taken by the firm in order to produce satisfactory evidence of the client's identity.

The regulations do not specify what amounts to satisfactory evidence for these purposes. However, regulation 2(5) and (6) do give further guidance. They provide:

> (5) For the purposes of these Regulations, and subject to paragraph (6), 'satisfactory evidence of identity' is evidence which is reasonably capable of establishing (and does in fact establish to the satisfaction of the person who obtains it) that the applicant for business is the person he claims to be.
>
> (6) Where the person who obtains the evidence mentioned in paragraph (5) knows or has reasonable grounds for believing that the applicant for business is a money service operator, satisfactory evidence of identity must also include the applicant's registered number (if any).

The Law Society's *Money Laundering Guidance* provides a commentary on these two paragraphs. In respect of sub-paragraph (5) it says:

> For evidence of identity to be satisfactory, the ML Regulations 2003 require it to pass two tests:
>
> - an objective test in that the evidence must be reasonably capable of establishing that the client is the person he or she claims to be; and
> - a subjective test in that the person who obtains the evidence must be satisfied that it does in fact establish that the client is the person he or she claims to be.

In relation to sub-paragraph (6) and the reference to money-service operators the Law Society has this to say:

> A money service operator is a person who carries on money service business but does not carry on relevant business falling within sub-paragraphs (a)-(c) of Regulation 2(2). With a few exceptions, a money service business is a business which operates a bureau de change, transmits money, or cashes cheques made payable to customers. Solicitors operating their client or office account would not usually be a money service business. Money service operators are not regulated by the FSA unless they carry on FSA regulated activities but were made subject to a Customs & Excise registration regime under the 2001 Regulations, and now under the ML Regulations 2003.

Detailed guidance on what amounts to satisfactory evidence of identity should appear in the firm's internal procedures. Partners and principals should not leave it to individual fee earners to decide what is and what is not satisfactory. A firm-wide policy should be adopted and the firm's nominated officer should be consulted where, in an individual case, a client is unable to satisfy the requirements of the policy.

The Law Society has provided detailed and comprehensive guidance in its *Money Laundering Guidance* on what might amount to satisfactory evidence. This guidance helpfully distinguishes between different categories of clients covering:

- Individuals: UK residents.
- Individuals: persons not resident in the UK.
- Individuals: no face-to-face meeting.
- Disadvantaged clients.
- Mentally incapacitated clients.
- Asylum seekers.
- Students and minors.
- Estates.
- Trusts.
- Corporate clients: listed on London Stock Exchange or UK recognised investment exchange.
- Corporate clients: listed on any other recognised, designated or approved exchange.
- Banks, investment firms and insurance companies.
- UK unlisted companies.
- Overseas unlisted companies.
- Subsidiaries.
- Partnerships, limited partnerships and limited liability partnerships.

The full Law Society guidance on evidence of identity appears in **Appendix B1**.

Firms should tailor this guidance to their own requirements, identifying the common categories of clients relevant to the firm's practice and setting out in the firm's money laundering manual details of the firm's policy regarding identification. Most firms will want to adopt a standard form for use by fee earners in the identification process. Examples of a simple money laundering manual and identification forms can be found in **Appendices C1** and **C2**.

Documentary evidence of identity is recommended for most situations, although in some circumstances firms may be prepared to accept evidence from third parties (e.g. credit reference agencies) or to make electronic searches of appropriate databases (e.g. the electoral roll). In each case it will be necessary for the firm to retain a record of the evidence of identity obtained (see below for details of this record). Consequently, the firm's system must ensure that original documentation is photocopied, third party evidence is retained and prints are taken of any electronic evidence relied upon.

> ... identification procedures ... must take into account the greater potential for money laundering which arises when B is not physically present when being identified ...

This requirement did not appear in the 1993 Regulations – it has been prompted by the concern that it is easier for criminals to obtain legal and other services if there is no face-to-face meeting between, for example, the solicitor and a criminal client. It is obviously not appropriate to ask a client to send a copy of his or her passport or driving licence for identification purposes if there is to be no face-to-face meeting.

The Law Society's *Money Laundering Guidance* on this suggests that where it is not possible physically to meet the client, the solicitor should consider requiring that someone else qualified and willing certifies the client's documentation. For example, a local solicitor, accountant, doctor or bank manager may be prepared to examine the original documents and send a certified copy to the firm. If the client is overseas, then original documents can be certified by an embassy or consulate, a qualified lawyer in the jurisdiction, or, in the case of international students, the registrar of a higher education establishment. In each case it is important for the solicitor to check the name and address of the third party by reference to a professional directory or otherwise.

If a third party certification is not available, where a face-to-face meeting is not possible, clients should send the original of the appropriate documents to the solicitor, who should then copy the documents before returning them to the client. Electronic checks might also be relevant in these circumstances.

When a firm is considering its policy on client identification, thought should be given to whether or not the firm is prepared to certify documents for other solicitors and, if so, who should be authorised by the firm to provide such certification.

> ... identification procedures ... must require that where satisfactory evidence of identity is not obtained, the business relationship or one-off transaction must not proceed any further ...

The Regulations do not require a solicitor to take reasonable steps to obtain client identification. Where the Regulations apply, it is an obligation to obtain satisfactory evidence of identity. If such evidence cannot be obtained the firm must not continue to act for the client.

Many firms will not want to commence work on a particular file until satisfactory evidence of identity has been obtained. Firms are advised not to accept money into client account until such evidence has been obtained.

Although there is nothing in the Regulations preventing a firm from starting work and accepting money before satisfactory evidence is obtained (the requirement is for such evidence to be obtained as soon as is reasonably practicable after first contact is made) it can be messy if subsequently, when such evidence is not made available, the firm has to withdraw and return the money held in client account.

As noted above, many firms will take the view that all new clients should be subject to identification procedures (regardless of whether or not the firm is undertaking relevant business). Further, most firms will adopt an identification procedure which specifies particular documents or checks. If a client cannot produce evidence strictly in accordance with the firm's procedures, this will not necessarily be fatal to the retainer. The firm's policy should insist that fee earners obtain evidence in accordance with the procedure but if this is not possible reference should be made to the firm's nominated officer.

The officer can decide on the particular facts of the case:

- Whether evidence is strictly necessary. Is the firm undertaking relevant business or is the transaction value of a one-off transaction less than €15,000? or
- If the firm is undertaking relevant business and there is need for identification, can the client supply information which is not strictly within the requirement of the firm's procedures but nevertheless meets the obligation imposed by the regulations?

One further important matter must be considered at this point. If, for any reason, a client cannot produce satisfactory evidence of identity, this failure might give rise to suspicion that the client or another is involved in money laundering. The requirements of PoCA 2002, ss.327–329 (the money laundering offences), section 330 (failure to disclose), and sections 333 (tipping off) or 342 (prejudicing an investigation) might be relevant. Consider the following scenario.

A client instructs a solicitor on the purchase of an asset (real property, shares etc). The client provides the solicitor with a cheque representing the purchase money or deposit (£20,000 – in excess of the €15,000 limit for one-off transactions). The money is paid into client account. The solicitor is undertaking relevant business and is acting within the regulated sector (the provision of legal services involving participation in a financial or real property transaction). Consequently, it will be necessary for the solicitor to obtain satisfactory evidence of identity. The client prevaricates – initially there appears to be a good reason why evidence cannot be produced immediately. Eventually, however, it is clear that the client is not going to produce satisfactory evidence within the time scale required by the Regulations. The solicitor must now consider the following points.

(a) Terminating the retainer immediately. Under the Regulations the one-off transaction must not proceed further. However, if the solicitor is likely to report the client (see (b) and (c) below) he must take care in explaining to the client the reason for termination. To explain that he cannot proceed without identification would appear to be acceptable. Any hint that the solicitor suspects the client of money laundering could be tipping off and/or prejudicing an investigation.

(b) Returning the £20,000 held in client account. However, if the fact that the client has been unable to produce evidence of identity gives rise to a suspicion that the client is benefiting from criminal conduct, then the holding of £20,000 in client account could mean the solicitor is guilty of:

   i.   concealing criminal property (PoCA 2002, s.327);

   ii. being concerned in an arrangement which facilitates the retention, use or control of criminal property (PoCA 2002, s.328); or

   iii. acquisition, use or possession of criminal property (PoCA 2002, s.329).

(c) To avoid committing the offence, an authorised report must be made and the £20,000 cannot be returned to the client without appropriate consent (i.e. the consent of NCIS).

(d) Even if no money was held in client account (and therefore the solicitor, by terminating the instructions, could not be guilty of a money laundering offence) any knowledge or suspicion (or reasonable grounds for knowledge or suspicion) of the client's involvement in money laundering would, potentially, have to be reported to prevent a criminal charge under PoCA 2002, s.330 since the solicitor is acting in the regulated sector. Consideration of appropriate defences (e.g. privilege) might be necessary.

> . . . identification procedures . . . must require that where B acts or appears to act for another person, reasonable measures must be taken for the purpose of establishing the identity of that person . . .

If the client instructing the solicitor acts or appears to be acting on behalf of another person (for example, the client might be an agent or nominee for another), then the Regulations require the solicitor to take 'reasonable measures' to establish the identity of that other person. This is less onerous than the obligation to obtain the client's identity. Whilst it would make sense for firms to adopt the same procedures for obtaining identity as those procedures used for clients, if reasonable steps have been taken and the third party's identity cannot be obtained, this fact does not automatically mean that the retainer cannot proceed. If reasonable steps have been taken and the third party's identity cannot be ascertained, the firm has complied with the Regulations. However, the same points as noted above regarding possible suspicion arising from the inability to obtain identification must be taken into account.

9.4.2   Exceptions: regulation 5

Regulation 5 contains a number of exceptional circumstances where, despite the requirements of regulation 4, no evidence of identity need be obtained. The exceptions will never apply if the circumstances are such that the solicitor knows or suspects that the transaction involved money laundering (regulation 5(1)). The Law Society's *Money Laundering Guidance* states:

> The exceptions are very narrowly drawn and solicitors will in most cases need to obtain satisfactory evidence of identity. Where a solicitor wishes to take advantage of an exception, but is in doubt as to whether or not it applies to the particular facts of a case, then expert legal advice should be taken.

Unless a particular exception applies to a number of clients or to a group of clients, it would appear to be more appropriate for solicitors to ignore the exceptions in individual client matters. It is imposing a burden upon individual fee earners to require them to consider complex exceptions at the outset of each new matter. However, for the sake of completeness, the exceptions are dealt with below:

There is no requirement to obtain evidence of any person's identity in any of the following circumstances.

Regulation 5(2)(a)

> Where A has reasonable grounds for believing that B carries on in the United Kingdom relevant business falling within any of sub-paragraphs (a) to (e) of regulation 2(2), is not a money service operator and, if carrying on an activity falling within regulation 2(2)(a), is an authorised person with permission under the 2000 Act to carry on that activity.

This would cover the situation where the client was a bank or stockbroker or other financial services provider (other than a money service operator).

Regulation 5(2)(b)

> Where A has reasonable grounds for believing that B does not carry on relevant business in the United Kingdom but does carry on comparable activities to those falling within sub-paragraph (a) and is covered by the Money Laundering Directive.

The Money Laundering Directive is defined in regulation 2(1) as meaning the Council Directive 91/308/EEC of 10 June 1991 on prevention of the use of the financial system for the purpose of money laundering as amended by Directive 2001/97/EC of the European Parliament and of the Council of 4 December 2000.

This exception would cover the situation where the client was a bank or stockbroker or other financial service provider (other than a money service operator) working from an EEA country. EEA countries cover members of the EU together with certain non-EU countries (notably Norway, Iceland and Liechtenstein). Details of non-EU countries which are EEA States can be found at the website: **http://europa.eu.int/comm/external_relations/eea/**.

Regulation 5(2)(c)

Where A has reasonable grounds for believing that B is regulated by an overseas regulatory authority (within the meaning given by section 82 of the Companies Act 1989) and is based or incorporated in a country (other than an EEA State) whose law contains comparable provisions to those contained in the Money Laundering Directive.

This would cover similar institutions and businesses operating outside the EEA but where the country's laws contain comparable provisions to those contained in the directive.

9.4.3   Regulation 5(3)

Where:

(a)   A carries out a one-off transaction with or for a third party pursuant to an introduction effected by a person who has provided a written assurance that evidence of the identity of all third parties introduced by him will have been obtained and recorded under procedures maintained by him;

(b)   that person identifies the third party; and

(c)   A has reasonable grounds for believing that that person falls within any of subparagraphs (a) to (c) of paragraph (2).

This exception only applies to one-off transactions. It allows a firm to ignore the requirement to obtain client identity where the client has been introduced by a person who the solicitor has reasonable grounds for believing falls within one of the three categories noted above. This means that this exception is likely to be limited to introductions from banking and financial service providers in the UK or from EEA countries or countries having equivalent money laundering laws. For the exception to apply, it is necessary for the introducer to have given the solicitor written assurance that all clients introduced will have had their identity obtained and recorded (a general assurance) and that the specific client has been identified by the introducer.

The Joint Money Laundering Steering Group has provided a specimen certificate for use in these circumstances. A copy of this appears in **Appendix B1**.

9.4.4 Regulation 5(4)

In relation to a contract of long-term insurance –

(a) in connection with a pension scheme taken out by virtue of a person's contract of employment or occupation where the contract of long-term insurance –

    (i) contains no surrender clause; and

    (ii) may not be used as collateral for a loan; or

(b) in respect of which a premium is payable –

    (i) in one instalment of an amount not exceeding 2,500 euro; or

    (ii) periodically and where the total payable in respect of any calendar year does not exceed 1,000 euro.

Long-term insurance catches such insurance contracts as endowment or pension policies, annuities and single premium bonds issued by insurance companies. It is highly unlikely that a solicitor's retainer would be restricted to the provision of a long-term insurance contract for a client. Although some solicitors undoubtedly make arrangements for clients to purchase such policies, in most cases these arrangements are linked with other services. As such this particular exception is unlikely to be of assistance to solicitors.

9.4.5 Regulation 5(5)

Where the proceeds of a one-off transaction are payable to B but are instead directly reinvested on his behalf in another transaction –

(a) of which a record is kept; and

(b) which can result only in another reinvestment made on B's behalf or in a payment made directly to B

Again, this exception only applies to a one-off transaction where the firm is acting on a disposal and the proceeds are payable to the client. The second condition appears to rule out a general application of this exception. The Treasury's view is that this exception is intended to apply to pension payments only, not to the sale and purchase of tangible assets. The second tangible asset, which was purchased by way of investment from the proceeds of the first asset, could be disposed of by gift and therefore would not satisfy the requirements of regulation 5(5)(*b*).

9.4.6 Conclusion

If a firm is relying on any of the exceptions, there will be no need for the firm to obtain client identification evidence and therefore no requirement for a record to be kept. However, it must be good practice to record on the client's file (or elsewhere) details of the exception relied upon and (if evidence of identity has been obtained by a third party) details of the evidence and how it was obtained.

9.5 TRANSITIONAL PROVISIONS

Regulation 30 states:

(1) Nothing in these Regulations obliges any person who carries on relevant business falling within any of sub-paragraphs (a) to (e) of regulation 2(2) to maintain identification procedures which require evidence to be obtained in respect of any business relationship formed by him before 1 April 1994.

(2) Nothing in these Regulations obliges any person who carries on relevant business falling within any of sub-paragraphs (f) to (n) of regulation 2(2) –

 (a) to maintain identification procedures which require evidence to be obtained in respect of any business relationship formed by him before 1 March 2004; . . .

There are two transitional provisions referred to in regulation 30. The first allows firms to avoid the need for identification procedures for clients who formed specified business relationships before 1 April 1994; the second for clients who formed specified business relationships before 1 March 2004.

Before looking at the details of these transitional provisions it must be stressed that they will only apply if the firm has had a business relationship with a client before either 1 April 1994 or 1 March 2004. It is a common mistake to take the view that there is no need to seek client identification where the firm acted for a client prior to 1 April 1994. If the only relationship with a client was a one-off transaction or series of one-off transactions sometime in the past, these transitional provisions will not apply. Further, if the firm has had a business relationship with a client formed, say, before 1 April 1994 and that business relationship has terminated, any new business relationship subsequently formed cannot benefit from these transitional provisions.

9.5.1 Pre-1 April 1994 business relationships

Where a firm has an on-going business relationship formed with the client before 1 April 1994 (the commencement date for the 1993 Money Laundering Regulations) and the retainer related to business falling within regulation 2(2)(a)–(e), there is no need for any identification procedure to be applied post-1 March 2004 under the terms of the 2003 Regulations. By way of reminder, regulation 2(2)(a)–(e) covers the following business:

(a) the regulated activity of –

 (i) accepting deposits;
 (ii) effecting or carrying out contracts of long-term insurance when carried on by a person who has received official authorisation pursuant to Article 4 or 51 of the Life Assurance Consolidation Directive;
 (iii) dealing in investments as principal or as agent;
 (iv) arranging deals in investments;

    (v)   managing investments;
    (vi) safeguarding and administering investments;
    (vii) sending dematerialised instructions;
    (viii) establishing (and taking other steps in relation to) collective investment schemes;
    (ix) advising on investments; or
    (x)   issuing electronic money;

(b) the activities of the National Savings Bank;

(c) any activity carried on for the purpose of raising money authorised to be raised under the National Loans Act 1968 under the auspices of the Director of Savings;

(d) the business of operating a bureau de change, transmitting money (or any representation of monetary value) by any means or cashing cheques which are made payable to customers;

(e) any of the activities in points 1 to 12 or 14 of Annex 1 to the Banking Consolidation Directive (which activities are, for convenience, set out in Schedule 1 to these Regulations) when carried on by way of business, ignoring an activity falling within any of sub-paragraphs (a) to (d);

The only relevant business affecting solicitors will be regulation 2(2)(a) regulated activities (although it was always a moot point as to whether the activities referred to in the Banking Consolidation Directive applied to solicitors). The following example is an illustration.

A solicitor was instructed on a particular trust administration in February 1990. The trust fund consists of listed securities. Since February 1990 the firm has arranged the purchase and sale of securities on behalf of the trustees, using the services of stockbrokers. The firm is still currently acting on the administration. On these facts:

(a) it would appear that there is a business relationship – an on-going relationship where the total payment to be made was not known or capable of being ascertained at the outset of the retainer;

(b) it is a relationship which is unbroken since February 1990;

(c) the relevant business undertaken as a result of this relationship would appear to be restricted to:

    i.   dealing as agent or arranging deals in investments;
    ii. safeguarding and administrating investments;
    iii. advising on investments;

(d) these activities all fall within regulation 2(2)(a).

Consequently, the transitional provisions would appear to apply to this case and no steps would have to be taken to obtain client identity as a result of the 2003 Regulations coming into force on 1 March 2004.

9.5.2   Pre-1 March 2004 business relationships

Where a firm has an on-going business relationship formed with the client before 1 March 2004 (the commencement date for the Money Laundering

Regulations 2003) and the retainer related to business falling within regulation 2(2)(f)–(n), there is no need for any identification procedure to be applied post-1 March 2004 under the terms of the 2003 Regulations. By way of reminder, regulation 2(2)(f)–(n) cover the following business:

(f)   estate agency work;

(g)   operating a casino by way of business;

(h)   the activities of a person appointed to act as an insolvency practitioner within the meaning of section 388 of the Insolvency Act 1986 or Article 3 of the Insolvency (Northern Ireland) Order 1989;

(i)   the provision by way of business of advice about the tax affairs of another person by a body corporate or unincorporate or, in the case of a sole practitioner, by an individual;

(j)   the provision by way of business of accountancy services by a body corporate or unincorporate or, in the case of a sole practitioner, by an individual;

(k)   the provision by way of business of audit services by a person who is eligible for appointment as a company auditor under section 25 of the Companies Act 1989 or Article 28 of the Companies (Northern Ireland) Order 1990;

(l)   the provision by way of business of legal services by a body corporate or unincorporate or, in the case of a sole practitioner, by an individual and which involves participation in a financial or real property transaction (whether by assisting in the planning or execution of any such transaction or otherwise by acting for, or on behalf of, a client in any such transaction);

(m)   the provision by way of business of services in relation to the formation, operation or management of a company or a trust; or

(n)   the activity of dealing in goods of any description by way of business (including dealing as an auctioneer) whenever a transaction involves accepting a total cash payment of 15,000 euro or more.

The common relevant business affecting solicitors will be regulation 2(2)(i), (l) and (m). The following example is an illustration.

A company client (a property developer) instructed a solicitor in March 2001. The solicitor entered into a general retainer with the client agreeing to act for the client on the sale of all future developments until either party determined the retainer. Since 2001 the solicitor has acted for the client on a number of sales – the retainer is still current. Post-1 March 2004, the client instructs the solicitor to act on the sale of a newly-developed site. On these facts:

• It would appear that there is a business relationship – an on-going relationship where the total payment to be made was not known or capable of being ascertained at the outset of the retainer.

• It is a relationship which is unbroken since March 2001.

• The relevant business undertaken as a result of this relationship would appear to be restricted to the provision by way of business of legal services involving the participation in a real property transaction.

• This activity falls within regulation 2(2)(l).

Consequently, the transitional provisions would appear to apply to this case and

---

no steps would have to be taken to obtain client identity as a result of instructions relating to the newly-developed site received after the coming into force on 1 March 2004 of the 2003 Regulations.

Because of the complexity of these provisions, firms may prefer to over comply and, post-1 March 2004 seek verification of all new clients' identities and all existing clients' identities on new matters (unless an existing client's evidence of identity is already on file).

9.6 RECORD-KEEPING PROCEDURES

Regulation 5 states:

(1) A must maintain procedures which require the retention of the records prescribed in paragraph (2) for the period prescribed in paragraph (3).

(2) The records are –

    (a) where evidence of identity has been obtained under the procedures stipulated by regulation 4 (identification procedures) . . . –

        i. a copy of that evidence;

        ii. information as to where a copy of that evidence may be obtained; or

        iii. information enabling the evidence of identity to be re-obtained, but only where it is not reasonably practicable for A to comply with paragraph (i) or (ii); and

    (b) a record containing details relating to all transactions carried out by A in the course of relevant business.

(3) In relation to the records mentioned in paragraph (2)(a), the period is –

    (a) where A and B have formed a business relationship, at least five years commencing with the date on which the relationship ends; or

    (b) in the case of a one-off transaction (or a series of such transactions), at least five years commencing with the date of the completion of all activities taking place in the course of that transaction (or, as the case may be, the last of the transactions).

(4) In relation to the records mentioned in paragraph (2)(b), the period is at least five years commencing with the date on which all activities taking place in the course of the transaction in question were completed.

As a result of regulation 5, firms must maintain two records as part of their money laundering procedures. A record must be kept of the evidence of the client identity and a record must be kept of details of the transaction which amounts to relevant business.

9.6.1 Evidence of client identity

The regulation permits two types of record to be kept, with a third type available where neither of the first two types are reasonably practicable. In most cases, firms will keep a copy of the evidence obtained. This can be by way of a photocopy, or the original document can be scanned and a digital copy maintained.

Since the Regulations require the evidence to be reasonably capable of establishing (and does, in fact, establish to the satisfaction of the person who obtains it) that the client is the person he claims to be, the onus is very much upon the individual fee earner who accepts the evidence to be satisfied. Consequently, to bring this point to the attention of all members of staff who are responsible for accepting evidence of identity, firms will frequently require members of staff personally to sign a statement confirming that they have seen the original of any document relied upon and that they are satisfied from the evidence that it is reasonably capable of establishing that the client is the person he claims to be. In the case of photographic evidence, the member of staff should certify the copy by way of confirming that the client appears to be the person shown in the photograph.

Where a passport is used for identification purposes, reference should be made to guidance from HMSO (Note 20) dated 5 December 2002. The Law Society's *Money Laundering Guidance* refers to this and it is reproduced below:

3.79 The HMSO guidance note no. 20 dated 5 December 2002 confirms that copies of the personal details page of a UK passport may be made for the purposes of record keeping by the following persons only:

(a)   the holder of the passport
(b)   notaries, solicitors, UK government departments and British consulates;
(c)   financial institutions and other persons and firms who are subject to the ML Regulations 2003; and
(d)   any person or firm for the purpose of certifying that identification checks have been made in accordance with the ML Regulations 2003.

3.80 The Guidance says that copies must be in black and white only so that they cannot be mistaken for a real passport page. Copying for these purposes includes photocopying, scanning, filming, reproduction in any other medium, including placing material on the Internet. The original document is the evidence of identity. The photocopy of the original is used to record and certify that identification checks have been made. There is no need to apply for a licence or pay a fee to take such copies.

If evidence is obtained from an electronic database, a print out of the evidence should be made and kept by way of evidence.

Since the Regulations do not specify what can and cannot be used as evidence of identity, firms may agree to accept personal knowledge of an individual partner or established member of staff as sufficient evidence of identity of clients introduced by them. It would appear to be over zealous to demand a passport or other formal evidence of identity from a partner's long-established friend or family member. However, in these circumstances, a record must still be retained in accordance with regulation 5: an appropriate written confirmation of the partner's knowledge of the client's identity should be retained.

If the firm does not hold the copy of the evidence, an alternative record that satisfies regulation 5 will be information as to where a copy of that evidence may be obtained. Only if it is not reasonably practicable to keep records in this form can a firm satisfy the requirements of regulation 5 by retaining information enabling the evidence of identity to be reobtained.

9.6.2 Evidence of transaction

The Law Society's *Money Laundering Guidance* indicates that, in most cases, keeping a copy of the client file and the accounting records for each client for whom the firm undertakes relevant business should satisfy this requirement of regulation 5.

In earlier guidance applicable to the Money Laundering Regulations 1993 (which imposed similar record-keeping requirements) the Law Society recommended that firms should keep a record of the origin of funds paid by the client to the firm (and, where appropriate, details of cheques should be noted). Whilst the client file is likely to contain general details of the origin of any funds, specific details such as the bank address and sort code, account name and number from which funds have been drawn may not necessarily have been recorded on the file. Consideration should be given to photocopying cheques before paying them into client account (if the volume of cheques makes this practicable). Alternatively, adjustments can be made to a firm's internal paying-in slip, used by fee earners to send cheques to the accounts department, requiring the paying bank's sort code and account number to be recorded.

9.6.3 Retention periods

The evidence of client identity must be retained for a period of at least five years from the date on which a business relationship ends or a period of at least five years from the date of completion of all activities carried out in the course of a one-off transaction. If there is a series of linked one-off transactions, the five-year period commences on completion of the activities carried out in the course of the last of the linked transactions.

The evidence of the transaction must be retained for the period of at least five years commencing with the date on which all activities taking place in the course of the transaction in question were completed.

Given that the five-year period commences in all cases at the end of the relationship or transaction, firms must recognise that in some cases the period might extend beyond the normal file retention period or accounting record retention. It is important for procedures to be maintained to ensure the money laundering records are not destroyed before the end of the retention period.

Further, given that most firms will use the client files for regulation 5 purposes, care must be taken at the end of a transaction not to simply hand over the client's file to the client or to a client's new solicitors without first creating a separate record of the transaction for regulation 5 purposes.

Although the Regulations do not specify where the records must be kept, there are compelling reasons for considering a central record of client identification evidence. If client identification records are kept on a client file, at the end of the transaction the file may be sent to storage (this will still satisfy the retention requirements, provided the firm is able to recover the file from storage). However, if after say, three years, the client returns to the firm, it is useful to have access to a central record of client identities to avoid the embarrassment of asking the client to provide verification details again, rather than to have to access a file in storage.

9.7 INTERNAL REPORTING PROCEDURES

Regulation 7 states:

(1) A must maintain internal reporting procedures which require that –

(a) a person in A's organisation is nominated to receive disclosures under this regulation ('the nominated officer');

(b) anyone in A's organisation to whom information or other matter comes in the course of relevant business as a result of which he knows or suspects or has reasonable grounds for knowing or suspecting that a person is engaged in money laundering must, as soon as is practicable after the information or other matter comes to him, disclose it to the nominated officer or a person authorised for the purposes of these Regulations by the Director General of the National Criminal Intelligence Service;

(c) where a disclosure is made to the nominated officer, he must consider it in the light of any relevant information which is available to A and determine whether it gives rise to such knowledge or suspicion or such reasonable grounds for knowledge or suspicion; and

(d) where the nominated officer does so determine, the information or other matter must be disclosed to a person authorised for the purposes of these Regulations by the Director General of the National Criminal Intelligence Service.

In this context, A means a person who carries on relevant business in the United Kingdom (reg. 4(1)).

A number of procedures are required as a result of this regulation.

9.7.1 Appointment of nominated officer: regulation 7(1)(*a*)

The firm must appoint someone as a nominated officer. His or her role is to receive disclosures from members of the firm. The nominated officer does not have to be a partner (or, in an incorporated practice, an officer) but should be of sufficient seniority to have access to the firm's clients' files and other internal business records.

A sole practitioner who does not employ staff or act in association with anyone else is not subject to regulation 7 and therefore does not have to appoint a nominated officer. Regulation 7(2) provides: 'Paragraph (1) does not apply where A is an individual who neither employs nor acts in association with any other person.'

Larger firms may wish to appoint deputy nominated officers who may undertake some of the functions of the nominated officer, subject to the nominated officer's overall supervision. All firms, whatever their size, should make arrangements covering the absence of the nominated officer as a result of holidays, sick leave or other reason.

Firms authorised under the Financial Services and Markets Act 2000 will have to seek approval of the Financial Services Authority to the appointment of the nominated officer.

9.7.2 Disclosure of knowledge or suspicion of money laundering: regulation 7(1)(*b*)

The Regulations impose an obligation on anyone in a firm to make a disclosure to the firm's nominated officer where they know or suspect (or have reasonable grounds for knowing or suspecting) that another is engaged in money laundering and where the information came into their possession as a result of relevant business. Alternatively, the disclosure can be made to NCIS, although most firms will require members to disclose internally.

This provision effectively replicates PoCA 2002, s.330 (see **Chapter 5**), since the definition of relevant business in the Money Laundering Regulations mirrors the definition of the regulated sector in section 330. Like PoCA 2002, s.330, regulation 7(1)(*b*) applies an objective test of knowledge or suspicion.

The Regulations provide for a defence of privilege (similar to the defence available in PoCA 2002, s.330). Regulation 7(3)–(6) provide:

(3) Paragraph (1)(b) does not apply in relation to a professional legal adviser where the information or other matter comes to him in privileged circumstances.

(4) Information or other matter comes to a professional legal adviser in privileged circumstances if it is communicated or given to him –

    (a) by (or by a representative of) a client of his in connection with the giving by the adviser of legal advice to the client;

(b) by (or by a representative of) a person seeking legal advice from the adviser; or

(c) by a person in connection with legal proceedings or contemplated legal proceedings.

(5) But paragraph (4) does not apply to information or other matter which is communicated or given with the intention of furthering a criminal purpose.

(6) 'Professional legal adviser' includes any person in whose hands information or other matter may come in privileged circumstances.

The wording of these subparagraphs is almost identical to the wording in PoCA 2002, s.330 except, as noted in **Chapter 5**, the definition of a professional legal adviser is extended to any person in whose hands information or other matter may come in privileged circumstances. For a full commentary on the defence of privilege, see **Chapter 5**.

9.7.3 Consideration and determination by the nominated officer: regulation 7(1)(*c*)

The Regulations require a nominated officer to consider any disclosures made by members of the firm in the light of all relevant information available in the firm. Hence there is a requirement for the nominated officer to be of sufficient seniority to gain access to this information. The Regulations do not specifically require the nominated officer to keep a record of this consideration but it would be good practice to do so. The information recorded can include:

(a) The name of the member of staff making the disclosure.
(b) The details of, and reasons for, the disclosure.
(c) The other relevant information taken into account by the nominated officer in making his determination.
(d) The decision whether or not to report to NCIS and the reason for the decision.

If the firm requires internal reports to be submitted to the nominated officer on specified forms, retention of these forms would satisfy the record-keeping requirements of (a) and (b) above although additional records would have to be kept to satisfy (c) and (d).

9.7.4 Disclosure to NCIS: regulation 7(1)(*d*)

If a nominated officer determines that the information gives rise to knowledge or suspicion (or reasonable grounds for knowledge or suspicion) that another is engaged in money laundering, the information must be disclosed to NCIS. This replicates the provisions of PoCA 2002, s.331 (see **Chapter 5**). Consequently, a nominated officer who does not comply with regulation

7(1)(*d*), in addition to any penalties for breaching the money laundering regulations, risks committing an offence under PoCA 2002, s.331.

9.7.5 Transitional provisions

Regulation 30(2) provides:

> (2) Nothing in these Regulations obliges any person who carries on relevant business falling within any of sub-paragraphs (f) to (n) of regulation 2(2) –
> ... (b) to maintain internal reporting procedures which require any action to be taken in respect of any knowledge, suspicion or reasonable grounds for knowledge or suspicion which came to that person before 1st March 2004.

Reference to subparagraphs (*f*) to (*n*) of regulation 2(2) can be found in **Paragraph 9.5.2**. This provision ensures that if, for example, information giving rise to knowledge or suspicion of another's engagement in money laundering came into the possession of a solicitor as a result of a property transaction (reg. 2(2)(l)) in February 2004 no action under the internal reporting procedures would be required. (No action under PoCA 2002, ss.330 or 331 would be required since the amendment to the definition of the regulated sector only came into force on 1 March 2004. Real property transactions were not within the regulated sector before that date.) However, if the property transaction continued into March 2004 and beyond, any information received after 1 March 2004 and giving rise to knowledge or suspicion of money laundering would be subject to regulation 7 (and to PoCA 2002, ss.330 and 331).

Note, however, that this transitional provision only applies to the requirements contained in the Money Laundering Regulations 2003. There may be obligations under the substantive law that would require disclosure by way of a defence to the money laundering offences.

9.8 PENALTIES

Regulation 3(2) states:

> (2) A person who contravenes this regulation is guilty of an offence and liable –
>
> (a) on conviction on indictment, to imprisonment for a term not exceeding 2 years, to a fine or to both;
> (b) on summary conviction, to a fine not exceeding the statutory maximum.

Further, regulation 27 provides that where it is shown that an offence under regulation 3 has been committed by a body corporate or partnership with the consent of or the connivance of an officer (in the case of an incorporated practice) or a partner (in the case of a partnership) or to be attributable to any neglect on their part, the officer as well as the body corporate or the partner as well as the partnership is guilty of an offence and liable to be proceeded against and punished accordingly. Partners and principals should note that personal liability can therefore arise where there is a failure to comply with the Regulations.

Regulation 3(3) states:

(3) In deciding whether a person has committed an offence under this regulation, the court must consider whether he followed any relevant guidance which was at the time concerned –

(a) issued by a supervisory authority or any other appropriate body;
(b) approved by the Treasury; and
(c) published in a manner approved by the Treasury as appropriate in their opinion to bring the guidance to the attention of persons likely to be affected by it.

A supervisory body is defined in regulation 2(8) and the term includes the Law Society.

As noted in previous chapters, The Law Society has issued Guidance to the solicitors' profession (*Money Laundering Guidance: Professional Ethics*, Pilot, January 2004). Extracts from the *Money Laundering Guidance* appear in the text of this book and in **Appendix B1**. The Law Society's *Money Laundering Guidance* is described as a pilot and has not been submitted to the Treasury for approval. Consequently, regulation 3(3) will not apply technically. However, as stated in the *Money Laundering Guidance*, a court 'may still take it into consideration' in deciding whether an offence has been committed under regulation 3.

PART 2

Practical Guidance

CHAPTER 10

Reporting suspicions

10.1 INTRODUCTION

The substantive law and the Money Laundering Regulations 2003 require disclosure of knowledge or suspicion of money laundering by way of defence and/or by way of obligation. In both cases, the disclosure can be internal (to the firm's nominated officer) or external. External authorised and protected disclosures need to be made to a constable, or a customs officer. Other external disclosures are made to a person authorised by the Director General of the National Criminal Intelligence Service (NCIS). In practice this means that all external disclosures are made to NCIS.

10.2 INTERNAL DISCLOSURES

Firms can decide themselves on the manner of internal disclosures. Although the Proceeds of Crime Act 2002 (PoCA 2002) s.339 provides that the form of disclosures (both internal and external) can be prescribed by order of the Secretary of State (see **Chapter 4**), at the time of writing no such order has been made. For internal disclosures, it is recommended that firms use an appropriate written form of disclosure. The consequences of making a disclosure are such that it is vital for firms to be able to recognise when a formal disclosure has been made internally – distinguishing this from an informal discussion with a more senior member of the firm. A precedent (which may be adapted depending upon the size and nature of the firm) can be found in **Appendix C3**.

As noted in **Chapter 9**, it is also recommended that nominated officers keep a record of internal disclosures and the steps taken by them in the light of such disclosures. This is particularly important where the decision is made not to report to NCIS.

If firms use an internal reporting form, it is vital that a copy of this form is not kept on the client's file. At the end of a transaction (or during a transaction, if a client chooses to change solicitors) and on the payment of a solicitor's costs, the client may require the firm to hand over the file (either to the client or to his new solicitors). If details of the internal disclosure remain, inadvertently, on the file, this could lead to a conviction for tipping off in extreme circumstances. (For details of the offence of tipping off, see **Chapter 7.**)

10.3 EXTERNAL DISCLOSURES

External disclosures by members of staff to NCIS should not be encouraged by way of a defence or compliance with an obligation. Members of staff will obtain the necessary defence or fulfil any obligation by making an internal disclosure to the firm's nominated officer. Complex questions of confidentiality and legal professional privilege can more easily be dealt with where the disclosure is internal. External reporting should be limited to the firm's nominated officer and will arise where the officer's obligations under PoCA 2002, ss.331 or 332 or regulation 7 of the Money Laundering Regulations 2003 apply. (For details of PoCA 2002, ss.331 and 332, see **Chapter 5**; for details of reg. 7, see **Chapter 9**.)

The Government has issued a white paper (March 2004) setting out proposals to merge NCIS with the National Crime Squad and parts of the Immigration Service and of Customs and Excise. The new body will be called the Serious and Organised Crime Agency (SOCA) and is likely to come into being in 2006. From sometime in that year it is likely that disclosures will be made to SOCA.

Disclosures by a nominated officer can be to NCIS using the form, available for downloading from the NCIS web-site (**www.ncis.gov.uk**). There are two forms available: one for standard disclosures (the standard report form) and one for limited intelligence disclosure reports. Full guidance notes on how to complete the forms are provided on the website. The forms for disclosure are reproduced in **Appendix C4** together with the guidance for their completion.

In addition, NCIS has issued guidance in relation to disclosure by the legal profession. This guidance has been updated in the light of the case of *P* v. *P* [2003] EWHC Fam 2260 (see **Chapter 7**). The guidance is reproduced in **Appendix B3**.

10.3.1 Standard report form

The standard report form should be used where firms are making protected or authorised disclosures under PoCA 2003, ss.337 and 338. The form can also be used where it is necessary to make a disclosure as a result of the Terrorism Act 2000 ss. 18 or 21A.

NCIS guidance states that although these forms are not mandatory, they are the preferred format and have been designed to facilitate the efficient and effective handling of disclosures by NCIS. The downloaded version of the report can be completed on the firm's own computer. NCIS have advised that the downloaded version must not be used for hand written reports. Hand written reports should only be completed on a special version of the form available by telephoning 020 7238 8282.

Where firms are using a computer-completed form (downloaded from the NCIS website) it will be necessary for the form to be printed and submitted by post or fax. The form cannot be submitted through the Internet. Forms should be faxed to 020 7238 8286 or sent by post to NCIS, PO Box 8000, London SE11 5EN.

The downloaded version is available in PDF format. Unless firms have the commercial version of the Acrobat Reader, the completed form cannot be saved to firms' computer files as a PDF document. It can, however, be printed and a hard copy retained. If firms wish to retain an electronic version, the completed PDF format document can be copied into a Word document and saved.

The standard form consists of five sheets and these can be submitted in different combinations depending upon the information disclosed. Since the form has been designed to be read by Image Character Recognition technology, amendments or additions outside the structure of the form will hamper the capability of NICS to process the form efficiently. The five sheets consist of:

- **Sheet 1: Summary section**. NCIS state that it is necessary for this sheet to be clearly completed enabling NCIS to check that it has received the correct number of sheets.
- **Sheet 2: Subject details**. This sets out the details of the subject of the report (victim or suspect).
- **Sheet 3: Additional details**. This sets out addresses of the subject.
- **Sheet 4: Transaction details**. This sets out the type of transaction and the amounts involved.
- **Sheet 5: Reasons for disclosure**. These must be set out in full.

In addition, the first time a firm submits a disclosure to NCIS or when the firm's contact details have changed, it will be necessary to submit the Source Registration Document.

10.3.2 Limited intelligence value reports

Dame Elizabeth Butler-Sloss in her judgment in *P* v. *P* stated:

> It is important for the legal profession to take into account . . . that the Act [PoCA 2002] makes no distinction between degrees of criminal property. An illegally obtained sum of £10 is no less susceptible to the definition of 'criminal property' than a sum of £1 million. Parliament clearly intended this to be the case. Whatever may be the resource implications, the legal profession would appear to be bound by the provisions of the Act in all cases, however big or small. If this approach is

scrupulously followed by the legal advisers, the result is likely to have a considerable and adverse impact upon NCIS . . .

Acknowledging the problem, NCIS has introduced a limited intelligence value report for use in certain specified circumstances. As with the standard report, the form of this report can be downloaded from the NCIS website and completed on the solicitor's own computer (see above for further details). Special versions of the form are available where the solicitor wishes to complete the form by hand. The form must be submitted by fax or post, and the contact fax number and address is the same as used to submit the standard form (see **Paragraph 10.3.1**).

The form itself is a single sheet. A copy, together with the guidance notes for completion, can be found in **Appendix C4**.

NCIS has issued guidance on the types of circumstances that are appropriate for abbreviated information to be provided in this form. It accepts that the provisions of PoCA 2002 mean that solicitors may be required to make disclosures but the information is likely to be of limited intelligence value to law enforcement agencies. However, NCIS reserves the right to ask solicitors to submit details on a standard form if it believes this is necessary.

The circumstances where a limited intelligence value report is appropriate can be found in the table included in the guidance notes at **Appendix C4**

10.3.3   Fast track

As noted in **Chapter 4**, on occasions solicitors may be under time constraints (e.g. completion of the transaction may be set for two or three days' time). In these circumstances, if an authorised disclosure is made, no further action which might facilitate the acquisition, retention, use or control of criminal property can be undertaken without appropriate consent. If the disclosure has been made internally, the firm's nominated officer cannot give appropriate consent unless NCIS has been notified and it has either consented to the action proposed or seven working days have elapsed during which NCIS has not given notice of refusal to act. (For details of these provisions, see **Chapter 3**.)

Where time is important, it is possible to ask NCIS to make a decision using the fast track procedure. To do so, the nominated officer should make the disclosure by fax indicating that the matter is urgent and giving details of the time critical issues so that consent can be given quickly. In most cases there is no need to telephone the duty desk at NCIS first to explain the urgency (telephone 020 7238 8282). The 'consent required' box should be marked on the standard form. Details of the timescale and the impact of a delayed response should be included in the report.

If NCIS agrees that the fast track procedure is appropriate it may refer the matter to the appropriate law enforcement agency immediately or otherwise determine the appropriate way forward. Once a decision has been reached the solicitor making the disclosure will be informed by fax.

10.3.4 Repeat disclosures

Dame Elizabeth Butler-Sloss, in her judgment in *P* v. *P* stated:

> I should like to remind legal advisers that it would not seem necessary to make repeated disclosures on the same facts, unless it is proposed to enter into a new arrangement or a variation of the same arrangement. Each time a further disclosure is made, time will start running again for 7 days or possibly 7 plus 31 days.

10.3.5 After the report

The Law Society has given guidance in relation to a solicitor's duty and obligations after making a report to NCIS. This guidance also deals with the tension between an obligation not to tip off and an individual's right to access to all of his personal data under the terms of the Data Protection Act 1998. The guidance is set out below.

> Even after a report has been made, firms should continue to be vigilant for any related transactions or instructions that cause the solicitor concern/suspicion and which may need to be reported. Follow up reports may need to be made because circumstances change or develop.
>
> If appropriate consent is withheld during the moratorium period, NCIS and/or law enforcement agencies will usually advise the organisation which made the report why this decision has been taken. Solicitors should not communicate these reasons to their clients or other parties.
>
> The submission of a report and/or the receipt of appropriate consent is not intended to override commercial judgement. It will be for solicitors to decide whether to continue to act. Terminating a retainer will not in itself amount to tipping off but the manner in which the retainer is terminated will be important. NCIS and/or law enforcement agencies may be able to provide some assistance to solicitors in explaining why they no longer wish to act for a client.
>
> There are concerns that reports may be revealed by the authorities to the suspected person or organisation, often a solicitor's own client. NCIS would prefer all information which they provide to law enforcement agencies to remain confidential, and for the reports to be included in the sensitive material bundle of any eventual prosecution papers. This means that the information will not automatically be disclosed by the prosecution to the defence lawyers. However, this is at the discretion of the prosecuting body. If the prosecuting body is sympathetic to the discloser's desire to remain anonymous they can mount Public Interest Immunity arguments. On occasion prosecuting bodies have discontinued cases rather than risk the identity of sources being revealed. The Law Society remains concerned that there should be official assurances about how this issue will be approached.
>
> Both NCIS and solicitors' firms are subject to the Data Protection Act 1998 which means that clients or others can make subject access requests under section 7. Such a request raises the question of whether a report to NCIS should be disclosed to the person making the subject access request. The tension between the

obligation not to tip off, and the individual's right of access to all of his personal data is addressed in guidance issued by HM Treasury in consultation with the Information Commissioner. Section 29 of the Data Protection Act provides an exemption from the need to provide personal data where disclosure would be likely to prejudice the prevention or detection of crime or the apprehension or prosecution of offenders. The guidance says that where disclosure would constitute a tipping off offence, the section 29 exemption would be likely to apply. The guidance applies even if a suspicion has been made internally within a solicitor's firm and not reported externally. Note that the Treasury guidance may be reviewed in the light of recent case law on the definition of personal data.

If solicitors receive a subject access request but are in doubt as to whether the provision of information, e.g. a copy report made to NCIS, would be likely to prejudice an investigation or potential investigation they should approach NCIS and the relevant law enforcement agency for guidance. Solicitors should keep records of any steps they take in determining whether disclosure would involve tipping off and/or the availability of a section 29 exemption. These records may be useful if the solicitor is asked to respond to enquiries made subsequently by the Information Commissioner or courts.

It is important to note that where a piece of information is not disclosed because of the section 29 exemption there is no obligation to tell the individual that the information has been withheld.

CHAPTER 11

Management of money laundering procedures

11.1 INTRODUCTION

This Chapter provides guidance on how firms can organise their management and administration of money laundering procedures to promote compliance with the Money Laundering Regulations 2003 and to avoid risking inadvertent involvement in money laundering offences. The dangers from the legislation of undertaking any legal services on behalf of clients are such that it is vital for even the smallest of firms to adopt anti-money laundering systems and policies.

11.2 POLICY DECISIONS

Firms should make a number of policy decisions in respect of their anti-money laundering procedures. It is vital to undertake all areas of practice within a framework of positive policy decisions rather than allowing the organisation to develop procedures in an unstructured way. Clear policy decisions allow all those involved in relevant business within the firm and those involved in other risk areas of the practice to understand their responsibilities and obligations. A senior partner (or officer) should be responsible for ensuring business decisions on anti-money laundering procedures. This partner (or officer) will frequently be the firm's nominated officer although where the nominated officer is not a partner (or officer) overall responsibility for the firm's policies should rest with a partner or officer.

The policy decisions required to be taken by the firm are listed below. This may not be an exhaustive list. Further details are provided on each heading in the paragraphs which follow. The policies include:

- Appointment of a nominated officer.
- Type of work at risk from money laundering activities.
- Amendments to the firm's Terms of Business.
- Internal reporting procedures.
- Client identification procedures.

- Record-keeping procedures.
- Branch or overseas offices.
- Staff training.

11.2.1 Appointment of a nominated officer

Regulation 7 of the Money Laundering Regulations 2003 requires firms to nominate a person to receive disclosures of knowledge or suspicion of money laundering. If the firm is undertaking relevant business, it is mandatory for such an officer to be appointed in accordance with regulation 7. A failure to do so will amount to a criminal offence under the terms of regulation 3.

However, even if the firm is not undertaking relevant business (in the light of the current definition of relevant business, this is likely to apply to a very small number of firms) the appointment of a nominated officer is still good practice. The substantive law contained in the Proceeds of Crime Act 2002 (PoCA 2002) and the Terrorism Act 2000 does not oblige firms to appoint a nominated officer, however, without the appointment authorised or protected disclosures could only be made to NCIS. The appointment of a nominated officer ensures that internal disclosures can be made. (The fact that a firm does not undertake relevant business under the Money Laundering Regulations 2003 does not avoid the risk that members of the firm may commit offences under PoCA 2002 or the Terrorism Act 2000.)

Most firms will appoint a partner to the role and this partner can then be made responsible for the overall anti-money laundering policies of the firm. However, there is no requirement that the nominated officer be a partner. The requirement in regulation 7 that the nominated officer should consider reports from members of staff 'in the light of any relevant information' which is available in the firm means the nominated officer should be of sufficient seniority to have access to this information.

The role is an important and onerous one. A nominated officer will be subject to PoCA 2002, ss. 331 and 332 (see **Chapter 6**) which give rise to criminal offences if the nominated officer fails to follow the requirements of the sections. Further criminal offences can arise under regulation 7 of the Money Laundering Regulations 2003. Consequently, individuals should be prepared to accept the role only if they are able to take on the responsibilities, which in many cases will be time consuming. Thought might be given to the role rotating between specified partners, with each individual partner undertaking the role for a period of, say, six months, providing those undertaking the role have sufficient knowledge.

One important part of the role is the ability to provide detailed advice to members of the firm on their responsibilities and compliance with the firm's procedures. Nominated officers will need to keep up to date with developments in this area making the necessary amendments to the firm's procedures.

Larger firms will frequently appoint deputy officers to whom certain duties can be delegated. The nominated officer should, however, remain in overall control and will be the person ultimately responsible for complying with the legal obligations of an officer.

All firms must ensure that temporary cover is provided when the nominated officer is absent from the firm, for whatever reason.

11.2.2 Type of work at risk from money laundering activities

There is probably no area of practice which is not at risk, to some extent, from involvement in money laundering activities. However, some areas of practice are undoubtedly at more risk than others and firms need to identify the high-risk areas to ensure proper risk management procedures are put in place for the fee earners and others operating in these areas. Details of individual practice areas and the common risks are contained in **Chapter 12**.

11.2.3 Terms of business

The firm's terms of business should be reconsidered in the light of the substantive law and money laundering regulations. It will not be tipping off or the offence of prejudicing an investigation for firms to amend their standard terms of business, thereby explaining to clients the basis on which the money laundering requirements apply to all retainers. Clauses to consider might include some or all of the following:

- **Client identification**
  This term can be to the effect that Government regulations now require firms to obtain details of clients' identity before acting for them and in the absence of satisfactory evidence of identity, the firm will not be able to act or continue to act for the client.
- **Reporting obligations**
  This term can indicate that the firm has an obligation to report knowledge or suspicion of certain criminal activities to the authorities and that in many cases this must be done without reference to, or the consent of, the client.
- **Terminating the retainer**
  This term can indicate that, in extreme cases, the firm might have to terminate the client's instructions in circumstances where the firm may not be able to communicate the reason for the termination to the client. (This could be relevant where an authorised disclosure is made to NCIS and the firm receives notice of refusal of consent to the firm continuing to act. The fee earner could be tipping off if the reason for the termination was communicated to the client.)

- **Limitation of liability**

  Theoretically, solicitors could be liable in civil law to clients (and others who might be victims of criminal activities). The Law Society's *Money Laundering Guidance* provides an excellent and comprehensive statement of the law on civil liability arising in the context of money laundering and offers practical guidance on how to reduce the risk of liability. Its guidance on this topic is printed in full in **Appendix B1**.

  Although an exclusion clause will not assist a solicitor where a victim who is not a client makes a civil claim, such a clause may assist in relation to claims by clients. If a completion is delayed as a result of an authorised disclosure and the client is consequently in breach of contract, the client may seek to obtain damages from the solicitor, particularly if it turns out that the suspected criminal conduct did not exist. A clause which seeks to limit liability from civil claims arising from a decision by a solicitor relating to his or her money laundering obligations may be helpful. Any such clause is likely to be subject to the reasonableness test in section 2(2) Unfair Contract Terms Act 1977. The Law Society's guidance on limitation of liability by contract is contained in paragraph 12.11 of *The Guide to The Professional Conduct of Solicitors* (8th edition 1999). This provides that solicitors may, by contract, seek to limit their liability provided such limitation is not below the minimum level of compulsory insurance cover (currently £1 million).

- **Source of funds**

  This term may specify that, as a result of Government regulations, the firm must have regard to the source of any funds to be used by the client in any transaction and that, consequently, the firm will require clients to fully disclose details of the source of funds. Failure to do may lead to the firm terminating the retainer.

  Where funds are sourced from abroad, consideration might be given to a requirement that such funds are brought into the UK through a UK clearing bank rather that directly into the solicitor's client account. In this way some comfort can be obtained from the bank's anti-money laundering procedures. However, it must be acknowledged that the use of a UK bank in these circumstances will not completely avoid any risks on the part of the solicitor. The solicitor may have information obtained in the course of acting which the bank does not have and which gives rise to suspicion or knowledge of criminal intent.

11.2.4 Internal reporting procedures

A key decision to be taken by firms is how members of staff should report their knowledge or suspicion of money laundering matters. For most firms, the decision will be that all members of staff should use the internal reporting procedures rather than external reporting. The name of the nominated officer together with the name of the deputy and/or alternative should be made known to all members of staff. Firms should consider using a standard form for internal reporting purposes, allowing for a clear distinction to be made between informal discussions with the nominated officer and formal disclosures.

A clear policy for post-disclosure requirements must be adopted and communicated. This policy should be that once an internal disclosure has been made:

- No further work should be undertaken on the file without the consent of the nominated officer. Failure to abide by this requirement could lead to the loss of any defence afforded by an authorised disclosure (see **Chapter 4**). Whilst in practice it may be possible for a limited amount of work to be undertaken on the file (i.e. that work which does not facilitate the acquisition, retention, use or control of criminal property) it is dangerous to allow individual fee earners to make a decision as to what might be possible and what activities might negate any defence. The nominated officer should take this decision centrally, after careful consideration of the facts.

- No communication should be made to anyone concerning the disclosure, without the consent of the nominated officer. Failure to comply with this requirement may lead to tipping off and/or the offence of prejudicing an investigation (see **Chapter 7**). Again, it makes sense to keep control of any subsequent communications centrally rather than to allow individual members of staff to make their own decisions. This restriction on communicating should be absolute. In other words, those making the disclosure should not communicate details to anyone, including other members of staff.

One problem arising from these policies (particularly the policy of restricting communications regarding the disclosure) is that if a fee earner leaves the firm or otherwise ceases to act on a file, any new fee earner may not be aware that concerns have been expressed regarding money laundering and that an authorised disclosure may have been made internally. To overcome this problem some firms operate a black book system. The nominated officer enters all reports (formal or otherwise) in a black book which he/she keeps confidential.

New fee earners can make a black book search by approaching the nominated officer who can simply confirm if any entry regarding that file has been made. Files which have given rise to a report could be tagged (extra number/letter on file reference) which would then indicate to any fee earner coming to the file that a black book search should be made. Tagging using a discreet indication should not give rise to any risk of tipping off where the client requires access to the file.

11.2.5   Client identification procedures

In addition to deciding exactly what evidence of identity is acceptable for different categories of client (for details see **Chapter 9** and, in particular, **Appendix B1**) a policy decision must be taken specifying which clients are subject to verification of their identity.

If firms wish to apply the Money Laundering Regulations 2003 strictly a complex new file opening procedure will have to be adopted which will have to be capable of ascertaining:

- Whether relevant business will be undertaken.
- If so, whether it is a business relationship or one-off transaction.
- If it is a one-off transaction, whether the amount involved is €15,000 or more or whether there is knowledge or suspicion of money laundering.
- Whether any of the exceptions apply.
- Whether the transitional provisions apply.

Even if, in the light of this complex checklist, a decision is taken that no identification procedures are necessary, the firm's procedures must be able to identify when a one-off transaction (which initially did not require identification) becomes a business relationship or when a transaction which starts as non-relevant business becomes relevant business (as a result perhaps of tax advice being sought and given).

There is a lot to be said for applying verification procedures to all clients regardless of the type of business.

The firm should also adopt a clear policy on what can and cannot be undertaken on behalf of clients before satisfactory evidence of identity is received. This should include reference to the holding of client money (see **Chapter 9** for further detail).

11.2.6   Record-keeping requirements

Details of the formal records required under the Money Laundering Regulations 2003 are contained in **Chapter 9**. However, the firm should consider keeping records (possibly using internally agreed forms) covering the following areas:

- Record of the evidence of the client's identity (as required by the Regulations).
- Record of the transaction (as required by the Regulations). In many cases this record can be satisfied by reference to the contents of the client file and accounting records.
- Copy of the client verification form (for an example, see **Appendix C1**).
- Details of the client's source of funds.
- Record of internal disclosures.

- Record of the nominated officer's consideration and determination regarding internal disclosures.
- Record of external disclosures.
- Record of staff training.

11.2.7 Branch or overseas offices

Where a firm has a branch and/or an overseas office, firms should consider how best to ensure compliance by those offices with their anti-money laundering procedures. If the firm has a branch office in England and Wales, staff at the branch office will be subject to the same obligations as those working in the main office. Effective control procedures must be devised in accordance with the firm's general procedures. Deputy nominated officers may be appointed in each branch office.

Overseas offices will not, strictly, be subject to UK law or to the Money Laundering Regulation 2003. However, many overseas jurisdictions impose similar anti-money laundering requirements on local practitioners. EU countries will be subject to the Second EU Money Laundering Directive and, as such, should have introduced similar provisions to the UK Regulations. As a general rule, however, it appears that the UK's legislation and money laundering regulations impose a greater obligation upon practitioners compared with overseas jurisdictions (with the possible exception of the Netherlands). Consequently, many English and Welsh firms with overseas offices have adopted a policy that their overseas offices should comply with the UK requirements to enable a common set of procedures throughout the firm's offices. Local nominated officers can be appointed in each office with similar roles to the nominated officer in the UK.

11.2.8 Staff training

The training requirements are contained in regulation 3 of the Money Laundering Regulations 2003 and are dealt with in **Chapter 9**.

Firms should determine their training policies so as to ensure that all relevant members of staff receive training in the substantive law, the Regulations, the firm's own procedures and in the recognition and dealing with transactions which may involve money laundering.

The firm's money laundering manual (see **Paragraph 11.3**) should be distributed to all relevant members of staff and, if appropriate, members of staff should be asked to sign a declaration that they have read and understood its contents.

Training should be a rolling programme, with regular updating sessions and sessions for newly joined members of staff. It should cover all members of staff, fee earning as well as support staff, but should be tailored to individual group requirements.

11.3 THE COMPLIANCE MANUAL

The PoCA 2002, the Terrorism Act 2000 and the Money Laundering Regulations 2003 require firms to comply with a fairly complex framework of rules. Full compliance with these requirements is essential.

Poor compliance in some circumstances can lead to a criminal conviction and the possibility of disciplinary action being taken against members of the firm. The firm's procedures for compliance with the requirements must therefore be given attention by high-level management within the firm. Once determined, the firm's policies and procedures must be communicated to all personnel who at any time may be involved in investment activities.

The most satisfactory method of recording and communicating the firm's procedures is by the use of a compliance manual. The manual should be in an easily readable form and should not attempt to reiterate all the provisions of PoCA 2002, the Terrorism Act 2000 or the Money Laundering Regulation 2003. Instead, it should seek to provide explanations and instructions in a practical way in respect of the anti-money laundering procedures adopted by the firm. The manual should be arranged in suitable sections. It is essential that the manual is kept up to date.

The contents of the manual will vary from firm to firm. It is suggested that the following should be included in the manual:

- **Policy decisions**
  The policies which have been determined by the firm should be clearly stated. The names of the nominated officer, deputies and alternative officer should be stated.
- **Brief explanation and illustration of the Acts and the Regulations as they apply to the firm**
  The manual should not seek to reiterate all the provisions of PoCA 2002 or the Terrorism Act 2002 and other material. However, the emphasis should be on explanation and illustration of how the Acts and Regulations apply to the firm's business.
- **The firm's procedures for compliance**
  The firm's procedures should be recorded to ensure that all personnel understand how clients must be identified, how internal reports should be made and which records need to be maintained and where they are held.
- **Specimen forms**
  All forms relating to the firm's anti-money laundering procedures should be included with instructions for their use.

- **Instructions to departments of the firm on procedures which relate specifically to work undertaken in those departments**
  Procedures to be followed when dealing with clients of the various departments should be recorded where possible using one subsection per department. The procedures should, of course, be consistent with the policy decisions made on the type and extent of any risk and the possibility of the work involving activities in the regulated sector.
- **A list of warnings**
  A simple list of warnings could be included to inform staff when they are stepping outside the firm's policies or their individual authority.
- **Help**
  No matter how well written the manual is, the Acts and the Regulations can present a considerable compliance problem. The manual should give clear instructions on how to obtain assistance and advice from within the firm. A call for help at a crucial point by a fee earner could prevent a breach of the firm's internal policies and prevent the inadvertent commission of a crime.

CHAPTER 12

How to spot money laundering activities in a solicitor's practice

12.1 INTRODUCTION

It should be clear from the previous chapters in this book that almost all areas of a solicitor's practice are at risk from possible involvement in money laundering transactions. This Chapter identifies specific practice areas and highlights the activities within those areas that could give rise to the risk.

It is impossible to define what amounts to a suspicion of involvement in criminal activities. Some parts of PoCA 2002 (e.g. the money laundering offences in ss. 327–329) require the test of whether the accused had knowledge or suspicion to be satisfied on a subjective basis. In other parts of the PoCA 2002 (notably failure to report, s.330) the test is a subjective and objective test. Some individuals are more suspicious than others, so in applying a subjective test, different results can be obtained using the same facts. Firms must encourage their staff to err on the side of caution; staff must be encouraged to consult with more senior members of the firm and, if necessary, with the firm's nominated officer. The Law Society's *Money Laundering Guidance* suggests that the thought processes which need to be undertaken after an initial cause for concern has been raised might include:

What is the cause for concern?

- Does your cause for concern relate to money, assets, or property which are the subject of a transaction?
- Is the cause for concern a lack of knowledge or understanding? If so, make enquiries, e.g. client does not appear wealthy but is buying a second home.
- Is your cause for concern based on fact, or rumour and gossip? For example, you may be aware that your client has a previous conviction for an acquisitive crime, which might lead you to question whether the money the client is using is profit from that crime. Alternatively, if the source of the information is more dubious, perhaps an obscure internet site, it may be necessary to verify the information through a better source.

Knowledge is likely to mean actual knowledge. In its *Money Laundering Guidance* the Law Society refers to *Archbold* (2004) at paragraphs 17–49 and reproduces the following quote:

There is some authority for the view that in the criminal law 'knowledge' includes 'wilfully shutting one's eyes to the truth': see, e.g. per Lord Reid in *Warner* v. *Metropolitan Police Commr* [1969] 2 AC 256 at 279, HL; *Atwal* v. *Massey*, 56 Cr.App.R. 6, DC. However such a proposition must be treated with great caution. The clear view of the courts at present is that this is a matter of evidence, and that nothing short of actual knowledge (or, in the case of dishonest handling, belief) will suffice.

12.2   CORPORATE DEPARTMENT

Activities in a firm's corporate department can give rise to a high risk of involvement in possible money laundering. Company formation services and financial transactions involving corporate clients will be within both the regulated sector for the purposes of the offence of failure to report (PoCA 2002, s.330) and within the definition of relevant business for the purposes of the Money Laundering Regulations 2003.

Consequently, corporate clients should be subject to identification procedures at the outset of new instructions (unless identification evidence is already held by the firm as a result of an earlier retainer). Further, members of staff will be required to report their knowledge or suspicion of criminal activities even if the retainer does not involve an arrangement which facilitates the acquisition, retention, use or control of criminal property or involve the holding in client account of possible criminal funds.

The following are specific areas of concern.

12.2.1   Formation of companies without any apparent commercial or other purpose

HM Treasury have identified front or shell companies as being a factor in many complex money laundering operations. Solicitors must be satisfied as to the commercial reason for a company formation transaction. They must understand why the client has come to the solicitor for assistance. In most cases, solicitors will be used because there will be an underlying legal service being provided along with the actual company formation: advising on the structure of the shareholding, the rights of shareholders, the constitution of the company etc. Instructions where a client (particularly one unknown to the firm) simply asks the firm to form a company should be treated with a degree of suspicion.

12.2.2   Formation of subsidiaries in circumstances where there appears to be no commercial or other purpose (particularly overseas subsidiaries)

For the same reason, formation of subsidiary companies should be treated with care where there appears to be no commercial or other proper purpose.

Any corporate transaction in an overseas jurisdiction should be considered carefully, particularly if the overseas jurisdiction is a country on the FATF's (Financial Action Task Force on Money Laundering) list of Non-Cooperative Countries and Territories (NCCTs). The FATF seeks to identify non-cooperative countries in the worldwide fight against money laundering. An up-to-date list of NCCTs can be found on the FATF's website: **www1.oecd.org/fatf/NCCT_en.htm#List**

The following list of non-cooperative countries and territories is current as of 24 March 2004 and was last changed on 27 February 2004:

- Cook Islands.
- Guatemala.
- Indonesia.
- Myanmar.
- Nauru.
- Nigeria.
- Philippines.

12.2.3 Appointment of solicitors as directors with little or no commercial involvement

It might be flattering for a solicitor to be asked to serve as a director of a client company and in many cases there may be compelling commercial reasons for such an appointment. However, those involved in money laundering will wish to project any company they use as a legitimate concern and having a reputable solicitor on the board of directors will assist in this aim. Solicitors must consider the possibility of involvement in money laundering before accepting any board appointment.

12.2.4 Purchase of private company using suspect funds

The purchase (or sale) of any asset can involve a money laundering transaction. The funds used to purchase the asset may fall within the definition of criminal property (see **Chapter 2**). Because of the wide definition, company shares may have been purchased in the past using criminal funds meaning that the shares could represent a person's benefit from criminal conduct and thus be criminal property. As with the purchase of any asset, solicitors should be concerned about the source of funds and/or the legitimacy of any asset.

12.2.5 Large payments for unspecified services to consultants, related parties, employees, etc

In the course of acting for a corporate client, solicitors are likely to become aware of many facts relating to the running of the company. Some of these facts (such as large payments for unspecified services or suspected tax evasion) may give rise to knowledge or suspicion of money laundering. Other examples might include the discovery of unauthorised transactions or improperly recorded transactions (particularly where the company has poor/inadequate accounting systems).

Even if the solicitor is not involved in a transaction relating to these payments, the fact that corporate work is likely to be within the regulated sector means that knowledge or suspicion of these matters could give rise to an obligation to report.

12.2.6 Unusual transactions (including purchase/sale transactions significantly above/below market price

Transactions may be unusual in themselves or because they are unusual by reference to the normal type of work done by the firm or for the particular client.

Fee earners should not act outside their normal range of expertise. Undoubtedly, money launderers play on the fact that firms might be persuaded to accept instructions (frequently at an attractive fee) in circumstances where the firm or fee earner has no in-depth knowledge of the type of transaction involved. In this way the money launderers will avoid detailed questions from the firm concerning the transaction.

Firms should be aware of the normal transactions their clients have been involved in over recent years. The most difficult transaction to identify involving money laundering is where the client has been a good client providing the firm with legitimate business over a number of years. Such clients who suddenly go rogue can be very difficult to identify as money launderers. Enquiries should be made where established clients instruct the firm in unusual circumstances.

Transactions which are unusual in themselves obviously give rise to concern and these will include any transaction which appears to be significantly over- or under-valued.

12.2.7 Long delays over the production of company accounts

Those using companies for unlawful purposes are unlikely to want to make public financial disclosures by filing accounts for the company. The penalties for late filing of company accounts are unlikely to concern the individuals behind the company – they will hope to have achieved their object and be well away before steps are taken to enforce the filing requirements.

12.2.8 Dubious businesses often use more than one set of professional advisers. Ask 'why me?'

Solicitors should be particularly concerned where they discover that a particular corporate client has instructed another firm of solicitors in similar circumstances, where, for example, there appears to be a parallel deal involving different advisers. One common approach used by money launderers is to split up a complex transaction into a number of smaller transactions, using different professional advisers in each of the smaller transactions. In this way, no one firm sees the overall picture. However, firms should be suspicious if the facts of a case suggest that this is what is going on. (An illustration of this method, where a corporate client uses a number of solicitors in a conveyancing transaction, is given in **Paragraph 12.3**.)

12.3 PROPERTY DEPARTMENT

Activities in a firm's property department also give rise to a high risk of involvement in possible money laundering. Real property transactions will be within both the regulated sector for the purposes of the offence of failure to report (PoCA 2002, s.330) and within the definition of relevant business for the purposes of the Money Laundering Regulations 2003.

Property clients should be subject to identification procedures at the outset of new instructions (unless identification evidence is already held by the firm as a result of an earlier retainer). Further, members of staff will be required to report their knowledge or suspicion of criminal activities even if the retainer does not involve an arrangement which facilitates the acquisition, retention, use or control of criminal property or involve the holding in client account of possible criminal funds.

The following are specific areas of concern.

12.3.1 Fictitious buyers (introduced by third party) and not known to the solicitor

Criminals commonly used the fictitious buyer scam to obtain mortgage advances by deception. Frequently, this involves individuals who claim to represent a large numbers of clients all of whom have suddenly decided to purchase houses and most of whom can never find time to meet the solicitor.

Mortgage applications would be made in fictitious names to many financial institutions (often using the same properties) using a number of innocent solicitors. The mortgage advance would clearly amount to criminal property (having been obtained by deception) and solicitors would clearly be at risk of involvement in money laundering activities. Any arrangement in which the solicitor was concerned (typically the completion of the mortgage) would facilitate the acquisition, retention, use or control of criminal property. This could apply where the client was involved in the criminal activity or where the solicitor was acting for the financial institution and another firm represented the perpetrator of the crime. Holding and/or dealing with the mortgage advance money in these circumstances could also give rise to the offence of acquisition, use or possession (PoCA 2002, s.329) or possibly the offence of concealing (PoCA 2002, s.327).

Whilst it is fair to say that the requirements for obtaining verification of the client's identity have undoubtedly reduced the number of frauds using this particular scam, solicitors must nonetheless be vigilant – this illustrates the importance of adopting proper and effective client identification procedures.

12.3.2 Payment of deposit directly to vendor (particularly where the deposit paid is excessive)

Another typical method of defrauding mortgage providers is to misrepresent the purchase price – using a price which appears to suggest that the value of the security is greater than it is in reality. Often this scam is achieved by a direct payment to the vendor by the purchaser, rather than making the payment through the solicitors.

By way of illustration, a client is purchasing property at an agreed price of £400,000. The client's building society agrees a maximum mortgage advance of 80 per cent of the purchase price, i.e. £320,000. Because of a poor survey report, the vendor agrees with the purchaser to reduce the price to £350,000. This would have the effect of reducing the mortgage advance if it came to the knowledge of the building society. The vendor and purchaser decide not to notify their own solicitors or the building society of the reduction. On exchange of contracts, the purchaser informs his solicitor that he has paid a deposit direct to the purchaser of £50,000, leaving only £350,000 to be paid on completion. Of course, no deposit has been paid and the property is purchased at a price of £350,000 albeit the paperwork shows a price of £400,000. The payment of a direct deposit (greater than the normal 10 per cent of the purchase price) should put the purchaser's solicitor on notice that the transaction needs to be considered with care.

12.3.3 Purchase of property using suspect funds

The purchase (or sale) of property can involve a money laundering transaction. The funds used to purchase the property may fall within the definition of criminal property (see **Chapter 2**). Further, because of the wide definition, property may have been purchased in the past using criminal funds meaning that the property could represent a person's benefit from criminal conduct and thus be criminal property. As with the purchase of any asset, solicitors should be concerned at the source of funds and/or the legitimacy of any asset.

12.3.4 Purchase of property using a corporate vehicle where there is no good commercial or other reason

As noted above, corporate vehicles are frequently used in money laundering transactions. It is sometimes easier to split complex transactions into smaller matters where companies are used. Firms must be satisfied that there are good commercial or legal reasons for using a company.

A group of criminal individuals intend purchasing a chain of 12 hotels. The total purchase price amounts to, say, £15 million. However, the individuals (perhaps using a crooked surveyor) intend applying for finance of £20 million using the hotels as security. To do this they will represent the value of the hotels as being in the region of £25 million.

The original purchase will go through at the legitimate price: £15 million. Rather than purchasing the group in the names of the individuals (or by way of a share purchase), the transaction will be an asset purchase, transferring the title to the 12 hotels into the name of a company (possibly an overseas company created using nominees for the individuals). This transaction will appear to be legitimate (although the purchase in the name of an off-shore company held by nominees might give rise to suspicion on the part of the purchaser's solicitor). Indeed, at this stage, it appears that no criminal activity has been undertaken. To avoid any further suspicion at the next stage (which will amount to criminal activity) the individuals are likely to instruct 12 different firms of solicitors, each of whom will be asked to act for the off-shore company on the sale of a single hotel to individuals (or other companies connected with them). The purchasers will also instruct 12 different firms of solicitors to act on their behalf. The total purchase price for these 12 transactions will be shown at £25 million, financed by loans of, in total, £20 million.

All solicitors acting in this scenario could be involved in an arrangement contrary to PoCA 2002, s.328 and guilty of a criminal offence if they knew or suspected that the arrangement facilitated the acquisition, retention, use or control of criminal property. The use of a company in the original transaction (solicitors acting on the second stage will be made aware that the individual hotels had been recently purchased by the off-shore company) and the possible knowledge that other professionals were involved in similar transactions could be sufficient to put the firms involved on notice that the circumstances were suspicious.

12.4 PRIVATE CLIENT DEPARTMENT

Activities in a firm's trust department can give rise to a high risk of involvement in possible money laundering. Probate work is less likely to give rise to a high risk of involvement but, nonetheless, since assets of various categories are involved, money laundering cannot be ruled out completely. Both trust administration and probate transactions are likely to be within both the regulated sector for the purposes of the offence of failure to report (PoCA 2002, s.330) and within the definition of relevant business for the purposes of the Money Laundering Regulations 2003.

In trust administration, the client will be the trustee(s). Unless the firm is acting for beneficiaries there is no need to establish the identity of beneficiaries for the purposes of the Money Laundering Regulations 2003. Trustees should be subject to identification procedures at the outset of new instructions (unless identification evidence is already held by the firm as a result of an earlier retainer) using the procedures for individual clients (or, if the trustee is a trust corporation, for companies). In probate matters, the client is the executor(s) or administrator(s) and again their identity should be established using the procedures for individuals or companies.

If the trust or estate administration work involves financial or real property transactions, tax advice, advice and arrangements relating to the purchase or sale of specified investments or acting on the formation, operation or management of a trust, the work will be in the regulated sector. This means that members of staff will be required to report their knowledge or suspicion of criminal activities even if the retainer does not involve an arrangement which facilitates the acquisition, retention, use or control of criminal property or involve the holding in client account of possible criminal funds.

The following are specific areas of concern.

12.4.1 The formation of trusts with no apparent commercial or other purpose

HM Treasury have identified trust funds as being a factor in many complex money laundering operations. Solicitors must be satisfied as to the commercial reason for a trust formation. They must understand why the client has come to the solicitor for assistance. In most cases, solicitors will be used because there will be an underlying legal service being provided along with the actual trust formation: administering the trust, or giving tax advice on the use of the trust. Instructions where a client (particularly one unknown to the firm) simply asks the firm to form a trust should be treated with a degree of suspicion. This is particularly so where the trust is intended to be an off-shore trust. Sometimes, the identity of off-shore trustees may be difficult to ascertain. Fee earners must be reminded that, where the firm is undertaking relevant business in the UK and satisfactory evidence of identification cannot be obtained, the business retainer must not proceed further.

If the intended trust fund is to be established in an NCCT (see **Paragraph 12.2.2**) particular care must be taken to ensure the identity of the trustees and the legitimacy of the trust fund.

12.4.2 The appointment of solicitors as trustees with little or no commercial involvement

As with the appointment of a solicitor as a director of a corporate client, it can be flattering for a solicitor to be asked by a settlor to act as a trustee of a trust. In many cases there may be compelling commercial or legal reasons for such an appointment. However, those involved in money laundering will wish to project any trust fund they use as a legitimate fund and having a reputable solicitor as a trustee will assist in this aim. Solicitors must consider the possibility of involvement in money laundering before accepting any trust appointment.

12.4.3 The receipt of suspect funds into the trust fund

The purchase (or sale) of any asset held in a trust fund can involve a money laundering transaction. The funds used to purchase the asset may fall within the definition of criminal property (see **Chapter 2**). Further, because of the wide definition, assets or investments held in the fund may have been purchased in the past using criminal funds meaning that those assets could represent a person's benefit from criminal conduct and thus be criminal property. As with the purchase of any asset, solicitors should be concerned at the source of funds and/or the legitimacy of any asset.

12.5 TAXATION ADVICE

The provision by way of business advice about the tax affairs of another will fall within the definition of relevant business (for the purposes of the Money Laundering Regulations 2003) and the regulated sector for the purposes of the offence of failure to report (PoCA 2002, s.330). Consequently, in any practice area where tax advice is given, clients should be subject to identification procedures at the outset of new instructions (unless identification evidence is already held by the firm as a result of an earlier retainer) even if the practice area itself would not involve relevant business. For example, drafting a will, or giving employment advice, will not be within the definition of relevant business. However, if in the course of will drafting, advice is given on inheritance tax planning, this advice will be sufficient to bring the matter within the definition of relevant business. Similarly, if in the course of employment advice, tax advice is given, this matter will then amount to relevant business.

Because tax advice will amount to business in the regulated sector, members of staff will be required to report their knowledge or suspicion of criminal activities even if the retainer does not involve an arrangement which facilitates the acquisition, retention, use or control of criminal property or involve the holding in client account of possible criminal funds.

Where a client admits tax evasion to a solicitor, that client is likely to be engaged in money laundering, that is, the client is in possession of criminal property, money or assets that represent money that should have been paid to the Revenue authorities. If the solicitor's transaction will involve any part of these fund or assets, the solicitor is in danger of being involved in an arrangement that will facilitate the retention, use or control of criminal property. It is likely that an authorised disclosure must be made. Even if the particular funds are not going to be used as part of a transaction, a report under PoCA 2002, s.330 will have to be made unless one of the appropriate defences applies (in particular, the information may have been passed on to the solicitor in privileged circumstances). Careful consideration must be given to the facts of the transaction.

There is a narrow dividing line between the concepts of tax evasion (which is a criminal offence) and tax avoidance (which is legitimate). Solicitors giving tax advice must take care not to cross that line so that the advice leads to tax evasion. The advice in these circumstances could amount to an arrangement which facilitates the acquisition of criminal property.

12.6   LITIGATION DEPARTMENT

Litigation (other than matrimonial disputes, for which see **Paragraph 12.6.3**) is likely to give rise to a smaller risk of involvement in money laundering than other departments within a firm. General litigation is unlikely to give rise to relevant business or to business in the regulated sector. The Treasury has confirmed that participation in litigation would not be viewed as participation in financial transactions. However, it is not inconceivable that litigation might involve a risk of money laundering and consequently firms should consider applying client identification procedures to all litigation clients.

12.6.1   Unusual settlements

The settlement of a dispute might give rise to money laundering concerns, particularly where the settlement is of an unusual amount or in unusual circumstances. It is not unknown for a dispute to be fabricated simply to provide a reason for the transfer of funds by way of settlement. Whilst involvement in litigation would not amount to relevant business or be within the regulated sector, participation in a financial settlement might amount to a financial transaction bringing the solicitor back within the regulatory regime.

12.6.2   Litigation involving suspect assets

It is quite possible that the assets which are subject to a dispute could be criminal property and thus the litigation itself could involve a risk of money laundering. The outcome of the litigation could be an arrangement facilitating the acquisition, retention, use or control of criminal property.

12.6.3   Matrimonial disputes

Matrimonial disputes are the one area where a high risk of involvement in money laundering exists. The judgment of Dame Elizabeth Butler-Sloss in *P* v. *P* [2003] EWHC Fam 2260 (which has been referred to in other parts of this book and which is the subject of Law Society Guidance, reproduced in **Appendix B2**) illustrates clearly the risks. A major problem arises from the enhanced duty of full and frank disclosure applying to solicitors and clients in relation to ancillary relief proceedings. Compliance with an ancillary relief order could amount to being concerned in an arrangement which facilitates the acquisition, retention, use or control of criminal property. The criminal property in these cases will frequently be the proceeds of tax evasion. However, if as a result of compliance with the full and frank disclosure requirements, a solicitor acquires information that suggests either his client or the client on the other side has benefited from any criminal conduct, steps must be taken to avoid committing an offence by making an authorised or protected disclosure.

It is not necessary for there to be ancillary relief proceedings. The act of negotiating a settlement between the parties in dispute could be an arrangement for the purposes of PoCA 2002, s.328.

12.6.4   Criminal litigation

In most cases, criminal litigation will not give rise to a high risk of involvement in money laundering. The litigation is unlikely to be within the regulated sector or amount to relevant business and, in any event, any information received from a client is likely to be privileged (the client will not be seeking the solicitor's services to further a criminal purpose).

The money laundering offences are unlikely to be relevant and even if the solicitor's costs represent criminal proceeds it should be possible to use the defence of adequate consideration under section 329(2)(c) (see **Chapter 3**).

One possible problem that could arise is in relation to bail. If a court requires a surety, then no money will pass and it is unlikely that the solicitor's involvement at this stage would be an arrangement which facilitates the acquisition, retention, use or control of criminal property, even if the solicitor suspects the only funds available to the person giving surety are criminal proceeds. However, if a sum is required to be paid into court, even if this sum does not pass through the solicitor's client account, it is arguable that the solicitor (if involved) is concerned in an arrangement and if the solicitor suspects that the payment from a third party represents criminal property, that arrangement could be said to be facilitating the use of criminal property.

12.7   CONCLUSION

In whatever practice area a solicitor works, there will be some element of risk from involvement in money laundering. The Law Society's Warning Card to Solicitors about money laundering highlights the following causes for concern.

Unusual settlement requests
Anything that is unusual or unpredictable or otherwise gives cause for concern should lead you to ask more questions about the source of the funds. Remember, proceeds of crime can arrive through the banking system as well.
Think carefully if any of the following are proposed or occur:

- Settlements by cash
- Surprise payments by way of third party cheque
- Money transfers where there is a variation between account holder or the signatory
- Requests to make regular payments out of client account
- Settlements which are reached too easily.

Unusual transactions

- Why has the client chosen your firm? Could the client find the same services nearer their home?
- Are you being asked to do something that does not fit in with the normal pattern of your business?
- Be cautious if instructions change without a reasonable explanation
- Be cautious about transactions which take an unusual turn

Use of your client account

- Using solicitors' client accounts to transmit money is useful to money launderers
- Do not provide a banking facility if you do not undertake any related legal work
- Be cautious if you are instructed to do legal work, receive funds into your client account, but then the instructions are cancelled and you are asked to return the money either to your client or a third party.

Remember you may still be assisting a money launderer even though money does not pass through your firm's bank accounts.

Suspect territory

- If you are instructed in transactions with an international element you can refer to the FATF who produce up to date information about different countries.

Finally, take heed of the contents of the following paragraph taken from the Law Society's *Money Laundering Guidance*:

Where appropriate, anti-money laundering procedures should place barriers between prospective clients and the services you provide. To cross those barriers successfully clients will need to provide sufficient information about themselves and their instructions to give you the confidence you need to act for them. The extent of the barriers you put in place will depend upon the assessed level of money laundering risk. If the initial information which clients provide is insufficient, more information will be needed. In some cases the information provided at the outset may lead to a suspicion of money laundering, in which case consideration will need to be given to whether a report should be made under POCA. In other cases the developments which happen in the client's matter might give rise to the solicitor asking more questions, or to form a suspicion. When sufficient information is known it is for the solicitor's own professional judgement whether he is suspicious.

PART 3

Appendices

A1

Extracts from the Proceeds of Crime Act 2002

[...]

PART 7
MONEY LAUNDERING

Offences

327 Concealing etc

(1) A person commits an offence if he–

    (a) conceals criminal property;
    (b) disguises criminal property;
    (c) converts criminal property;
    (d) transfers criminal property;
    (e) removes criminal property from England and Wales or from Scotland or from Northern Ireland.

(2) But a person does not commit such an offence if–

    (a) he makes an authorised disclosure under section 338 and (if the disclosure is made before he does the act mentioned in subsection (1)) he has the appropriate consent;
    (b) he intended to make such a disclosure but had a reasonable excuse for not doing so;
    (c) the act he does is done in carrying out a function he has relating to the enforcement of any provision of this Act or of any other enactment relating to criminal conduct or benefit from criminal conduct.

(3) Concealing or disguising criminal property includes concealing or disguising its nature, source, location, disposition, movement or ownership or any rights with respect to it.

328 Arrangements

(1) A person commits an offence if he enters into or becomes concerned in an arrangement which he knows or suspects facilitates (by whatever means) the acquisition, retention, use or control of criminal property by or on behalf of another person.

(2) But a person does not commit such an offence if–

    (a) he makes an authorised disclosure under section 338 and (if the disclosure is made before he does the act mentioned in subsection (1)) he has the appropriate consent;

    (b) he intended to make such a disclosure but had a reasonable excuse for not doing so;

    (c) the act he does is done in carrying out a function he has relating to the enforcement of any provision of this Act or of any other enactment relating to criminal conduct or benefit from criminal conduct.

329 Acquisition, use and possession

(1) A person commits an offence if he–

    (a) acquires criminal property;

    (b) uses criminal property;

    (c) has possession of criminal property.

(2) But a person does not commit such an offence if–

    (a) he makes an authorised disclosure under section 338 and (if the disclosure is made before he does the act mentioned in subsection (1)) he has the appropriate consent;

    (b) he intended to make such a disclosure but had a reasonable excuse for not doing so;

    (c) he acquired or used or had possession of the property for adequate consideration;

    (d) the act he does is done in carrying out a function he has relating to the enforcement of any provision of this Act or of any other enactment relating to criminal conduct or benefit from criminal conduct.

(3) For the purposes of this section–

    (a) a person acquires property for inadequate consideration if the value of the consideration is significantly less than the value of the property;

    (b) a person uses or has possession of property for inadequate consideration if the value of the consideration is significantly less than the value of the use or possession;

    (c) the provision by a person of goods or services which he knows or suspects may help another to carry out criminal conduct is not consideration.

330 Failure to disclose: regulated sector

(1) A person commits an offence if each of the following three conditions is satisfied.

(2) The first condition is that he–

    (a) knows or suspects, or

    (b) has reasonable grounds for knowing or suspecting,

that another person is engaged in money laundering.

(3) The second condition is that the information or other matter—

    (a) on which his knowledge or suspicion is based, or
    (b) which gives reasonable grounds for such knowledge or suspicion,
    came to him in the course of a business in the regulated sector.

(4) The third condition is that he does not make the required disclosure as soon as is practicable after the information or other matter comes to him.

(5) The required disclosure is a disclosure of the information or other matter—

    (a) to a nominated officer or a person authorised for the purposes of this Part by the Director General of the National Criminal Intelligence Service;
    (b) in the form and manner (if any) prescribed for the purposes of this subsection by order under section 339.

(6) But a person does not commit an offence under this section if—

    (a) he has a reasonable excuse for not disclosing the information or other matter;
    (b) he is a professional legal adviser and the information or other matter came to him in privileged circumstances;
    (c) subsection (7) applies to him.

(7) This subsection applies to a person if—

    (a) he does not know or suspect that another person is engaged in money laundering, and
    (b) he has not been provided by his employer with such training as is specified by the Secretary of State by order for the purposes of this section.

(8) In deciding whether a person committed an offence under this section the court must consider whether he followed any relevant guidance which was at the time concerned—

    (a) issued by a supervisory authority or any other appropriate body,
    (b) approved by the Treasury, and
    (c) published in a manner it approved as appropriate in its opinion to bring the guidance to the attention of persons likely to be affected by it.

(9) A disclosure to a nominated officer is a disclosure which—

    (a) is made to a person nominated by the alleged offender's employer to receive disclosures under this section, and
    (b) is made in the course of the alleged offender's employment and in accordance with the procedure established by the employer for the purpose.

(10) Information or other matter comes to a professional legal adviser in privileged circumstances if it is communicated or given to him—

    (a) by (or by a representative of) a client of his in connection with the giving by the adviser of legal advice to the client,

155

(b) by (or by a representative of) a person seeking legal advice from the adviser, or

(c) by a person in connection with legal proceedings or contemplated legal proceedings.

(11) But subsection (10) does not apply to information or other matter which is communicated or given with the intention of furthering a criminal purpose.

(12) Schedule 9 has effect for the purpose of determining what is–

(a) a business in the regulated sector;
(b) a supervisory authority.

(13) An appropriate body is any body which regulates or is representative of any trade, profession, business or employment carried on by the alleged offender.

331 Failure to disclose: nominated officers in the regulated sector

(1) A person nominated to receive disclosures under section 330 commits an offence if the conditions in subsections (2) to (4) are satisfied.

(2) The first condition is that he–

(a) knows or suspects, or
(b) has reasonable grounds for knowing or suspecting,
that another person is engaged in money laundering.

(3) The second condition is that the information or other matter–

(a) on which his knowledge or suspicion is based, or
(b) which gives reasonable grounds for such knowledge or suspicion,
came to him in consequence of a disclosure made under section 330.

(4) The third condition is that he does not make the required disclosure as soon as is practicable after the information or other matter comes to him.

(5) The required disclosure is a disclosure of the information or other matter–

(a) to a person authorised for the purposes of this Part by the Director General of the National Criminal Intelligence Service;
(b) in the form and manner (if any) prescribed for the purposes of this subsection by order under section 339.

(6) But a person does not commit an offence under this section if he has a reasonable excuse for not disclosing the information or other matter.

(7) In deciding whether a person committed an offence under this section the court must consider whether he followed any relevant guidance which was at the time concerned–

(a) issued by a supervisory authority or any other appropriate body,
(b) approved by the Treasury, and

(c) published in a manner it approved as appropriate in its opinion to bring the guidance to the attention of persons likely to be affected by it.

(8) Schedule 9 has effect for the purpose of determining what is a supervisory authority.

(9) An appropriate body is a body which regulates or is representative of a trade, profession, business or employment.

332   Failure to disclose: other nominated officers

(1) A person nominated to receive disclosures under section 337 or 338 commits an offence if the conditions in subsections (2) to (4) are satisfied.

(2) The first condition is that he knows or suspects that another person is engaged in money laundering.

(3) The second condition is that the information or other matter on which his knowledge or suspicion is based came to him in consequence of a disclosure made under section 337 or 338.

(4) The third condition is that he does not make the required disclosure as soon as is practicable after the information or other matter comes to him.

(5) The required disclosure is a disclosure of the information or other matter–

> (a) to a person authorised for the purposes of this Part by the Director General of the National Criminal Intelligence Service;
> (b) in the form and manner (if any) prescribed for the purposes of this subsection by order under section 339.

(6) But a person does not commit an offence under this section if he has a reasonable excuse for not disclosing the information or other matter.

333   Tipping off

(1) A person commits an offence if–

> (a) he knows or suspects that a disclosure falling within section 337 or 338 has been made, and
> (b) he makes a disclosure which is likely to prejudice any investigation which might be conducted following the disclosure referred to in paragraph (a).

(2) But a person does not commit an offence under subsection (1) if–

> (a) he did not know or suspect that the disclosure was likely to be prejudicial as mentioned in subsection (1);
> (b) the disclosure is made in carrying out a function he has relating to the enforcement of any provision of this Act or of any other enactment relating to criminal conduct or benefit from criminal conduct;
> (c) he is a professional legal adviser and the disclosure falls within subsection (3).

(3) A disclosure falls within this subsection if it is a disclosure–

(a) to (or to a representative of) a client of the professional legal adviser in connection with the giving by the adviser of legal advice to the client, or
(b) to any person in connection with legal proceedings or contemplated legal proceedings.

(4) But a disclosure does not fall within subsection (3) if it is made with the intention of furthering a criminal purpose.

334 Penalties

(1) A person guilty of an offence under section 327, 328 or 329 is liable–

(a) on summary conviction, to imprisonment for a term not exceeding six months or to a fine not exceeding the statutory maximum or to both, or
(b) on conviction on indictment, to imprisonment for a term not exceeding 14 years or to a fine or to both.

(2) A person guilty of an offence under section 330, 331, 332 or 333 is liable–

(a) on summary conviction, to imprisonment for a term not exceeding six months or to a fine not exceeding the statutory maximum or to both, or
(b) on conviction on indictment, to imprisonment for a term not exceeding five years or to a fine or to both.

Consent

335 Appropriate consent

(1) The appropriate consent is–

(a) the consent of a nominated officer to do a prohibited act if an authorised disclosure is made to the nominated officer;
(b) the consent of a constable to do a prohibited act if an authorised disclosure is made to a constable;
(c) the consent of a customs officer to do a prohibited act if an authorised disclosure is made to a customs officer.

(2) A person must be treated as having the appropriate consent if–

(a) he makes an authorised disclosure to a constable or a customs officer, and
(b) the condition in subsection (3) or the condition in subsection (4) is satisfied.

(3) The condition is that before the end of the notice period he does not receive notice from a constable or customs officer that consent to the doing of the act is refused.

(4) The condition is that–

(a) before the end of the notice period he receives notice from a constable or customs officer that consent to the doing of the act is refused, and
(b) the moratorium period has expired.

(5) The notice period is the period of seven working days starting with the first working day after the person makes the disclosure.

(6) The moratorium period is the period of 31 days starting with the day on which the person receives notice that consent to the doing of the act is refused.

(7) A working day is a day other than a Saturday, a Sunday, Christmas Day, Good Friday or a day which is a bank holiday under the Banking and Financial Dealings Act 1971 (c. 80) in the part of the United Kingdom in which the person is when he makes the disclosure.

(8) References to a prohibited act are to an act mentioned in section 327(1), 328(1) or 329(1) (as the case may be).

(9) A nominated officer is a person nominated to receive disclosures under section 338.

(10) Subsections (1) to (4) apply for the purposes of this Part.

336 Nominated officer: consent

(1) A nominated officer must not give the appropriate consent to the doing of a prohibited act unless the condition in subsection (2), the condition in subsection (3) or the condition in subsection (4) is satisfied.

(2) The condition is that–

  (a) he makes a disclosure that property is criminal property to a person authorised for the purposes of this Part by the Director General of the National Criminal Intelligence Service, and
  (b) such a person gives consent to the doing of the act.

(3) The condition is that–

  (a) he makes a disclosure that property is criminal property to a person authorised for the purposes of this Part by the Director General of the National Criminal Intelligence Service, and
  (b) before the end of the notice period he does not receive notice from such a person that consent to the doing of the act is refused.

(4) The condition is that–

  (a) he makes a disclosure that property is criminal property to a person authorised for the purposes of this Part by the Director General of the National Criminal Intelligence Service,
  (b) before the end of the notice period he receives notice from such a person that consent to the doing of the act is refused, and
  (c) the moratorium period has expired.

(5) A person who is a nominated officer commits an offence if–

(a) he gives consent to a prohibited act in circumstances where none of the conditions in subsections (2), (3) and (4) is satisfied, and
(b) he knows or suspects that the act is a prohibited act.

(6) A person guilty of such an offence is liable–

(a) on summary conviction, to imprisonment for a term not exceeding six months or to a fine not exceeding the statutory maximum or to both, or
(b) on conviction on indictment, to imprisonment for a term not exceeding five years or to a fine or to both.

(7) The notice period is the period of seven working days starting with the first working day after the nominated officer makes the disclosure.

(8) The moratorium period is the period of 31 days starting with the day on which the nominated officer is given notice that consent to the doing of the act is refused.

(9) A working day is a day other than a Saturday, a Sunday, Christmas Day, Good Friday or a day which is a bank holiday under the Banking and Financial Dealings Act 1971 (c. 80) in the part of the United Kingdom in which the nominated officer is when he gives the appropriate consent.

(10) References to a prohibited act are to an act mentioned in section 327(1), 328(1) or 329(1) (as the case may be).

(11) A nominated officer is a person nominated to receive disclosures under section 338.

Disclosures

337   Protected disclosures

(1) A disclosure which satisfies the following three conditions is not to be taken to breach any restriction on the disclosure of information (however imposed).

(2) The first condition is that the information or other matter disclosed came to the person making the disclosure (the discloser) in the course of his trade, profession, business or employment.

(3) The second condition is that the information or other matter–

(a) causes the discloser to know or suspect, or
(b) gives him reasonable grounds for knowing or suspecting,
that another person is engaged in money laundering.

(4) The third condition is that the disclosure is made to a constable, a customs officer or a nominated officer as soon as is practicable after the information or other matter comes to the discloser.

(5) A disclosure to a nominated officer is a disclosure which–

(a) is made to a person nominated by the discloser's employer to receive disclosures under this section, and

(b) is made in the course of the discloser's employment and in accordance with the procedure established by the employer for the purpose.

338   Authorised disclosures

(1) For the purposes of this Part a disclosure is authorised if–

(a) it is a disclosure to a constable, a customs officer or a nominated officer by the alleged offender that property is criminal property,

(b) it is made in the form and manner (if any) prescribed for the purposes of this subsection by order under section 339, and

(c) the first or second condition set out below is satisfied.

(2) The first condition is that the disclosure is made before the alleged offender does the prohibited act.

(3) The second condition is that–

(a) the disclosure is made after the alleged offender does the prohibited act,

(b) there is a good reason for his failure to make the disclosure before he did the act, and

(c) the disclosure is made on his own initiative and as soon as it is practicable for him to make it.

(4) An authorised disclosure is not to be taken to breach any restriction on the disclosure of information (however imposed).

(5) A disclosure to a nominated officer is a disclosure which–

(a) is made to a person nominated by the alleged offender's employer to receive authorised disclosures, and

(b) is made in the course of the alleged offender's employment and in accordance with the procedure established by the employer for the purpose.

(6) References to the prohibited act are to an act mentioned in section 327(1), 328(1) or 329(1) (as the case may be).

339   Form and manner of disclosures

(1) The Secretary of State may by order prescribe the form and manner in which a disclosure under section 330, 331, 332 or 338 must be made.

(2) An order under this section may also provide that the form may include a request to the discloser to provide additional information specified in the form.

(3) The additional information must be information which is necessary to enable the person to whom the disclosure is made to decide whether to start a money laundering investigation.

(4) A disclosure made in pursuance of a request under subsection (2) is not to be taken to breach any restriction on the disclosure of information (however imposed).

(5) The discloser is the person making a disclosure mentioned in subsection (1).

(6) Money laundering investigation must be construed in accordance with section 341(4).

(7) Subsection (2) does not apply to a disclosure made to a nominated officer.

Interpretation

340 Interpretation

(1) This section applies for the purposes of this Part.

(2) Criminal conduct is conduct which–

  (a) constitutes an offence in any part of the United Kingdom, or
  (b) would constitute an offence in any part of the United Kingdom if it occurred there.

(3) Property is criminal property if–

  (a) it constitutes a person's benefit from criminal conduct or it represents such a benefit (in whole or part and whether directly or indirectly), and
  (b) the alleged offender knows or suspects that it constitutes or represents such a benefit.

(4) It is immaterial–

  (a) who carried out the conduct;
  (b) who benefited from it;
  (c) whether the conduct occurred before or after the passing of this Act.

(5) A person benefits from conduct if he obtains property as a result of or in connection with the conduct.

(6) If a person obtains a pecuniary advantage as a result of or in connection with conduct, he is to be taken to obtain as a result of or in connection with the conduct a sum of money equal to the value of the pecuniary advantage.

(7) References to property or a pecuniary advantage obtained in connection with conduct include references to property or a pecuniary advantage obtained in both that connection and some other.

(8) If a person benefits from conduct his benefit is the property obtained as a result of or in connection with the conduct.

(9) Property is all property wherever situated and includes–

  (a) money;
  (b) all forms of property, real or personal, heritable or moveable;
  (c) things in action and other intangible or incorporeal property.

(10) The following rules apply in relation to property–

    (a) property is obtained by a person if he obtains an interest in it;

    (b) references to an interest, in relation to land in England and Wales or Northern Ireland, are to any legal estate or equitable interest or power;

    (c) references to an interest, in relation to land in Scotland, are to any estate, interest, servitude or other heritable right in or over land, including a heritable security;

    (d) references to an interest, in relation to property other than land, include references to a right (including a right to possession).

(11) Money laundering is an act which–

    (a) constitutes an offence under section 327, 328 or 329,

    (b) constitutes an attempt, conspiracy or incitement to commit an offence specified in paragraph (a),

    (c) constitutes aiding, abetting, counselling or procuring the commission of an offence specified in paragraph (a), or

    (d) would constitute an offence specified in paragraph (a), (b) or (c) if done in the United Kingdom.

(12) For the purposes of a disclosure to a nominated officer–

    (a) references to a person's employer include any body, association or organisation (including a voluntary organisation) in connection with whose activities the person exercises a function (whether or not for gain or reward), and

    (b) references to employment must be construed accordingly.

(13) References to a constable include references to a person authorised for the purposes of this Part by the Director General of the National Criminal Intelligence Service.

PART 8
INVESTIGATIONS
CHAPTER 1
INTRODUCTION

341 Investigations

(1) For the purposes of this Part a confiscation investigation is an investigation into–

    (a) whether a person has benefited from his criminal conduct, or

    (b) the extent or whereabouts of his benefit from his criminal conduct.

(2) For the purposes of this Part a civil recovery investigation is an investigation into–

    (a) whether property is recoverable property or associated property,

    (b) who holds the property, or

    (c) its extent or whereabouts.

(3) But an investigation is not a civil recovery investigation if–

(a) proceedings for a recovery order have been started in respect of the property in question,

(b) an interim receiving order applies to the property in question,

(c) an interim administration order applies to the property in question, or

(d) the property in question is detained under section 295.

(4) For the purposes of this Part a money laundering investigation is an investigation into whether a person has committed a money laundering offence.

342 Offences of prejudicing investigation

(1) This section applies if a person knows or suspects that an appropriate officer or (in Scotland) a proper person is acting (or proposing to act) in connection with a confiscation investigation, a civil recovery investigation or a money laundering investigation which is being or is about to be conducted.

(2) The person commits an offence if–

(a) he makes a disclosure which is likely to prejudice the investigation, or

(b) he falsifies, conceals, destroys or otherwise disposes of, or causes or permits the falsification, concealment, destruction or disposal of, documents which are relevant to the investigation.

(3) A person does not commit an offence under subsection (2)(a) if–

(a) he does not know or suspect that the disclosure is likely to prejudice the investigation,

(b) the disclosure is made in the exercise of a function under this Act or any other enactment relating to criminal conduct or benefit from criminal conduct or in compliance with a requirement imposed under or by virtue of this Act, or

(c) he is a professional legal adviser and the disclosure falls within subsection (4).

(4) A disclosure falls within this subsection if it is a disclosure–

(a) to (or to a representative of) a client of the professional legal adviser in connection with the giving by the adviser of legal advice to the client, or

(b) to any person in connection with legal proceedings or contemplated legal proceedings.

(5) But a disclosure does not fall within subsection (4) if it is made with the intention of furthering a criminal purpose.

(6) A person does not commit an offence under subsection (2)(b) if–

(a) he does not know or suspect that the documents are relevant to the investigation, or

(b) he does not intend to conceal any facts disclosed by the documents from any appropriate officer or (in Scotland) proper person carrying out the investigation.

(7) A person guilty of an offence under subsection (2) is liable–

    (a) on summary conviction, to imprisonment for a term not exceeding six months or to a fine not exceeding the statutory maximum or to both, or

    (b) on conviction on indictment, to imprisonment for a term not exceeding five years or to a fine or to both.

(8) For the purposes of this section–

    (a) 'appropriate officer' must be construed in accordance with section 378;

    (b) 'proper person' must be construed in accordance with section 412.

A2

Extracts from the Terrorism Act 2000 (as amended)

[. . .]

Offences

15   Fund-raising

(1) A person commits an offence if he–

  (a) invites another to provide money or other property, and
  (b) intends that it should be used, or has reasonable cause to suspect that it may be used, for the purposes of terrorism.

(2) A person commits an offence if he–

  (a) receives money or other property, and
  (b) intends that it should be used, or has reasonable cause to suspect that it may be used, for the purposes of terrorism.

(3) A person commits an offence if he–

  (a) provides money or other property, and
  (b) knows or has reasonable cause to suspect that it will or may be used for the purposes of terrorism.

(4) In this section a reference to the provision of money or other property is a reference to its being given, lent or otherwise made available, whether or not for consideration.

16   Use and possession

(1) A person commits an offence if he uses money or other property for the purposes of terrorism.

(2) A person commits an offence if he–

  (a) possesses money or other property, and
  (b) intends that it should be used, or has reasonable cause to suspect that it may be used, for the purposes of terrorism.

17 Funding arrangements

A person commits an offence if–

(a) he enters into or becomes concerned in an arrangement as a result of which money or other property is made available or is to be made available to another, and

(b) he knows or has reasonable cause to suspect that it will or may be used for the purposes of terrorism.

18 Money laundering

(1) A person commits an offence if he enters into or becomes concerned in an arrangement which facilitates the retention or control by or on behalf of another person of terrorist property–

(a) by concealment,

(b) by removal from the jurisdiction,

(c) by transfer to nominees, or

(d) in any other way.

(2) It is a defence for a person charged with an offence under subsection (1) to prove that he did not know and had no reasonable cause to suspect that the arrangement related to terrorist property.

[. . .]

(As inserted by the Anti-Terrorism, Crime and Security Act 2001, s.3, Sched.2, Part 3, para. 5(1), (2))

21A Failure to disclose: regulated sector

(1) A person commits an offence if each of the following three conditions is satisfied.

(2) The first condition is that he–

(a) knows or suspects, or

(b) has reasonable grounds for knowing or suspecting,

that another person has committed an offence under any of sections 15 to 18.

(3) The second condition is that the information or other matter–

(a) on which his knowledge or suspicion is based, or

(b) which gives reasonable grounds for such knowledge or suspicion,

came to him in the course of a business in the regulated sector.

(4) The third condition is that he does not disclose the information or other matter to a constable or a nominated officer as soon as is practicable after it comes to him.

(5) But a person does not commit an offence under this section if–

(a) he has a reasonable excuse for not disclosing the information or other matter;

(b) he is a professional legal adviser and the information or other matter came to him in privileged circumstances.

(6) In deciding whether a person committed an offence under this section the court must consider whether he followed any relevant guidance which was at the time concerned–

    (a) issued by a supervisory authority or any other appropriate body,

    (b) approved by the Treasury, and

    (c) published in a manner it approved as appropriate in its opinion to bring the guidance to the attention of persons likely to be affected by it.

(7) A disclosure to a nominated officer is a disclosure which–

    (a) is made to a person nominated by the alleged offender's employer to receive disclosures under this section, and

    (b) is made in the course of the alleged offender's employment and in accordance with the procedure established by the employer for the purpose.

(8) Information or other matter comes to a professional legal adviser in privileged circumstances if it is communicated or given to him–

    (a) by (or by a representative of) a client of his in connection with the giving by the adviser of legal advice to the client,

    (b) by (or by a representative of) a person seeking legal advice from the adviser, or

    (c) by a person in connection with legal proceedings or contemplated legal proceedings.

(9) But subsection (8) does not apply to information or other matter which is communicated or given with a view to furthering a criminal purpose.

(10) Schedule 3A has effect for the purpose of determining what is–

    (a) a business in the regulated sector;

    (b) a supervisory authority.

(11) For the purposes of subsection (2) a person is to be taken to have committed an offence there mentioned if–

    (a) he has taken an action or been in possession of a thing, and

    (b) he would have committed the offence if he had been in the United Kingdom at the time when he took the action or was in possession of the thing.

(12) A person guilty of an offence under this section is liable–

    (a) on conviction on indictment, to imprisonment for a term not exceeding five years or to a fine or to both;

    (b) on summary conviction, to imprisonment for a term not exceeding six months or to a fine not exceeding the statutory maximum or to both.

(13) An appropriate body is any body which regulates or is representative of any trade, profession, business or employment carried on by the alleged offender.

(14) The reference to a constable includes a reference to a person authorised for the purposes of this section by the Director General of the National Criminal Intelligence Service.

A3

Money Laundering Regulations, SI 2003/3075

2003 No. 3075
FINANCIAL SERVICES
The Money Laundering Regulations 2003

Made	*28th November 2003*
Laid before Parliament	*28th November 2003*
Coming into force in accordance with	
regulation 1(2)	

ARRANGEMENT OF REGULATIONS

PART I:
GENERAL

PART II:
OBLIGATIONS ON PERSONS WHO CARRY ON RELEVANT BUSINESS

PART III:
MONEY SERVICE OPERATORS AND HIGH VALUE DEALERS
Registration

9. Registers of money service operators and high value dealers

10. Requirement to be registered

11. Supplementary information

12. Determination of application to register

13. Cancellation of registration

14. Fees

Powers of the Commissioners

15. Entry, inspection etc.

16. Order for access to recorded information

17. Procedure where recorded information is removed

18. Failure to comply with requirements under regulation 17

19. Entry, search etc.

Penalties, review and appeals

20. Power to impose penalties

21. Review procedure

22. Appeals to a VAT and duties tribunal

Miscellaneous

23. Prosecution of offences by the Commissioners

24. Recovery of fees and penalties through the court

25. Authorised persons operating a bureau de change

PART IV:
MISCELLANEOUS

26. Supervisory authorities etc. to report evidence of money laundering

27. Offences by bodies corporate etc.

28. Prohibitions in relation to certain countries

SCHEDULES

Whereas the Treasury are a government department designated[1] for the purposes of section 2(2) of the European Communities Act 1972[2] in relation to measures relating to preventing the use of the financial system for the purpose of money laundering;

Now therefore the Treasury, in exercise of the powers conferred on them by –

(i) section 2(2) of the European Communities Act 1972, and
(ii) sections 168(4)(b), 402(1)(b), 417(1)[3] and 428(3) of the Financial Services and Markets Act 2000[4],

hereby make the following Regulations:

PART I
GENERAL

1. Citation, commencement etc.

(1) These Regulations may be cited as the Money Laundering Regulations 2003.

(2) These Regulations come into force –

(a) for the purposes of regulation 10 in so far as it relates to a person who acts as a high value dealer, on 1st April 2004;
(b) for the purposes of regulation 2(3)(h), on 31st October 2004;
(c) for the purposes of regulation 2(3)(i), on 14th January 2005;
(d) for all other purposes, on 1st March 2004.

(3) These Regulations are prescribed for the purposes of sections 168(4)(b) and 402(1)(b) of the 2000 Act.

(4) The following Regulations are revoked –

(a) the Money Laundering Regulations 1993[5];
(b) the Financial Services and Markets Act 2000 (Regulations Relating to Money Laundering) Regulations 2001[6];
(c) the Money Laundering Regulations 2001[7].

2. Interpretation

(1) In these Regulations –

"the 2000 Act" means the Financial Services and Markets Act 2000;

"applicant for business" means a person seeking to form a business relationship, or carry out a one-off transaction, with another person acting in the course of relevant business carried on by that other person in the United Kingdom;

"applicant for registration" means an applicant for registration as a money service operator, or as a high value dealer;

"the appropriate judicial authority" means –

    (a) in England and Wales, a magistrates' court,
    (b) in Scotland, the sheriff,
    (c) in Northern Ireland, a court of summary jurisdiction;

"authorised person" has the meaning given by section 31(2) of the 2000 Act;

"the Authority" means the Financial Services Authority;

"the Banking Consolidation Directive" means Directive 2000/12/EC of the European Parliament and of the Council of 20th March 2000 relating to the taking up and pursuit of the business of credit institutions as last amended by Directive 2002/87/EC of the European Parliament and of the Council of 16th December 2002[8];

"business relationship" means any arrangement the purpose of which is to facilitate the carrying out of transactions on a frequent, habitual or regular basis where the total amount of any payments to be made by any person to any other in the course of the arrangement is not known or capable of being ascertained at the outset;

"cash" means notes, coins or travellers' cheques in any currency;

"the Commissioners" means the Commissioners of Customs and Excise;

"constable" includes a person commissioned by the Commissioners and a person authorised for the purposes of these Regulations by the Director General of the National Criminal Intelligence Service;

"EEA State" means a State which is a contracting party to the agreement on the European Economic Area signed at Oporto on 2nd May 1992 as it has effect for the time being;

"estate agency work" has the meaning given by section 1 of the Estate Agents Act 1979[9] save for the omission of the words "(including a business in which he is employed)" in subsection (1) and includes a case where, in relation to a disposal or acquisition, the person acts as principal;

"high value dealer" means a person who carries on the activity mentioned in paragraph (2)(n);

"the Life Assurance Consolidation Directive" means Directive 2002/83/EC of the European Parliament and of the Council of 5th November 2002 concerning life assurance[10];

"justice" means a justice of the peace or, in relation to Scotland, a justice within the meaning of section 307 of the Criminal Procedure (Scotland) Act 1995[11];

"money laundering" means an act which falls within section 340(11) of the Proceeds of Crime Act 2002[12] or an offence under section 18 of the Terrorism Act 2000[13];

"the Money Laundering Directive" means Council Directive 91/308/EEC of 10th June 1991 on prevention of the use of the financial system for the purpose of money laundering as amended by Directive 2001/97/EC of the European Parliament and of the Council of 4th December 2001[14];

"money service business" means any of the activities mentioned in paragraph (2)(d) (so far as not excluded by paragraph (3)) when carried on by way of business;

"money service operator" means a person who carries on money service business other than a person who carries on relevant business falling within any of sub-paragraphs (a) to (c) of paragraph (2);

"nominated officer" has the meaning given by regulation 7;

"officer" (except in regulations 7, 10 and 27) has the meaning given by section 1(1) of the Customs and Excise Management Act 1979[15];

"officer in overall charge of the investigation" means the person whose name and address are endorsed on the order concerned as being the officer so in charge;

"one-off transaction" means any transaction other than one carried out in the course of an existing business relationship;

"operator" means a money service operator;

"recorded information" includes information recorded in any form and any document of any nature whatsoever;

"registered number" has the meaning given by regulation 9(2);

"relevant business" has the meaning given by paragraph (2);

"the review procedure" means the procedure under regulation 21;

"satisfactory evidence of identity" has the meaning given by paragraphs (5) and (6);

"supervisory authority" has the meaning given by paragraphs (7) and (8);

"tribunal" means a VAT and duties tribunal.

(2) For the purposes of these Regulations, "relevant business" means –

    (a) the regulated activity of –

        (i)   accepting deposits;

      (ii) effecting or carrying out contracts of long-term insurance when carried on by a person who has received official authorisation pursuant to Article 4 or 51 of the Life Assurance Consolidation Directive;

      (iii) dealing in investments as principal or as agent;

      (iv) arranging deals in investments;

      (v) managing investments;

      (vi) safeguarding and administering investments;

      (vii) sending dematerialised instructions;

      (viii)establishing (and taking other steps in relation to) collective investment schemes;

      (ix) advising on investments; or

      (x) issuing electronic money;

(b) the activities of the National Savings Bank;

(c) any activity carried on for the purpose of raising money authorised to be raised under the National Loans Act 1968[16] under the auspices of the Director of Savings;

(d) the business of operating a bureau de change, transmitting money (or any representation of monetary value) by any means or cashing cheques which are made payable to customers;

(e) any of the activities in points 1 to 12 or 14 of Annex 1 to the Banking Consolidation Directive (which activities are, for convenience, set out in Schedule 1 to these Regulations) when carried on by way of business, ignoring an activity falling within any of sub-paragraphs (a) to (d);

(f) estate agency work;

(g) operating a casino by way of business;

(h) the activities of a person appointed to act as an insolvency practitioner within the meaning of section 388 of the Insolvency Act 1986[17] or Article 3 of the Insolvency (Northern Ireland) Order 1989[18];

(i) the provision by way of business of advice about the tax affairs of another person by a body corporate or unincorporate or, in the case of a sole practitioner, by an individual;

(j) the provision by way of business of accountancy services by a body corporate or unincorporate or, in the case of a sole practitioner, by an individual;

(k) the provision by way of business of audit services by a person who is eligible for appointment as a company auditor under section 25 of the Companies Act 1989[19] or Article 28 of the Companies (Northern Ireland) Order 1990[20];

(l) the provision by way of business of legal services by a body corporate or unincorporate or, in the case of a sole practitioner, by an individual and which involves participation in a financial or real property transaction (whether by assisting in the planning or execution of any such transaction or otherwise by acting for, or on behalf of, a client in any such transaction);

(m) the provision by way of business of services in relation to the formation, operation or management of a company or a trust; or

(n) the activity of dealing in goods of any description by way of business (including dealing as an auctioneer) whenever a transaction involves accepting a total cash payment of 15,000 euro or more.

(3) Paragraph (2) does not apply to –

(a) the issue of withdrawable share capital within the limit set by section 6 of the Industrial and Provident Societies Act 1965[21] by a society registered under that Act;

   (b) the acceptance of deposits from the public within the limit set by section 7(3) of that Act by such a society;

   (c) the issue of withdrawable share capital within the limit set by section 6 of the Industrial and Provident Societies Act (Northern Ireland) 1969[22] by a society registered under that Act;

   (d) the acceptance of deposits from the public within the limit set by section 7(3) of that Act by such a society;

   (e) activities carried on by the Bank of England;

   (f) any activity in respect of which an exemption order under section 38 of the 2000 Act has effect if it is carried on by a person who is for the time being specified in the order or falls within a class of persons so specified;

   (g) any activity (other than one falling within sub-paragraph (f)) in respect of which a person was an exempted person for the purposes of section 45 of the Financial Services Act 1986[23] immediately before its repeal;

   (h) the regulated activities of arranging deals in investments or advising on investments, in so far as the investment consists of rights under a regulated mortgage contract;

   (i) the regulated activities of dealing in investments as agent, arranging deals in investments, managing investments or advising on investments, in so far as the investment consists of rights under, or any right to or interest in, a contract of insurance which is not a qualifying contract of insurance; or

   (j) the Official Solicitor to the Supreme Court when acting as trustee in his official capacity.

(4) The following must be read with section 22 of the 2000 Act, any relevant order under that section and Schedule 2 to that Act –

   (a) paragraphs (2)(a) and (3)(h) and (i);

   (b) regulation 25 (authorised persons operating a bureau de change);

   (c) references in these Regulations to a contract of long-term insurance.

(5) For the purposes of these Regulations, and subject to paragraph (6), "satisfactory evidence of identity" is evidence which is reasonably capable of establishing (and does in fact establish to the satisfaction of the person who obtains it) that the applicant for business is the person he claims to be.

(6) Where the person who obtains the evidence mentioned in paragraph (5) knows or has reasonable grounds for believing that the applicant for business is a money service operator, satisfactory evidence of identity must also include the applicant's registered number (if any).

(7) For the purposes of these Regulations, each of the following is a supervisory authority –

   (a) the Bank of England;

   (b) the Authority;

   (c) the Council of Lloyd's;

   (d) the Office of Fair Trading;

   (e) the Occupational Pensions Regulatory Authority;

   (f) a body which is a designated professional body for the purposes of Part 20 of the 2000 Act;

   (g) the Gaming Board for Great Britain.

(8) The Secretary of State and the Treasury are each a supervisory authority in the exercise, in relation to a person carrying on relevant business, of their respective functions under the enactments relating to companies or insolvency or under the 2000 Act.

(9) In these Regulations, references to amounts in euro include references to equivalent amounts in another currency.

(10) For the purpose of the application of these Regulations to Scotland, "real property" means "heritable property".

PART II
OBLIGATIONS ON PERSONS WHO CARRY ON RELEVANT BUSINESS

3. Systems and training etc. to prevent money laundering

(1) Every person must in the course of relevant business carried on by him in the United Kingdom –

  (a) comply with the requirements of regulations 4 (identification procedures), 6 (record-keeping procedures) and 7 (internal reporting procedures);
  (b) establish such other procedures of internal control and communication as may be appropriate for the purposes of forestalling and preventing money laundering; and
  (c) take appropriate measures so that relevant employees are –

    (i) made aware of the provisions of these Regulations, Part 7 of the Proceeds of Crime Act 2002 (money laundering) and sections 18 and 21A of the Terrorism Act 2000[24]; and
    (ii) given training in how to recognise and deal with transactions which may be related to money laundering.

(2) A person who contravenes this regulation is guilty of an offence and liable –

  (a) on conviction on indictment, to imprisonment for a term not exceeding 2 years, to a fine or to both;
  (b) on summary conviction, to a fine not exceeding the statutory maximum.

(3) In deciding whether a person has committed an offence under this regulation, the court must consider whether he followed any relevant guidance which was at the time concerned –

  (a) issued by a supervisory authority or any other appropriate body;
  (b) approved by the Treasury; and
  (c) published in a manner approved by the Treasury as appropriate in their opinion to bring the guidance to the attention of persons likely to be affected by it.

(4) An appropriate body is any body which regulates or is representative of any trade, profession, business or employment carried on by the alleged offender.

(5) In proceedings against any person for an offence under this regulation, it is a defence for that person to show that he took all reasonable steps and exercised all due diligence to avoid committing the offence.

(6) Where a person is convicted of an offence under this regulation, he shall not also be liable to a penalty under regulation 20 (power to impose penalties).

4. Identification procedures

(1) In this regulation and in regulations 5 to 7 –

    (a) "A" means a person who carries on relevant business in the United Kingdom; and

    (b) "B" means an applicant for business.

(2) This regulation applies if –

    (a) A and B form, or agree to form, a business relationship;

    (b) in respect of any one-off transaction –

        (i) A knows or suspects that the transaction involves money laundering; or

        (ii) payment of 15,000 euro or more is to be made by or to B; or

    (c) in respect of two or more one-off transactions, it appears to A (whether at the outset or subsequently) that the transactions are linked and involve, in total, the payment of 15,000 euro or more by or to B.

(3) A must maintain identification procedures which –

    (a) require that as soon as is reasonably practicable after contact is first made between A and B –

        (i) B must produce satisfactory evidence of his identity; or

        (ii) such measures specified in the procedures must be taken in order to produce satisfactory evidence of B's identity;

    (b) take into account the greater potential for money laundering which arises when B is not physically present when being identified;

    (c) require that where satisfactory evidence of identity is not obtained, the business relationship or one-off transaction must not proceed any further; and

    (d) require that where B acts or appears to act for another person, reasonable measures must be taken for the purpose of establishing the identity of that person.

5. Exceptions

(1) Except in circumstances falling within regulation 4(2)(b)(i), identification procedures under regulation 4 do not require A to take steps to obtain evidence of any person's identity in any of the following circumstances.

(2) Where A has reasonable grounds for believing that B –

    (a) carries on in the United Kingdom relevant business falling within any of sub-paragraphs (a) to (e) of regulation 2(2), is not a money service operator and, if carrying on an activity falling within regulation 2(2)(a), is an authorised person with permission under the 2000 Act to carry on that activity;

    (b) does not carry on relevant business in the United Kingdom but does carry on comparable activities to those falling within sub-paragraph (a) and is covered by the Money Laundering Directive; or

(c) is regulated by an overseas regulatory authority (within the meaning given by section 82 of the Companies Act 1989) and is based or incorporated in a country (other than an EEA State) whose law contains comparable provisions to those contained in the Money Laundering Directive.

(3) Where –

(a) A carries out a one-off transaction with or for a third party pursuant to an introduction effected by a person who has provided a written assurance that evidence of the identity of all third parties introduced by him will have been obtained and recorded under procedures maintained by him;

(b) that person identifies the third party; and

(c) A has reasonable grounds for believing that that person falls within any of sub-paragraphs (a) to (c) of paragraph (2).

(4) In relation to a contract of long-term insurance –

(a) in connection with a pension scheme taken out by virtue of a person's contract of employment or occupation where the contract of long-term insurance –

(i) contains no surrender clause; and

(ii) may not be used as collateral for a loan; or

(b) in respect of which a premium is payable –

(i) in one instalment of an amount not exceeding 2,500 euro; or

(ii) periodically and where the total payable in respect of any calendar year does not exceed 1,000 euro.

(5) Where the proceeds of a one-off transaction are payable to B but are instead directly reinvested on his behalf in another transaction –

(a) of which a record is kept; and

(b) which can result only in another reinvestment made on B's behalf or in a payment made directly to B.

6. Record-keeping procedures

(1) A must maintain procedures which require the retention of the records prescribed in paragraph (2) for the period prescribed in paragraph (3).

(2) The records are –

(a) where evidence of identity has been obtained under the procedures stipulated by regulation 4 (identification procedures) or pursuant to regulation 8 (casinos) –

(i) a copy of that evidence;

(ii) information as to where a copy of that evidence may be obtained; or

(iii) information enabling the evidence of identity to be re-obtained, but only where it is not reasonably practicable for A to comply with paragraph (i) or (ii); and

(b) a record containing details relating to all transactions carried out by A in the course of relevant business.

(3) In relation to the records mentioned in paragraph (2)(a), the period is –

    (a) where A and B have formed a business relationship, at least five years commencing with the date on which the relationship ends; or

    (b) in the case of a one-off transaction (or a series of such transactions), at least five years commencing with the date of the completion of all activities taking place in the course of that transaction (or, as the case may be, the last of the transactions).

(4) In relation to the records mentioned in paragraph (2)(b), the period is at least five years commencing with the date on which all activities taking place in the course of the transaction in question were completed.

(5) Where A is an appointed representative, his principal must ensure that A complies with this regulation in respect of any relevant business carried out by A for which the principal has accepted responsibility pursuant to section 39(1) of the 2000 Act.

(6) Where the principal fails to do so, he is to be treated as having contravened regulation 3 and he, as well as A, is guilty of an offence.

(7) "Appointed representative" has the meaning given by section 39(2) of the 2000 Act and "principal" has the meaning given by section 39(1) of that Act.

7. Internal reporting procedures

(1) A must maintain internal reporting procedures which require that –

    (a) a person in A's organisation is nominated to receive disclosures under this regulation ("the nominated officer");

    (b) anyone in A's organisation to whom information or other matter comes in the course of relevant business as a result of which he knows or suspects or has reasonable grounds for knowing or suspecting that a person is engaged in money laundering must, as soon as is practicable after the information or other matter comes to him, disclose it to the nominated officer or a person authorised for the purposes of these Regulations by the Director General of the National Criminal Intelligence Service;

    (c) where a disclosure is made to the nominated officer, he must consider it in the light of any relevant information which is available to A and determine whether it gives rise to such knowledge or suspicion or such reasonable grounds for knowledge or suspicion; and

    (d) where the nominated officer does so determine, the information or other matter must be disclosed to a person authorised for the purposes of these Regulations by the Director General of the National Criminal Intelligence Service.

(2) Paragraph (1) does not apply where A is an individual who neither employs nor acts in association with any other person.

(3) Paragraph (1)(b) does not apply in relation to a professional legal adviser where the information or other matter comes to him in privileged circumstances.

(4) Information or other matter comes to a professional legal adviser in privileged circumstances if it is communicated or given to him –

179

(a) by (or by a representative of) a client of his in connection with the giving by the adviser of legal advice to the client;

(b) by (or by a representative of) a person seeking legal advice from the adviser; or

(c) by a person in connection with legal proceedings or contemplated legal proceedings.

(5) But paragraph (4) does not apply to information or other matter which is communicated or given with the intention of furthering a criminal purpose.

(6) "Professional legal adviser" includes any person in whose hands information or other matter may come in privileged circumstances.

8. Casinos

(1) A person who operates a casino by way of business in the United Kingdom must obtain satisfactory evidence of identity of any person before allowing that person to use the casino's gaming facilities.

(2) A person who fails to do so is to be treated as having contravened regulation 3.

PART III
MONEY SERVICE OPERATORS AND HIGH VALUE DEALERS
Registration

9. Registers of money service operators and high value dealers

(1) The Commissioners must maintain a register of operators.

(2) The Commissioners must allocate to every registered operator a number, which is to be known as his registered number.

(3) The Commissioners must maintain a register of high value dealers.

(4) The Commissioners may keep the registers in any form they think fit.

10. Requirement to be registered

(1) A person who acts as an operator or as a high value dealer must first be registered by the Commissioners.

(2) An applicant for registration must –

(a) make an application to be registered in such manner as the Commissioners may direct; and

(b) furnish the following information to the Commissioners –

(i) his name and (if different) the name of the business;

(ii) his VAT registration number or, if he is not registered for VAT, any other reference number issued to him by the Commissioners;

(iii) the nature of the business;

(iv) the address of each of the premises at which he proposes to carry on the business;

(v) any agency or franchise agreement relating to the business, and the names and addresses of all relevant principals, agents, franchisors or franchisees;

(vi) the name of the nominated officer (if any); and

(vii) whether any person concerned (or proposed to be concerned) in the management, control or operation of the business has been convicted of money laundering or an offence under these Regulations.

(3) At any time after receiving an application for registration and before determining it, the Commissioners may require the applicant for registration to furnish them, within 21 days beginning with the date of being requested to do so, with such further information as they reasonably consider necessary to enable them to determine the application.

(4) Any information to be furnished to the Commissioners under this regulation must be in such form or verified in such manner as they may specify.

(5) In this regulation, "the business" means money service business (or, in the case of a high value dealer, the business of dealing in goods) which the applicant for registration carries on or proposes to carry on.

(6) In paragraph (2)(b)(vii), the reference to "money laundering or an offence under these Regulations" includes an offence referred to in regulation 2(3) of the Money Laundering Regulations 1993 or an offence under regulation 5 of those Regulations.

11. Supplementary information

(1) If at any time after a person has furnished the Commissioners with any information under regulation 10 –

(a) there is a change affecting any matter contained in that information; or

(b) it becomes apparent to that person that the information contains an inaccuracy;

he must supply the Commissioners with details of the change or, as the case may be, a correction of the inaccuracy (hereafter "supplementary information") within 30 days beginning with the date of the occurrence of the change (or the discovery of the inaccuracy) or within such later time as may be agreed with the Commissioners.

(2) The supplementary information must be supplied in such manner as the Commissioners may direct.

(3) The obligation in paragraph (1) applies also to changes affecting any matter contained in any supplementary information supplied pursuant to this regulation.

12. Determination of application to register

(1) The Commissioners may refuse to register an applicant for registration if, and only if –

(a) any requirement of –

(i) paragraphs (2) to (4) of regulation 10 (requirement to be registered);

(ii) regulation 11 (supplementary information); or

(iii) regulation 14 (fees);

has not been complied with; or

(b) it appears to them that any information furnished pursuant to regulation 10 or 11 is false or misleading in a material particular.

(2) The Commissioners must, by the end of the period of 45 days beginning with the date on which they receive the application or, where applicable, the date on which they receive any further information required under regulation 10(3), give notice in writing to the applicant for registration of –

(a) their decision to register him and, in the case of an applicant for registration as an operator, his registered number; or

(b) the following matters –

(i) their decision not to register him;

(ii) the reasons for their decision;

(iii) the review procedure; and

(iv) the right to appeal to a tribunal.

13. Cancellation of registration

(1) The Commissioners may cancel the registration of an operator or high value dealer if, at any time after registration, it appears to them that they would have had grounds to refuse registration under paragraph (1) of regulation 12 (determination of application to register).

(2) Where the Commissioners decide to cancel the registration of an operator or high value dealer, they must forthwith inform him, in writing, of –

(a) their decision and the date from which the cancellation takes effect;

(b) the reasons for their decision; .

(c) the review procedure; and

(d) the right to appeal to a tribunal.

14. Fees

(1) The Commissioners may charge a fee –

(a) to an applicant for registration; and

(b) to an operator or high value dealer annually on the anniversary of his registration by them under these Regulations.

(2) The Commissioners may charge under paragraph (1) such fees as they consider will enable them to meet any expenses incurred by them in carrying out any of their functions under these Regulations or for any incidental purpose.

(3) Without prejudice to the generality of paragraph (2), a fee may be charged in respect of each of the premises at which the operator, high value dealer or applicant for registration carries on (or proposes to carry on) money service business or relevant business falling within regulation 2(2)(n).

Powers of the Commissioners

15. Entry, inspection etc.

(1) Where an officer has reasonable cause to believe that any premises are used in connection with money service business or relevant business falling within regulation 2(2)(n), he may at any reasonable time enter and inspect the premises and inspect any recorded information or currency found on the premises.

(2) An operator or high value dealer must –

(a) furnish to an officer, within such time and in such form as the officer may reasonably require, such information relating to the business as the officer may reasonably specify; and

(b) upon demand made by the officer, produce or cause to be produced for inspection by the officer at such place, and at such time, as the officer may reasonably require, any recorded information relating to the business.

(3) An officer may take copies of, or make extracts from, any recorded information produced under paragraph (2).

16. Order for access to recorded information

(1) Where, on an application by an officer, a justice is satisfied that there are reasonable grounds for believing –

(a) that an offence under these Regulations is being, has been or is about to be committed by an operator or high value dealer; and

(b) that any recorded information which may be required as evidence for the purpose of any proceedings in respect of such an offence is in the possession of any person;

he may make an order under this regulation.

(2) An order under this regulation is an order that the person who appears to the justice to be in possession of the recorded information to which the application relates must –

(a) give an officer access to it;

(b) permit an officer to take copies of, or make extracts from, any information produced; or

(c) permit an officer to remove and take away any of it which he reasonably considers necessary;

not later than the end of the period of 7 days beginning with the date of the order or the end of such longer period as the order may specify.

(3) Where the recorded information consists of information stored in any electronic form, an order under this regulation has effect as an order to produce the information in a form in which it is visible and legible, or from which it can readily be produced in a visible and legible form, and, if the officer wishes to remove it, in a form in which it can be removed.

17. Procedure where recorded information is removed

(1) An officer who removes any recorded information in the exercise of a power conferred by regulation 16 must, if so requested by a person showing himself –

    (a) to be the occupier of premises from which the information was removed; or
    (b) to have had custody or control of the information immediately before the removal;

provide that person with a record of what he has removed.

(2) The officer must provide the record within a reasonable time from the making of the request for it.

(3) Subject to paragraph (7), if a request for permission to be granted access to anything which –

    (a) has been removed by an officer; and
    (b) is retained by the Commissioners for the purposes of investigating an offence;

is made to the officer in overall charge of the investigation by a person who had custody or control of the thing immediately before it was so removed or by someone acting on behalf of such a person, that officer must allow the person who made the request access to it under the supervision of an officer.

(4) Subject to paragraph (7), if a request for a photograph or copy of any such thing is made to the officer in overall charge of the investigation by a person who had custody or control of the thing immediately before it was so removed, or by someone acting on behalf of such a person, that officer must –

    (a) allow the person who made the request access to it under the supervision of an officer for the purpose of photographing it or copying it; or
    (b) photograph or copy it, or cause it to be photographed or copied.

(5) Where anything is photographed or copied under paragraph (4)(b), the photograph or copy must be supplied to the person who made the request.

(6) The photograph or copy must be supplied within a reasonable time from the making of the request.

(7) There is no duty under this regulation to grant access to, or supply a photograph or a copy of, anything if the officer in overall charge of the investigation for the purposes of which it was removed has reasonable grounds for believing that to do so would prejudice –

    (a) that investigation;
    (b) the investigation of an offence other than the offence for the purposes of the investigation of which the recorded information was removed; or
    (c) any criminal proceedings which may be brought as a result of –

        (i) the investigation of which he is in charge; or
        (ii) any such investigation as is mentioned in sub-paragraph (b).

18.   Failure to comply with requirements under regulation 17

(1) Where, on an application made as mentioned in paragraph (2), the appropriate judicial authority is satisfied that a person has failed to comply with a requirement imposed by regulation 17, the authority may order that person to comply with the requirement within such time and in such manner as may be specified in the order.

(2) An application under paragraph (1) may only be made –

  (a) in the case of a failure to comply with any of the requirements imposed by regulation 17(1) and (2), by the occupier of the premises from which the thing in question was removed or by the person who had custody or control of it immediately before it was so removed;

  (b) in any other case, by the person who had such custody or control.

(3) In England and Wales and Northern Ireland, an application for an order under this regulation is to be made by complaint; and sections 21 and 42(2) of the Interpretation Act (Northern Ireland) 1954[25] apply as if any reference in those provisions to any enactment included a reference to this regulation.

19.   Entry, search etc.

(1) Where a justice is satisfied on information on oath that there is reasonable ground for suspecting that an offence under these Regulations is being, has been or is about to be committed by an operator or high value dealer on any premises or that evidence of the commission of such an offence is to be found there, he may issue a warrant in writing authorising any officer to enter those premises, if necessary by force, at any time within one month from the time of the issue of the warrant and search them.

(2) A person who enters the premises under the authority of the warrant may –

  (a) take with him such other persons as appear to him to be necessary;

  (b) seize and remove any documents or other things whatsoever found on the premises which he has reasonable cause to believe may be required as evidence for the purpose of proceedings in respect of an offence under these Regulations; and

  (c) search or cause to be searched any person found on the premises whom he has reasonable cause to believe to be in possession of any such documents or other things; but no woman or girl may be searched except by a woman.

(3) The powers conferred by a warrant under this regulation may not be exercised –

  (a) outside such times of day as may be specified in the warrant; or

  (b) if the warrant so provides, otherwise than in the presence of a constable in uniform.

(4) An officer seeking to exercise the powers conferred by a warrant under this regulation or, if there is more than one such officer, that one of them who is in charge of the search must provide a copy of the warrant endorsed with his name as follows –

  (a) if the occupier of the premises concerned is present at the time the search is to begin, the copy must be supplied to the occupier;

185

(b) if at that time the occupier is not present but a person who appears to the officer to be in charge of the premises is present, the copy must be supplied to that person;

(c) if neither sub-paragraph (a) nor (b) applies, the copy must be left in a prominent place on the premises.

Penalties, review and appeals

20. Power to impose penalties

(1) The Commissioners may impose a penalty of such amount as they consider appropriate, not exceeding £5,000, on a person to whom regulation 10 (requirement to be registered) applies, where that person fails to comply with any requirement in regulation 3 (systems and training etc. to prevent money laundering), 10, 11 (supplementary information), 14 (fees) or 15 (entry, inspection etc.).

(2) The Commissioners must not impose a penalty on a person where there are reasonable grounds for them to be satisfied that the person took all reasonable steps for securing that the requirement would be complied with.

(3) Where the Commissioners decide to impose a penalty under this regulation, they must forthwith inform the person, in writing, of –

(a) their decision to impose the penalty and its amount;
(b) their reasons for imposing the penalty;
(c) the review procedure; and
(d) the right to appeal to a tribunal.

(4) Where a person is liable to a penalty under this regulation, the Commissioners may reduce the penalty to such amount (including nil) as they think proper.

21. Review procedure

(1) This regulation applies to the following decisions of the Commissioners –

(a) a decision under regulation 12 to refuse to register an applicant;
(b) a decision under regulation 13 to cancel the registration of an operator or high value dealer;
(c) a decision under regulation 20 to impose a penalty.

(2) Any person who is the subject of a decision as mentioned in paragraph (1) may by notice in writing to the Commissioners require them to review that decision.

(3) The Commissioners need not review any decision unless the notice requiring the review is given before the end of the period of 45 days beginning with the date on which written notification of the decision was first given to the person requiring the review.

(4) A person may give a notice under this regulation to require a decision to be reviewed for a second or subsequent time only if –

(a) the grounds on which he requires the further review are that the Commissioners did not, on any previous review, have the opportunity to consider certain facts or other matters; and

(b) he does not, on the further review, require the Commissioners to consider any facts or matters which were considered on a previous review except in so far as they are relevant to any issue to which the facts or matters not previously considered relate.

(5) Where the Commissioners are required under this regulation to review any decision they must either –

(a) confirm the decision; or
(b) withdraw or vary the decision and take such further steps (if any) in consequence of the withdrawal or variation as they consider appropriate.

(6) Where the Commissioners do not, within 45 days beginning with the date on which the review was required by a person, give notice to that person of their determination of the review, they are to be assumed for the purposes of these Regulations to have confirmed the decision.

22.   Appeals to a VAT and duties tribunal

On an appeal from any decision by the Commissioners on a review under regulation 21, the tribunal have the power to –

(a) quash or vary any decision of the Commissioners, including the power to reduce any penalty to such amount (including nil) as they think proper; and
(b) substitute their own decision for any decision quashed on appeal.

Miscellaneous

23.   Prosecution of offences by the Commissioners

(1) Proceedings for an offence under these Regulations may be instituted by order of the Commissioners.

(2) Such proceedings may be instituted only against an operator or high value dealer or, where such a person is a body corporate, a partnership or an unincorporated association, against any person who is liable to be proceeded against under regulation 27 (offences by bodies corporate etc.).

(3) Any such proceedings which are so instituted must be commenced in the name of an officer.

(4) In the case of the death, removal, discharge or absence of the officer in whose name any such proceedings were commenced, those proceedings may be continued by another officer.

(5) Where the Commissioners investigate, or propose to investigate, any matter with a view to determining –

(a) whether there are grounds for believing that an offence under these Regulations has been committed by any person mentioned in paragraph (2); or
(b) whether such a person should be prosecuted for such an offence;

that matter is to be treated as an assigned matter within the meaning of the Customs and Excise Management Act 1979.

(6) In exercising their power to institute proceedings for an offence under these Regulations, the Commissioners must comply with any conditions or restrictions imposed in writing by the Treasury.

(7) Conditions or restrictions may be imposed under paragraph (6) in relation to –

(a) proceedings generally; or
(b) such proceedings, or categories of proceedings, as the Treasury may direct.

24. Recovery of fees and penalties through the court

Where any fee is charged, or any penalty is imposed, by virtue of these Regulations –

(a) if the person from whom it is recoverable resides in England and Wales or Northern Ireland, it is recoverable as a civil debt; and
(b) if that person resides in Scotland, it may be enforced in the same manner as an extract registered decree arbitral bearing a warrant for execution issued by the sheriff court of any sheriffdom in Scotland.

25. Authorised persons operating a bureau de change

(1) No authorised person may, as from 1st April 2004, carry on the business of operating a bureau de change unless he has first informed the Authority that he proposes to do so.

(2) Where an authorised person ceases to carry on that business, he must inform the Authority forthwith.

(3) Any information to be supplied to the Authority under this regulation must be in such form or verified in such manner as the Authority may specify.

(4) Any requirement imposed by this regulation is to be treated as if it were a requirement imposed by or under the 2000 Act.

(5) Any function of the Authority under this regulation is to be treated as if it were a function of the Authority under the 2000 Act.

PART IV
MISCELLANEOUS

26. Supervisory authorities etc. to report evidence of money laundering

(1) Where a supervisory authority, in the light of any information obtained by it, knows or suspects, or has reasonable grounds for knowing or suspecting, that someone has or may have been engaged in money laundering, the supervisory authority must disclose the information to a constable as soon as is reasonably practicable.

(2) Where a supervisory authority passes the information to any other person who has such knowledge or suspicion or such reasonable grounds for knowledge or suspicion as is mentioned in paragraph (1), he may disclose the information to a constable.

(3) Where any person within paragraph (6), in the light of any information obtained by him, knows or suspects or has reasonable grounds for knowing or suspecting that someone has or may have been engaged in money laundering, he must, as soon as is reasonably practicable, disclose that information either to a constable or to the supervisory authority by whom he was appointed or authorised.

(4) Where information has been disclosed to a constable under this regulation, he (or any person obtaining the information from him) may disclose it in connection with the investigation of any criminal offence or for the purpose of any criminal proceedings, but not otherwise.

(5) A disclosure made under this regulation is not to be taken to breach any restriction on the disclosure of information (however imposed).

(6) Persons within this paragraph are –

(a) a person or inspector appointed under section 65 or 66 of the Friendly Societies Act 1992[26];
(b) an inspector appointed under section 49 of the Industrial and Provident Societies Act 1965 or section 18 of the Credit Unions Act 1979[27];
(c) an inspector appointed under section 431, 432, 442 or 446 of the Companies Act 1985[28] or under Article 424, 425, 435 or 439 of the Companies (Northern Ireland) Order 1986[29];
(d) a person or inspector appointed under section 55 or 56 of the Building Societies Act 1986[30];
(e) a person appointed under section 167, 168(3) or (5), 169(1)(b) or 284 of the 2000 Act, or under regulations made as a result of section 262(2)(k) of that Act, to conduct an investigation; and
(f) a person authorised to require the production of documents under section 447 of the Companies Act 1985, Article 440 of the Companies (Northern Ireland) Order 1986 or section 84 of the Companies Act 1989.

27. Offences by bodies corporate etc.

(1) If an offence under regulation 3 committed by a body corporate is shown –

(a) to have been committed with the consent or the connivance of an officer; or
(b) to be attributable to any neglect on his part;

the officer as well as the body corporate is guilty of an offence and liable to be proceeded against and punished accordingly.

(2) If an offence under regulation 3 committed by a partnership is shown –

(a) to have been committed with the consent or the connivance of a partner; or
(b) to be attributable to any neglect on his part;

the partner as well as the partnership is guilty of an offence and liable to be proceeded against and punished accordingly.

(3) If an offence under regulation 3 committed by an unincorporated association (other than a partnership) is shown –

- (a) to have been committed with the consent or the connivance of an officer of the association or a member of its governing body; or
- (b) to be attributable to any neglect on the part of such an officer or member;

that officer or member as well as the association is guilty of an offence and liable to be proceeded against and punished accordingly.

(4) If the affairs of a body corporate are managed by its members, paragraph (1) applies in relation to the acts and defaults of a member in connection with his functions of management as if he were a director of the body.

(5) In this regulation –

- (a) "partner" includes a person purporting to act as a partner; and
- (b) "officer", in relation to a body corporate, means a director, manager, secretary, chief executive, member of the committee of management, or a person purporting to act in such a capacity.

28. Prohibitions in relation to certain countries

(1) The Treasury may direct any person who carries on relevant business –

- (a) not to enter a business relationship;
- (b) not to carry out any one-off transaction; or
- (c) not to proceed any further with a business relationship or one-off transaction;

in relation to a person who is based or incorporated in a country (other than an EEA State) to which the Financial Action Task Force has decided to apply counter-measures.

(2) A person who fails to comply with a Treasury direction is to be treated as having contravened regulation 3.

29. Minor and consequential amendments

The provisions mentioned in Schedule 2 to these Regulations have effect subject to the amendments there specified, being minor amendments and amendments consequential on the provisions of these Regulations.

30. Transitional provisions

(1) Nothing in these Regulations obliges any person who carries on relevant business falling within any of sub-paragraphs (a) to (e) of regulation 2(2) to maintain identification procedures which require evidence to be obtained in respect of any business relationship formed by him before 1st April 1994.

(2) Nothing in these Regulations obliges any person who carries on relevant business falling within any of sub-paragraphs (f) to (n) of regulation 2(2) –

    (a) to maintain identification procedures which require evidence to be obtained in respect of any business relationship formed by him before 1st March 2004; or

    (b) to maintain internal reporting procedures which require any action to be taken in respect of any knowledge, suspicion or reasonable grounds for knowledge or suspicion which came to that person before 1st March 2004.

John Heppell

Nick Ainger
Two of the Lords Commissioners of Her Majesty's Treasury

28th November 2003

SCHEDULE 1

Regulation 2(2)(e)

ACTIVITIES LISTED IN ANNEX 1 TO THE BANKING CONSOLIDATION DIRECTIVE

1. Acceptance of deposits and other repayable funds.

2. Lending.

3. Financial leasing.

4. Money transmission services.

5. Issuing and administering means of payment (eg credit cards, travellers' cheques and bankers' drafts).

6. Guarantees and commitments.

7. Trading for own account or for account of customers in –

    (a) money market instruments (cheques, bills, certificates of deposit, etc.);
    (b) foreign exchange;
    (c) financial futures and options;
    (d) exchange and interest-rate instruments;
    (e) transferable securities.

8. Participation in securities issues and the provision of services related to such issues.

9. Advice to undertakings on capital structure, industrial strategy and related questions and advice as well as services relating to mergers and the purchase of undertakings.

10. Money broking.

11. Portfolio management and advice.

12. Safekeeping and administration of securities.

13. Credit reference services.

14. Safe custody services.

SCHEDULE 2

Regulation 29

MINOR AND CONSEQUENTIAL AMENDMENTS

PART I
Primary Legislation
Value Added Tax Act 1994 (c. 23)

1. – (1) Section 83 of the Value Added Tax Act 1994 is amended as follows.

(2) In paragraph (zz), for "regulation 16 of the Money Laundering Regulations 2001", substitute "regulation 21 of the Money Laundering Regulations 2003".

Northern Ireland Act 1998 (c. 47)

2. – (1) Paragraph 25 of Schedule 3 (reserved matters) to the Northern Ireland Act 1998 is amended as follows.

(2) For "1993" substitute "2003".

PART II
Secondary Legislation
The Cross-Border Credit Transfers Regulations 1999 (S.I. 1999/1876)

3. – (1) Regulation 12 of the Cross-Border Credit Transfers Regulations 1999 is amended as follows.

(2) For paragraph (2) substitute –

" (2) In this regulation "enactments relating to money laundering" means section 18 of the Terrorism Act 2000, section 340(11) of the Proceeds of Crime Act 2002 and the Money Laundering Regulations 2003.".

The Terrorism Act 2000 (Crown Servants and Regulators) Regulations 2001 (S.I. 2001/192)

4. – (1) The Terrorism Act 2000 (Crown Servants and Regulators) Regulations 2001 are amended as follows.

(2) In regulation 2, for the definition of "relevant financial business" substitute –

" 'relevant business' has the meaning given by regulation 2(2) of the Money Laundering Regulations 2003.".

(3) In regulation 3, for "relevant financial business" substitute "relevant business".

The Representation of the People (England and Wales) Regulations 2001
(S.I. 2001/341)

5. – (1) The Representation of the People (England and Wales) Regulations 2001 are amended as follows.

(2) In regulation 114(3)(b)[31] –

> (i)   for "1993" substitute "2003"; and
> (ii) omit ", the Money Laundering Regulations 2001".

The Representation of the People (Northern Ireland) Regulations 2001
(S.I. 2001/400)

6. – (1) The Representation of the People (Northern Ireland) Regulations 2001 are amended as follows.

(2) In regulation 107(3)(b)[32] –

> (i)   in paragraph (i), for "1993" substitute "2003";
> (ii) omit paragraph (ii); and
> (iii) in paragraph (iii), omit the words "either of" and "sets of".

The Representation of the People (Scotland) Regulations 2001 (S.I. 2001/497)

7. – (1) The Representation of the People (Scotland) Regulations 2001 are amended as follows.

(2) In regulation 113(3)(b)[33] –

> (i)   for "1993" substitute "2003"; and
> (ii) omit ", the Money Laundering Regulations 2001".

The Proceeds of Crime Act 2002 (Failure to Disclose Money Laundering: Specified Training) Order 2003 (S.I. 2003/171)

8. – (1) The Proceeds of Crime Act 2002 (Failure to Disclose Money Laundering: Specified Training) Order 2003 is amended as follows.

(2) In article 2, for "regulation 5(1)(c) of the Money Laundering Regulations 1993" substitute "regulation 3(1)(c)(ii) of the Money Laundering Regulations 2003".

EXPLANATORY NOTE

(This note is not part of the Regulations)

These Regulations replace the Money Laundering Regulations 1993 and 2001 with updated provisions which reflect Directive 2001/97/EC of the European Parliament and of the Council amending Council Directive 91/308/EEC on prevention of the use of the financial system for the purpose of money laundering. A Transposition Note setting out how the main elements of Directive 2001/97/EC will be transposed into

UK law is available from the Financial Systems and International Standards Team, HM Treasury, 1 Horse Guards Road, London SW1A 2HQ. The Transposition Note is also on HM Treasury's website (**www.hm-treasury.gov.uk**). A regulatory impact assessment has been prepared and placed in the library of each House of Parliament. A copy is likewise available from the Treasury and can be found on the Treasury's website.

Where business relationships are formed, or one-off transactions are carried out, in the course of relevant business (defined in regulation 2), the persons carrying out such relevant business are required to maintain certain identification procedures (regulation 4), record-keeping procedures (regulation 6) and internal reporting procedures (regulation 7) and to establish other appropriate procedures for the purpose of forestalling or preventing money laundering (regulation 3(1)(b)). They are also required to train their employees in those procedures and, more generally, in the recognition of money laundering transactions and the law relating to money laundering (regulation 3(1)(c)). A person who fails to maintain the procedures or carry out the training is guilty of a criminal offence (regulation 3(2)). Casino operators must obtain satisfactory evidence of the identity of all people using their gaming facilities (regulation 8).

Regulation 9 requires the Commissioners of Customs and Excise to keep a register of money service operators and a register of high value dealers and regulations 10–11 state the registration requirements placed on such persons. Regulation 12 lists the grounds on which registration may be refused by the Commissioners, including where information which has been supplied is incomplete, false or misleading. Regulation 13 lists the circumstances in which registration may be cancelled by the Commissioners. Regulation 14 allows the Commissioners to charge fees.

Regulations 15 to 19 state the powers of the Commissioners in relation to money service operators and high value dealers, including a power to enter and inspect premises. Where there are reasonable grounds for believing that an offence under the Regulations is being, has been or is about to be committed by a money service operator or high value dealer, the Commissioners may seek a court order requiring any person in possession of certain information to allow them access to it. Regulation 19 allows the Commissioners to enter premises with a warrant, to search persons and to take away documents. Regulation 20 allows the Commissioners to impose a civil penalty in certain circumstances. Regulation 21 provides a mechanism for a formal review by the Commissioners of their decisions. Regulation 22 provides for appeals against the Commissioners' decisions to be heard by a VAT tribunal. Regulation 23 allows the Commissioners to prosecute offences under the Regulations. Regulation 24 allows fees and penalties to be recovered as a civil debt. Regulation 25 requires people who are authorised by the Financial Services Authority ("the FSA") to inform the FSA before they operate bureaux de change.

Regulation 26 requires supervisory authorities (defined in regulation 2) and various other people who obtain information indicative of money laundering to inform a constable. Regulation 28 allows the Treasury to require people who carry on relevant business to refrain from doing business with people in certain non-EEA States.

Notes:

[1] S.I. 1992/1711.
[2] 1972 c. 68. By virtue of the amendment of section 1(2) made by section 1 of the European Economic Area Act 1993 (c. 51) regulations may be made under section

2(2) to implement obligations of the United Kingdom created by or arising under the Agreement on the European Economic Area signed at Oporto on 2nd May 1992 (Cm 2073) and the Protocol adjusting that Agreement signed at Brussels on 17th March 1993 (Cm 2183).

[3] See the definition of "prescribed".

[4] 2000 c. 8.

[5] S.I. 1993/1933, amended by S.I. 1994/1696, S.I. 1998/1129, S.I. 2000/2952, S.I. 2001/3641 and 3649.

[6] S.I. 2001/1819.

[7] S.I. 2001/3641.

[8] OJ L 126, 26.5.2000, p.1; OJ L 35, 11.2.2003, p.1.

[9] 1979 c. 38. Section 1 was amended by the Law Reform (Miscellaneous Provisions) (Scotland) Act 1985 (c. 73), Schedule 1, Pt I, para. 40, the Planning (Consequential Provisions) Act 1990 (c. 11), Schedule 2, para. 42, the Planning (Consequential Provisions) (Scotland) Act 1997 (c. 11), Schedule 2, para. 28 and by S.I. 2001/1283.

[10] OJ L 345, 19.12.2002, p.1.

[11] 1995 c. 46.

[12] 2002 c. 29.

[13] 2000 c. 11.

[14] OJ L 166, 28.6.1991, p.77; OJ L 344, 28.12.2001, p.76.

[15] 1979 c. 2.

[16] 1968 c. 13.

[17] 1986 c. 45.

[18] S.I. 1989/2405 (N.I. 19).

[19] 1989 c. 40.

[20] S.I. 1990/593 (N.I. 5).

[21] 1965 c. 12.

[22] 1969 c. 24 (N.I.).

[23] 1986 c. 60. This Act was repealed as from 1st December 2001 by S.I. 2001/3649, art. 3(1)(c).

[24] Section 21A was inserted by the Anti-terrorism, Crime and Security Act 2001 (c. 24), Schedule 2, Part 3, para. 5.

[25] 1954 c. 33 (N.I.).

[26] 1992 c. 40.

[27] 1979 c. 34.

[28] 1985 c. 6.

[29] S.I. 1986/1032 (N.I. 6).

[30] 1986 c. 53.

[31] Inserted by regulation 15 of the Representation of the People (England and Wales) (Amendment) Regulations 2002 (S.I. 2002/1871).

[32] Inserted by regulation 21 of the Representation of the People (Northern Ireland) (Amendment) Regulations 2002 (S.I. 2002/1873).

[33] Inserted by regulation 14 of the Representation of the People (Scotland) (Amendment) Regulations 2002 (S.I. 2002/1872).

B1

Extracts from the Law Society's Guidance on Money Laundering (Pilot Edition – January 2004)

[. . .]

PART 2 – HOW CAN IDENTITY BE ESTABLISHED?

General principles

3.66　Solicitors must be satisfied that they are dealing with a real person or organisation (natural, corporate or legal), and obtain satisfactory evidence of identity
to establish that the client is that person or organisation. For the purpose of the
ML Regulations 2003, 'satisfactory evidence of identity' is evidence which is
reasonably capable of establishing (and does in fact establish to the satisfaction
of the person obtaining it) that the client is the person he or she claims to be.

3.67　Some firms may wish to produce standard forms for use by their staff in
relation to evidence of identity.

3.68　In deciding what evidence is satisfactory, and how much evidence is required,
a common sense approach should be applied. There will be circumstances
when it will be both necessary and permissible to apply commercial judgement
to the extent of the initial identification requirements. Decisions will need to
be taken on the number of persons to be identified within the client organisation, the identification evidence required, and whether additional evidence is
necessary.

3.69　The first step in the identification process is to think about exactly who your
client is. In some cases it will be immediately obvious but in others it may be
necessary to consider the position and, on occasion, to discuss and agree this
with the client(s). For example, if you are acting for one of a group of companies, exactly which company or companies will you be acting for? If another
professional firm or a bank asks you for advice, are you acting for them or for
their underlying client? If acting on a domestic house purchase, are you acting
for one individual or for both partners within a relationship? You must obtain
satisfactory evidence of identity in relation to all persons for whom you intend
to act. In the case of joint instructions from two or more clients, the identity of

all the clients must be checked (but see paragraph 3.120 below in relation to partnerships).

3.70   You must also consider whether your client is instructing you as principal or agent. Where the client is or appears to act for another person then, in addition to obtaining evidence of identity in relation to the client, under Regulation 4(3)(d), you must also take reasonable measures to establish the identity of any principal for whom that client is acting, and under Regulation 6 you must maintain records in relation to that evidence. This obligation to take reasonable measures is rather less than the obligation to obtain satisfactory evidence in relation to the client, but it must still be complied with.

3.71   You may make checks by looking at actual documentary evidence such as passports and certificates of incorporation issued by Companies House, or by making electronic checks of suitable databases such as the FSA register, the Law Society database of practising solicitors, and the electoral register. Where you rely on an electronic check it may be advisable to print out and retain a copy of the evidence with your records. [...]

3.72   You may also ask third parties, such as investigation and information service providers, and credit reference agencies, to obtain the evidence for you as long as you are reasonably satisfied that they are reputable, and that the evidence they produce will be reliable, and that you ensure that your records of the evidence are complete. For example, you may rely on a copy of the details page of a passport as part of the evidence of identity if it has been certified by a reputable lawyer (for details as to who may photocopy UK passports see paragraphs 3.79–3.80).

3.73   When using a combination of electronic and documentary checks, you must ensure that different original sources of information are used. For example, a physical check of a mortgage statement and an electronic check of the same mortgage account come from the same source, so one does not corroborate the other.

3.74   Some clients may object to providing evidence of identity. It may be helpful to explain the reason for requiring evidence of identity in the initial interview or client care letter. More people in the UK are now used to being asked for evidence of identity by their bank or building society, so it will be increasingly rare to find a client who objects to such a request from a solicitor. If a client is unwilling to provide evidence it will be for the solicitor to assess whether this in itself is a cause for concern.

Copying and certifying original identification documents

3.75   As already mentioned, usually you should keep a printed or other copy of any evidence of identification obtained as you may be required to produce the evidence in the future. It may be helpful to make a note on the retained copy as to when the original document was seen and by whom. If reliance is being placed on copies provided by others these should be certified.

3.76   Such a copy may be made in several ways, including fax copying, photocopying, scanning, filming and reproduction in any other medium, including the placing of materials on the Internet.

197

3.77 Certified copies of original identification evidence should be made by checking the copy against the original and then signing and dating the copy as a true copy of the original. In the case of photographic evidence of an individual's identity the person certifying should confirm that the individual is the person shown in the photograph. When copying a passport or national identity card, only the personal details pages need to be copied and kept as evidence.

3.78 If the client cannot meet you to produce the original identification document, you should think carefully before asking the client to send valuable personal identity documents, such as passports, driving licences and identity cards by normal post because of the dangers of interception and fraud. These dangers can even exist with registered or other guaranteed postal services. The client should be warned of the dangers and given a choice as to another method. You should arrange an appointment when the client can produce the documents required or, if you are not able to meet the client, you should follow the guidance in paragraphs 3.90 to 3.94 below.

3.79 The HMSO guidance note no. 20 dated 5 December 2002 confirms that copies of the personal details page of a UK passport may be made for the purposes of record keeping by the following persons only:

(a) the holder of the passport
(b) notaries, solicitors, UK government departments and British consulates;
(c) financial institutions and other persons and firms who are subject to the ML Regulations 2003; and
(d) any person or firm for the purpose of certifying that identification checks have been made in accordance with the ML Regulations 2003.

3.80 The guidance says that copies must be in black and white only so that they cannot be mistaken for a real passport page. Copying for these purposes includes photocopying, scanning, filming, reproduction in any other medium, including placing material on the Internet. The original document is the evidence of identity. The photocopy of the original is used to record and certify that identification checks have been made. There is no need to apply for a licence or pay a fee to take such copies.

Individuals

3.81 In general, an individual's identity is made up of both full name and current address, including the postcode where available and in most cases you should obtain satisfactory evidence in relation to both name and address, and a combination of checks should be carried out. Where an EEA member state identity card is produced showing name, address, and with a photograph this may be accepted as satisfactory evidence without further corroboration. The previous address should be confirmed if the client has moved recently.

3.82 Where evidence of identity is required in relation to an individual, and that individual is known to a solicitor or qualified EEA or US lawyer who confirms in writing (a) that s/he has known the individual for over two years and (b) the individual's private or trading address, then no further evidence of identity is usually required, unless there are circumstances which increase risk.

3.83 Where you are reasonably satisfied that an individual is nationally or internationally known a record of identification can include a file note of your satisfaction about identity, usually including an address.

Individuals: documentary evidence of personal identity: UK residents

3.84 The following is a list of examples of suitable documentary evidence of name for UK resident private individuals. You should be satisfied that any documents offered are originals to guard against forged or counterfeit documents and that photographs, if any, provide a likeness to the client:

- current signed passport;
- EEA member state identity card (which can also be used as evidence of address if it gives this);
- cheque drawn on an account in the name of the client with a bank in the UK or EEA;
- residence permit issued by Home Office to EEA nationals on sight of own country passport;
- current UK or EEA photo-card driving licence;
- current full UK driving licence – old-style provisional driving licences should not be accepted;
- benefit book or original notification letter from the Benefits Agency confirming the right to benefits;
- photographic registration cards for self-employed individuals and partnerships in the construction industry C1S4 (the card does not contain an issue or expiry date and is renewed only if the individual's appearance changes dramatically);
- firearms or shotgun certificate;
- national identity card containing a photograph of the client; and
- an entry in a local or national telephone directory confirming name and address.

Documentary evidence of address

3.85 The following is a list of examples of suitable documentary evidence of address for UK resident private individuals. Do not use any of these documents if you have already used them as evidence of name:

- confirmation from an electoral register search that a person of that name lives at that address;
- a recent utility bill or statement, or a certificate from a utilities supplier confirming an arrangement to pay for services on pre-payment terms (do not accept mobile telephone bills which can be sent to different addresses);
- local council tax bill for current year;
- current full UK driving licence – old-style provisional driving licences should not be accepted;
- bank, building society or credit union statement or passbook containing current address;
- a recent original mortgage statement from a recognised lender;
- solicitor's letter confirming recent house purchase or land registry confirmation of address;
- local council or housing association rent card or tenancy agreement;

- benefit book or original notification letter from the Benefits Agency confirming the right to benefits;
- EEA member state identity card;
- Inland Revenue self-assessment statement or tax demand;
- house or motor insurance certificate;
- record of any home visit made; and
- an entry confirming name and address in a local or national telephone directory.

Individuals: persons not resident in the UK

3.86 If you meet the client, you should be able to see a passport or national identity card as evidence of name and, if it gives it, an address. You can take copies of the pages containing the relevant information (reference numbers, date and country of issue) in which case you should certify the copy examined against the original and the date of the examination, or record that information in your records as part of the identification evidence. You must be reasonably satisfied that the document is a genuine passport or national identity card, and if in doubt as to whether it is genuine you could ask advice from an embassy or consulate official for the country concerned.

3.87 Where a prospective client is a national of, or resident in, a country on the FATF list of non-co-operative countries and territories, solicitors should consider whether they need to carry out further checks to find out exactly who the client is and what his or her business is before accepting instructions.

3.88 In addition, separate evidence of the client's permanent residential address (or, for business clients, principal business address) should usually be obtained, preferably from a national identity card, an official source, a reputable directory or from a qualified lawyer who confirms that the client is known to him and that he lives or works at the address given. A post box number alone is not normally sufficient evidence of address (although there are some countries, such as Hong Kong and the Gulf States, where post box addresses are commonly used) and if you accept a box number as evidence of address you should satisfy yourself (personally or through an agent) that the address can be physically located by way of a recorded description or other means.

3.89 Evidence of name and address could be obtained from a credit or financial institution in the client's home country or country of residence or through a reputable investigation and information service provider or credit reference agency. For professionals, evidence of name and practising address may be obtained from reputable professional directories.

Individuals: when you do not meet the client

3.90 There may be difficulties in verifying identity if the client is unable to visit your office (for example if he or she is disabled or lives at a distance from you or is overseas). In such cases you must satisfy yourself that your instructions have been given to you by the client or an authorised person on his or her behalf. A client who is unwilling to meet you without a good reason may be cause for concern [...]

3.91 Where you are so satisfied, you should enquire whether it is possible for the client to produce the documentary evidence you require to someone else qualified and willing to take and certify copies on your behalf. This would enable you to obtain evidence from valuable documents such as his or her passport. For a person physically within the UK, copies of evidence should be certified, for example, by a UK solicitor, accountant, doctor or high street bank manager, whose name and address should be noted and checked by reference to a professional directory or, for solicitors, the Law Society database of practising solicitors. The person undertaking the certification must be capable of being contacted if necessary. The certified copies should be kept with your other records of identity.

3.92 For a person not resident within the UK, the copy of the passport, national identity card and documentary evidence of address can be certified by:

- an embassy, consulate or high commission of the country of issue;
- a qualified lawyer or notary; or
- in the case of international students, the registrar of a UK higher education institution.

3.93 Where reliance is placed on certification by a qualified lawyer or notary, you should verify that his or her name and practice address appear in a reputable professional directory, or that the professional is currently on record with the appropriate professional body as practising at the address shown on the certificate or practice notepaper, and you should keep a note of this name and address with the evidence of identity.

3.94 Where it is not possible either to meet the client or for someone else to take and certify copies for you as set out above, you may not wish to ask the client to post valuable identity documents to you so, in practice, you may not see documents such as a passport, driving licence or identity card. You could, however, ask to see a combination of other less valuable documents which might satisfy you as to identity. You might also wish to make some electronic checks or arrange for evidence to be obtained though a reputable investigation and information service provider or credit reference agency. In all cases you must satisfy yourself that you have evidence which is reasonably capable of establishing (and does in fact establish to your satisfaction) that the client is the person he or she claims to be.

Disadvantaged clients

3.95 It is not the intention of the ML Regulations 2003 to exclude those who are already at a disadvantage from access to legal advice and financial services. Some disadvantaged clients may not be able to produce detailed evidence of identity (for example, they may not have a passport or driving licence and their name may not appear on utility bills). You might consider accepting as identification evidence a letter or statement from someone in a position of responsibility who knows the client (for example, a solicitor, doctor, minister of religion, teacher, hostel manager, social worker) which tends to show that the client is who he or she says he or she is and, if applicable, to confirm his or her permanent address.

3.96 Evidence of address might include:

- correspondence from a relevant government agency, including a benefits payment book or giro cheque;
- a tenancy agreement from a local housing association;
- a letter from the householder with whom the client is living who is named on a current council tax bill;
- a letter from the matron of a nursing or residential care home or the client's care worker;
- a letter from a hostel manager confirming temporary residence; or
- a letter from the Home Office confirming refugee status and granting permission to work, or a Home Office travel document for refugees.

Mentally incapacitated clients

3.97 Solicitors unsure as to whether a client is mentally incapacitated should refer to Principle 24.04 of the *Guide to the Professional Conduct of Solicitors 1999*.

3.98 Where solicitors are unable to comply with normal identification requirements because of their clients' mental health problems medical workers, hostel staff, social workers, or Receivers or Guardians appointed by a court, may assist with locating and producing identification documents. It is recognised that confirming the identity of clients whose personal affairs are in some disarray can be difficult, and so solicitors must exercise extra flexibility in the ways identification checks are done, e.g. in some circumstances oral confirmation of identity from a person who knows the client well may suffice.

Asylum seekers

3.99 An applicant's registration card could be used in conjunction with other evidence. The details in the card should, wherever possible, be verified by a passport, identity card or birth certificate. Please note that the registration card does not contain a signature as the Home Office relies on a biometric check (fingerprint held on microchip) to confirm identity.

3.100 Evidence of address can be obtained in the way suggested for disadvantaged clients.

Students and minors

3.101 The normal identification procedures should be used but if they do not provide satisfactory evidence, verification could be obtained in the following ways:

- through the home address of the parents;
- once the student is in residence, confirmation of the UK address from the registrar of the client's higher education institution;
- looking at a tenancy agreement or student accommodation contract; or
- confirmation of a temporary address and documentary evidence from the householder with whom the student is living (for example, by seeing the council tax bill in the householder's name).

3.102 If instructions are given by a family member or guardian, you should check the identity of that adult as well as the minor.

Estates

3.103 When acting for an estate, the firm's client will be the executor(s) or administrator(s) of that estate. Their identities will need to be established using the procedures for individuals or companies set out in this chapter. When acting for more than one executor or administrator it will normally be necessary to establish the identity of at least two. In addition to the will, solicitors should obtain copies of the grant of probate or letters of administration, and in the case of an existing executorship or administration obtain a copy of the death certificate. If a will trust is created, and the trustees are different from the executors the procedures in relation to trusts (see below) need to be followed in relation to the trustees when the will trust comes into operation.

Trusts

3.104 Trusts do not, of course, have separate legal personality. There are many different types of trust. Firms are advised to adopt a risk based approach in determining what evidence should be obtained and the nature of the evidence that is appropriate, recognising that trusts are popular vehicles for money launderers. The classic long established family settlement may raise different issues to an offshore discretionary trust.

3.105 When acting for trusts, the firm's client will be the trustees whose position can be checked by referring to the document establishing the trust (and, if appropriate, documents dealing with the appointment of the current trustees). Their identities need to be established using procedures for individuals or companies summarised elsewhere in this Guidance. When acting for more than one trustee it will be necessary to establish the identity of at least two individual trustees. Whether all the trustees, and/or the identity of any living settlor should also be established will depend on your assessment of the risk which will itself depend on your knowledge of the nature, purpose and original source of the funding for the trust. When acting for trustees who are based in offshore jurisdictions with strict bank secrecy and confidentiality rules or in jurisdictions without equivalent money laundering procedures, you may need to make fuller enquiries of the trustees to obtain details (for example, full name and business or home address) of the settlor.

3.106 When acting for the settlor to form the trust, it will be necessary to establish his or her identity using procedures already mentioned.

3.107 Except where the firm is acting for beneficiaries, there is no need to establish the identity of beneficiaries for the purpose of the ML Regulations 2003, although it would be normal practice for a firm of solicitors to check the identity of beneficiaries before making any distribution.

Employee and Pension Trusts

3.108 Such trusts would normally be low risk. Where the client is the sponsoring employer or settlor of a pensions trust or employee benefits trust, only the identity of that sponsoring employer or the settlor need be verified. Where the client is the trustee(s) of a tax approved pension scheme trust, identification of the sponsoring employer would normally be sufficient.

CORPORATE CLIENTS

3.109 Company structures are attractive to money launderers and firms should take a risk based approach in determining what evidence should be obtained, and the nature of the evidence that is appropriate. Dealing with a listed company presents a different risk to a private company. The following paragraphs set out minimum requirements, and firms may need to seek further evidence in higher risk situations.

Companies listed on the London Stock Exchange or a UK recognised investment exchange

3.110 Where a company is:

- listed on the London Stock Exchange or another recognised UK investment exchange; or
- a member of a UK recognised investment exchange; or
- the subsidiary of such a company;

no further evidence is required of identity beyond evidence of listing (such as a copy of the relevant dated page from the Financial Times or the London Stock Exchange's list of companies (which can be found at **www.londonstock exchange.com**) and, for subsidiaries, a copy of the latest annual return or comparable evidence such as an extract from a reputable online information provider showing the parent/subsidiary relationship.

Corporates listed or traded on any other recognised, designated or approved exchange

3.111 A list of these exchanges is published by the FSA (**www.fsa.gov.uk stock exchanges**) and the JMLSG website: **www.jmlsg.org.uk** also sets out a list. Where a company or corporation is listed or traded on a recognised, designated or approved exchange, or is one whose shares or securities are traded there, or is a subsidiary of such an entity, no further evidence is required of identity beyond evidence of such listing or trading and, for subsidiaries, a copy of the latest annual return or comparable evidence such as an extract from a reputable online information provider showing the parent/subsidiary relationship.

Banks, investment firms and insurance companies carrying on relevant business in the UK or subsidiaries of such entities (see Regulation 2(2) for the definition of relevant business)

3.112 In such cases you may obtain satisfactory evidence of identity by taking a copy of the relevant dated page from the on-line FSA register (**www.fsa.gov.uk**) showing that the bank, investment firm or company is authorised by the FSA to carry on relevant business, and for subsidiaries, a copy of the latest annual return or comparable evidence such as an extract from a reputable online information provider showing the parent/subsidiary relationship.

Banks, investment firms and insurance companies regulated in another EU or FATF member country, or for subsidiaries of such entities

3.113 In such cases you may obtain satisfactory evidence of identity by checking the regulated status of the prospective client with the relevant regulatory or supervisory authority, for example, by taking a copy of the relevant page from the regulator's website, and, for subsidiaries, a copy of the latest annual return or comparable evidence such as an extract from a reputable online information provider showing the parent/subsidiary relationship.

Other corporate clients: general

3.114 For UK companies not within paragraphs 3.109 to 3.111 above, and where reasonably practicable for overseas corporations not within those paragraphs, evidence of identity should be obtained as set out below.

UK companies

3.115 Evidence of identity will be required in relation to the company itself, usually comprising:

- a copy of the certificate of incorporation
- a list of directors
- a list of shareholders
- the registered address

which can be obtained from an official, or recognised independent source including an extract from a reputable online information provider.

3.116 In addition, where it is reasonably practicable, you should obtain evidence of identity in relation to one of its directors or shareholders, one of whom should usually be the person instructing you or alternatively appears to you, on the face of it, to be active in the management or control of the company. Note that lists of Directors and Shareholders should contain details of home addresses for the relevant individuals and so provide the documentary evidence of address (see paragraph 3.85). Where it is not reasonably practicable to obtain such additional identification evidence you might consider establishing a list of any shareholders holding 20% or more of the shares in the company or, if there are none, the principal owners. It may be necessary for further checks to be made about beneficial ownership if the initial information obtained is of the identity of mere nominees. By way of exception where the company is a well established household name there is no need to obtain the additional identification referred to in this subparagraph;

Overseas corporations (unlisted)

3.117 Evidence of identity will be required in relation to the company itself. Where it is obtainable in the relevant country this will usually include the certificate of incorporation, but can also include the lists referred to above in relation to UK companies. In countries where there is no certificate of incorporation, or equivalent, other evidence that reasonably satisfies you that the corporation is in existence should be obtained (for example a copy of the most recent audited accounts).

3.118 You may use an extract from a reputable online information provider, or the services of a reputable directory or information search agency. In addition, where it is reasonably practicable, you should obtain evidence of identity in relation to one of its directors or shareholders, one of whom should usually be the person instructing you or alternatively appears to you, on the face of it, to be active in the management or control of the company. Where it is not reasonably practicable to obtain such additional identification evidence you might consider establishing a list of any shareholders holding 20% or more of the shares in the company or, if there are none, the principal owners.

Subsidiaries (and sister companies) whether in the UK or elsewhere

3.119 Where the new client is a subsidiary of an existing client, in respect of whom an identification check has been carried out recently, evidence of the subsidiary or other relationship will be required and may be sufficient, provided that the record of the identification of the existing client is kept for the correct time period in relation not only for that existing client but also for the new client.

Partnerships, limited partnerships and Limited Liability Partnerships

3.120 For partnerships and limited partnerships you should obtain evidence of identity in respect of the partner who is instructing you and one other partner together with satisfactory evidence of the trading address (possibly obtained from a directory or similar). UK LLPs should obtain evidence in line with the requirements for other corporate clients set out above.

3.121 If preferred, where you are instructed on behalf of a partnership, limited partnership or a LLP formed under the Limited Liability Partnerships Act 2000, of lawyers, chartered or certified accountants or chartered surveyors, satisfactory evidence of identity may be obtained in the form of (a) confirmation of the firm's existence from a reputable directory or information or search agency or from the appropriate professional body (for example a copy of the relevant page from the Law Society's on-line directory of solicitors) and (b) confirmation of the firm's trading address, such as a copy of the relevant page from a reputable directory (such as Chambers, The Legal 500 or Martindale Hubble). For these professional partnerships it is not usually necessary to obtain evidence in relation to individual partners or members of the limited partnership or LLP.

CHAPTER 4 – PRIVILEGE AND CONFIDENTIALITY – PARAGRAPHS 4.1–4.14

The solicitor's duty of client confidentiality

4.1   A solicitor is under a *professional* and *legal* obligation to keep the affairs of clients confidential and to ensure that his or her staff do likewise. This duty of confidentiality is fundamental to the solicitor/client relationship.

4.2   It extends to all matters divulged to a solicitor by a client or (on his behalf) from whatever source.

4.3   Whilst there may be exceptional circumstances in which this general obligation of confidence can be overridden, the common law has long recognised its importance by providing protection to ensure that certain of these communications are immune from disclosure unless statute expressly, or by necessary implication, overrides that protection.

Protecting client confidentiality – legal professional privilege – LPP

4.4   The protection is provided by way of *a privilege against disclosure* and is called legal professional privilege (LPP).

> The policy of legal professional privilege requires that the client should be secure in the knowledge that protected documents and information will not be disclosed at all. [1]

4.5   Both the Government and the courts recognise its importance, describing LPP respectively as,

> . . .*a cornerstone of the legal system. It serves the public interest because it recognises that it is in the interests of justice that a person consulting his legal adviser should be able to do so in confidence, since otherwise he may not feel able to be fully open about his position. This might impede his ability either to protect his rights or to defend himself properly in any subsequent action.* [2]

and as

> . . .*a fundamental human right long established in the common law. It is a necessary corollary of the right of any person to obtain skilled advice about the law. Such advice cannot be effectively obtained unless the client is able to put all the facts before the advisor without fear that they may be afterwards disclosed and used to his prejudice.* [3]

What communications are privileged?

4.6   Not everything that lawyers have a duty to keep confidential is privileged. Only those confidential communications falling under either of the two heads of privilege –'advice privilege' or 'litigation privilege', are protected by LPP.

Who is a 'lawyer' for such purposes?

4.7   This includes solicitors and their employees, barristers, in-house lawyers but not accountants, even if they give legal advice (subject to one very limited exception). However POCA, when dealing with communications in privileged circumstances adopts the narrower term – 'professional legal adviser'. [. . .]

Advice privilege

4.8   Communications between a lawyer (acting in his capacity as a lawyer), and a client, are privileged if they are *confidential* and *for the purpose of seeking legal advice from a lawyer or providing legal advice to a client*. Case law gives some help in showing what is, or is not, covered by advice privilege. For example:

- conveyancing documents are not communications [4]
- neither is a client account ledger maintained in relation to the client's money [5]
- nor an appointments diary or time record on an attendance note, time sheet or fee record relating to a client [6]
- whereas a solicitor's bill of costs and statement of account is privileged [7]
- and notes of open court proceedings [8], or conversations, correspondence or meetings with opposing lawyers [9] are not privileged, as the content of the communication is not confidential.

4.9 Merely because a client is speaking or writing to his or her solicitor does not make that communication privileged – it is only those communications that directly seek or provide advice or 'where information is passed by the solicitor or the client to the other in the course of keeping each other informed so that advice may be sought or given as required' [10]. This will include advice as to what should prudently and sensibly be done in the relevant legal context [11].

Litigation privilege

4.10 Under this head the following are privileged:–

Confidential communications made, *after litigation has started*, or is *'reasonably in prospect'*, between

- a lawyer and a client,
- a lawyer and an agent (whether or not that agent is a lawyer), or
- a lawyer and a third party,

for the *sole or dominant purpose* of litigation, whether

- for seeking or giving advice in relation to it, or
- for obtaining evidence to be used in it, or
- for obtaining information leading to obtaining such evidence.

Pre-existing documents

4.11 An original document which is not brought into existence for either of these privileged purposes and so is not already privileged, does not acquire privileged status merely by being given to a lawyer for advice or otherwise for a privileged purpose.

Fraud or illegality – the crime/fraud exception

4.12 It is proper for a lawyer to advise a client on how to stay within the law and avoid committing a crime [12] or to warn a client that proposed actions could attract prosecution [13] and such advice will be protected by privilege.

4.13 LPP does not however exist in respect of documents which themselves form part of a criminal or fraudulent act or communications which take place in order to obtain advice with the intention of carrying out an offence [14]. It is irrelevant whether or not the lawyer is aware that he is being used for that purpose [15]. If the lawyer suspects that he is unwittingly being involved by his client in a fraud, before he can consider himself released from his duty of confidentiality, the courts require there to be strong prima facie evidence before LPP can be displaced [16]. Whilst he may release himself if such evidence exists, he may also raise the issue with the Court for an order authorising him to make disclosure to the victim [17].

4.14 The general 'crime fraud exception' principle is restated in the Police and Criminal Evidence Act 1984 (PACE) [18] at section 10(2) where items held with the intention of furthering a criminal purpose are declared not to be items subject to LPP. It is important to note that the intention to further a criminal purpose need not be that of the client (or the lawyer) – it is sufficient that a third party intends the lawyer/client communication to be made with that purpose (e.g. where the innocent client is being 'used' by a third party) [19].

Notes:

1. Lord Hoffman in *R* v. *Special Commissioner and Anor, ex p Morgan Grenfell & Co Ltd* [2002] UKHL 21.
2. *'In the public interest?'* Lord Chancellor's Department consultation paper issued following publication of the OFT's report on competition in the professions.
3. *Morgan Grenfell.*
4. *R* v. *Inner London Crown Court ex p Baines & Baines* [1988] QB 579.
5. *Nationwide Building Society* v. *Various Solicitors* [1999] PNLR 53. Such entries are not created for the purpose of giving legal advice to a client but are internal records maintained in part to discharge a solicitor's professional and disciplinary obligations under the Solicitors' Accounts Rules.
6. *R* v. *Manchester Crown Court, ex p. Rogers* [1999] 1 WLR 832.
7. *Chant* v. *Brown* (1852) 9 Hare 790.
8. *Parry* v. *News Group Newspapers* (1990) 140 New Law Journal 1719.
9. *Parry.*
10. In *re Konigsberg (a bankrupt)* [1989] 1 WLR 1257.
11. See generally the judgment of Taylor LJ in *Balabel* v. *Air India* [1988] Ch at 330.
12. *Bullivant* v. *Att-Gen of Victoria* [1901] AC 196.
13. *Butler* v. *Board of Trade* [1971] Ch 680.
14. *R* v. *Cox & Railton* (1884) 14 QBD 153.
15. *Banque Keyser Ullman* v. *Skandia* [1986] 1 Lloyds Rep 336.
16. *O'Rourke* v. *Darbishire* [1920] AC 581.
17. *Finers* v. *Miro* [1991] 1 WLR 35.
18. It is also reflected in numerous other criminal statutes – including POCA section 330 (failure to disclose) and section 333 (tipping off) – [...].
19. *R* v. *Central Criminal Court ex p Francis & Francis* [1989] 1 AC 346.

CHAPTER 5 – CIVIL LIABILITY – PARAGRAPHS 5.1–5.23

Introduction to liabilities under civil law

5.1 The principal focus of recent legislation on money laundering has been to ensure that businesses, which can include solicitors, have in place effective AML systems and controls in order to reduce opportunities for money laundering and to provide for the forfeiture of the profits of crime. That legislation does not seek to recompense the victim of criminal activity but to take away the proceeds. By contrast, under civil law in England & Wales, a victim of crime may have a claim against those who became involved in or provided assistance in the process of laundering money. Such a claim may be attractive where the victim is seeking a 'deep pocket' from which a recovery can be made, particularly in situations where the wrongdoer cannot be found or is not able to repay. Recent examples include the high profile frauds such as the BCCI, Maxwell and Polly Peck affairs, all of which involved claims against professionals. This trend is likely to continue. Solicitors should therefore be alive to the possibility of a civil claim.

5.2   There are no civil claims that equate directly to the criminal offences of theft and handling stolen property but there are established legal principles that can be used to recover money or property. In particular, a victim may have claims against third parties involved in money laundering for constructive trusteeship; money had and received; and tracing in equity or conspiracy.

5.3   The law of constructive trust and the circumstances in which liability can arise are complicated. This chapter aims to give guidance on how civil liability for breach of a constructive trust can arise and offers practical guidance on how to reduce the risk of liability. This Guidance is no substitute for appropriate legal advice.

Constructive trusteeship

5.4   'Trusteeship' here does not connote an orthodox trust involving a trust deed or a settlor and beneficiaries. Rather, in certain circumstances the courts will impose on an intermediary a liability to repay, as constructive trustee, the monies claimed by a claimant. For liability to arise, there must be 'trust' monies. A trust relationship arises whenever a person, the trustee, is compelled in equity to hold property for the benefit of some person or persons, the beneficiary, or for some purpose other than his own. *In certain situations (but by no means all) there will be a fiduciary relationship between a solicitor and his client.* [1] *Further, negligence or breach of contract by a fiduciary will not necessarily amount to breach of a fiduciary duty – it is breach of a fiduciary obligation (often by disloyalty or infidelity by the fiduciary) that gives rise to a constructive trust.*

5.5   Conventionally, liability as a constructive trustee can arise in two situations:

(a)   where a person 'receives and becomes chargeable' with trust property – commonly called *'knowing receipt'*;

(b)   where a person 'assists with knowledge of a fraudulent and dishonest design on the part of the trustees' – historically referred to as 'knowing assistance', but more accurately referred to as *'dishonest assistance'*.

5.6   There are differences between these two heads of liability. The main difference concerns 'knowledge' for the purposes of founding liability and in particular whether or not an element of dishonesty is required. An intermediary will be trustee of funds laundered after acquiring the requisite degree of knowledge.

Knowing receipt

5.7   Liability for 'knowing receipt' is receipt-based. The cause of action is restitutionary and is available only where the defendant received or applied the monies in breach of trust *for his own use and benefit.* Dishonesty is not an essential ingredient of the claim. The claimant must show:

(a) a disposal of his assets in breach of fiduciary duty or breach of trust;

(b) the beneficial receipt by the defendant of assets which are traceable as representing the assets of the claimant; and

(c) knowledge on the part of the defendant that the assets received are traceable to a breach of fiduciary duty which makes it unconscionable for the defendant to retain the benefit of those assets.

5.8 Element (b) is perhaps the most significant, since in many cases a solicitor will not be in receipt of the monies for his own benefit. A solicitor receiving money into client account and therefore effectively acting as agent for the client and paying it away as part of a transaction does not receive the trust monies for his own benefit. He must also account to the client for interest earned on those monies whilst in his hands. The position is different where the solicitor receives the money and applies it in payment of fees – this would constitute beneficial receipt of the monies.

5.9 Element (c) requires a defendant to have knowledge that the funds received are traceable to a breach of trust. The level of knowledge required has given rise to a substantial body of case law – in particular, whether actual knowledge is required or whether constructive knowledge is enough. That case law suggests that knowledge could derive from:

(a) actual knowledge;

(b) wilfully shutting one's eyes to the obvious;

(c) wilfully and recklessly failing to make such inquiries as an honest and reasonable man would have made;

(d) knowledge of circumstances which would indicate the facts to an honest and reasonable man;

(e) knowledge of circumstances which would put an honest and reasonable man on inquiry.

The first three categories are regarded as constituting actual knowledge, the latter two as constructive knowledge. However, more recently the courts have moved away from the distinction between actual and constructive knowledge, preferring instead to adopt a test of whether the recipient's state of knowledge was such as to 'make it unconscionable for him to retain the benefit of the receipt.' [2]

5.10 As a general rule, solicitors are entitled to act on the basis that their customers are honest. In relation to a bank it has been stated that:

> Account officers are not detectives. Unless and until they are alerted to the possibility of wrongdoing, they proceed, and are entitled to proceed, on the assumption that they are dealing with honest men. [3]

Dishonest assistance

5.11 This head of liability is also commonly referred to as 'knowing assistance' or 'accessory liability.' The elements of liability are:

(a) a breach of trust or fiduciary duty by someone other than the defendant in which the defendant assisted;

(b) where in doing so the defendant acted dishonestly;

(c) resulting in loss.

5.12 There are any number of ways in which a breach of trust or of fiduciary duty might arise. The breach of trust can be innocent rather than dishonest[4], although in the context of money laundering this is unlikely.

5.13 Assistance is essentially a factual issue, involving an examination of the accessory's conduct and state of knowledge. The case of *Agip (Africa) Ltd* v. *Jackson* [5] concerned a firm of accountants but illustrates that assistance for these purposes is likely to include activities that give rise to liability under section 328 POCA. In this case the defendant accountants formed companies in the Isle of Man with nominal share capital and served as directors. The companies opened bank accounts, received and made payments and were then liquidated. These were considered to be types of assistance for the purpose of this liability.

5.14 It is now clear that the accessory must have acted dishonestly [6] in the sense that his conduct falls below what is required of an honest solicitor in the circumstances. Honesty is judged objectively and inferences can be drawn where, for example, someone deliberately closes his eyes or ears, or deliberately fails to ask questions in case he learns something he would rather not know. [7]

5.15 Suspicion falls a long way short of knowledge required to establish constructive trust liability. In a recent court decision a judge made clear that the bank's suspicions about its customer, based on intelligence but not hard evidence, were not sufficient to give rise to constructive trust liability even though a report to NCIS was considered necessary. [8] However, each case must be judged on its own facts and there are risks which are difficult to quantify until this issue is finally determined in court.

5.16 Care is needed when acting for Politically Exposed Persons (PEPs) which includes senior political figures, their immediate family and close associates. A broad definition of PEPs is that they are individuals who are or have been entrusted with prominent public functions. Such persons may abuse their public powers. Business relationships with individuals holding important public positions and with persons or companies clearly related to them may expose a service provider to significant legal and/or reputational risks. Particular care should be taken if the amounts involved are in excess of the expected legitimate wealth of the person in question and where that person is from a country where corruption is said to be prevalent.

Practical issues

5.17 It is obviously difficult to prove a defendant's state of knowledge. A disclosure report to NCIS will provide useful evidence and it has been suggested that the fact that a disclosure report has been made could increase the risk of constructive trust claims. This risk cannot be completely ruled out. It is the Law Society's view that a solicitor's risk of constructive liability will be lowered rather than increased by making an immediate disclosure to NCIS. This is because the disclosure report is likely to be seen as a badge of honesty. Similarly, assessing money laundering risk and reacting appropriately are likely to be regarded as badges of honesty and reduce the risk of constructive trust liability.

5.18 The courts may give directions to trustees as to the administration of the trust. It is unlikely that a firm acting in accordance with such directions would be liable as constructive trustees. The case of *Finers* v. *Miro* [9] is an example of where this procedure was followed. This procedure should only be used in cases of real need. This is because the danger for solicitors making such applications is that they have to furnish the Court with evidence that they are constructive trustees. This could be relied on by the victim of the wrong in mounting a claim against a solicitor. An alternative is that solicitors consider seeking a binding declaration under Civil Procedure Rules, Part 40.20.

5.19 Two further notes of caution should also be considered:

(a) A solicitor should not as a matter of knee-jerk reaction report a matter to NCIS, simply in order to provide protection against a claim in constructive trust. If in fact there is no reasonable basis for the solicitor's suspicions of money laundering then a report to NCIS should not be made.

(b) Even where an NCIS report is appropriately made, appropriate consent to continue dealings does not by itself absolve solicitors of the need to satisfy themselves that they are conducting themselves as an honest person would.

Negligence

5.20 Delays between making a report to NCIS and receiving appropriate consent can lead to solicitors fearing that their client's matter may be damaged or lost, which in turn might lead to fears of a negligence claim.

5.21 The only reported case of which we are aware of a civil action instituted by a customer against an intermediary as a result of delays in processing instructions is *A* v. *Bank of Scotland* [2002] 1 WLR 751. In that case the delay was exceptional and arose after the bank obtained an order freezing the customer's bank account. The bank was concerned about tipping off liability. The guidelines in this case and in the case of *C* v. *S* [1999] 2 All ER 343 promulgated by the Court of Appeal for dealing with the risk of tipping off liability could be equally relevant to situations where there is a perceived risk of civil action.

5.22 The absence of reported decisions about cases involving claims against intermediaries may suggest that the risks of civil action consequent upon delay should not be overstated. The risk will be minimised by making NCIS aware as soon as possible of concerns over a possible civil action or complaint. These concerns should be explained to NCIS over the telephone and the disclosure report should be submitted by fax under a covering letter which explains the concerns and the reasons for it. NCIS should be told of any developments which affect the risk of a complaint or civil action and should be pressed on a regular basis to deal with the disclosure [. . .]. NCIS will fast track the disclosure and try to ensure that it is processed within a shorter timescale than usual. If despite your efforts appropriate consent is not provided within the timescale you require you should consider seeking legal advice, and whether you should notify your insurers. Insurance companies have their own nominated officer, and if possible solicitors should contact the nominated officer to explain the reasons for the notification. In case of doubt, particularly in relation to the tipping-off offence, contact Professional Ethics.

5.23 [...]

Notes:

1. *Bristol & West Building Society* v. *Mothew* [1996] 4 All ER 698 at 710 where this issue is examined at some length.
2. *BCCI* v. *Akindele* [2000] 4 All ER 221 at 235.
3. *Macmillan Inc* v. *Bishopsgate Investment Trust plc (No 3)* [1995] 1 All ER 747 at 783.
4. *Royal Brunei Airlines* v. *Tan* [1995] 2 AC 378.
5. [1990] Ch 265.
6. *Royal Brunei Airlines* v. *Tan* [1995] 2 AC 378.
7. *Twinsectra Ltd* v. *Yardley* [2002] 2 AC 164.
8. *The Governor and Company of the Bank of Scotland* v. *A Limited* [2000] All ER (D) 864.
9. [1991] 1 All ER 182.

ANNEX 11

MONEY LAUNDERING

APPENDIX 1

INTRODUCTION CERTIFICATE

For Completion by Intermediaries Regulated in the UK, the EEA or in non-EEA Countries with Equivalence Status

---

FULL NAME OF APPLICANT:

DATE OF BIRTH:
(*if applicant is an individual*)

ADDRESS OF APPLICANT:
(*including [postcode/zip code]*)

INTRODUCER:

ADDRESS OF INTRODUCER:

REGULATOR:

WE CERTIFY THAT:

A.   we have verified the identity and address of the applicant stated above in accordance with the anti-money laundering laws of the jurisdiction in which we are regulated and that documentary evidence has been obtained and checks have been undertaken to confirm the client's name and address shown above is true and correct, and

EITHER:

B.1   certified copies of the documentary evidence obtained in respect of the applicant stated above are attached to this certificate.

OR:

B.2   copies of the documentary evidence obtained in respect of the applicant stated above will be retained in our records and, upon request, certified copies of such documentary evidence will be made available to you.

(please circle B1 or B2)

WE CERTIFY THAT we have no knowledge, suspicion or reasonable grounds to believe that the applicant stated above is or has been involved in criminal conduct or otherwise engaged in money laundering. Should we subsequently have knowledge or suspicion that the applicant may be involved in any such activities, subject to any legal constraints we shall inform you as soon as reasonably practicable.

Signed   Full Name:

....
Authorised Signatory

Job Title: ....   Date: ....

NOTES TO A *REGULATED PERSON* OR *FIRM* ON COMPLETING THE CLIENT INTRODUCTION CERTIFICATE

1.   The full name and address of the Client must be given at the top of the Certificate. [Where the client is a Trust, a separate Certificate must be completed in respect of each Trustee or settlor whose identity has been verified.]

2.   Part A should be completed where the *Introducer* has fully verified the identity and address of the client in accordance with the Regulations/EU directive or equivalent provisions. The Certificate may be used by you as evidence of the identity and address of the client(s) and should be retained on file for the required period. Where this Certificate has been completed by the Introducer you are not obliged to undertake any further verification of identity.

3.   Part B.1 or B.2 should be completed to state whether the client is acting on his/her own behalf or as trustees or nominee on behalf of one or more third

parties. If a trust/nominee relationship applies it is important that the client confirms that the identity of the person who has provided the funds together with any named beneficiary have been verified. If there are anonymous principals, these should be declared in Part C.

4.   Part C should be completed where the Introducer has not confirmed the identity of the client. A reason should be given, for example, transaction exempt from the Introducer viewpoint.

5.   The Certificate must be signed by the Introducer and details of the Introducer's firm, etc., inserted as shown. If an incomplete Certificate is received, it should be returned immediately to the Introducer for completion.

6.   The information given in the draft certificate may be submitted by the Introducer in a variety of forms as long as the document(s) include all the information detailed in the certificate overleaf and it has been completed in accordance with above.

7.   The Certificate should be completed by an intermediary which is regulated by an "overseas regulatory authority" which exercises "regulatory functions". These terms are defined in the money laundering regulations to include functions similar to the Financial Services Authority and the Bank of England.

Law Society's guidance on *P* v. *P*

INTRODUCTION

The judgment in this case arose out of ancillary relief proceedings in which a party's legal adviser had reported the other side to the National Criminal Intelligence Service (NCIS) for apparent tax evasion. The report had been made, and appropriate consent sought, in order to obtain a defence to the s.328 arrangement offence under the Proceeds of Crime Act 2002 (PoCA). The matter was brought to the court's attention because the legal advisers were unsure how to proceed, particularly in the light of the fact that the advice from NCIS appeared to conflict with the professional obligations of the legal advisers.

The Law Society's Money Laundering Task Force, in consultation with family lawyers, has, on behalf of the Law Society, prepared the following guidance for family solicitors on the effect of the judgment. However, solicitors should be aware that this is a new and developing area of law. This should therefore be regarded as interim guidance: further guidance will be published as necessary.

GUIDANCE

The arrangement offence under PoCA

1. It is an offence under s.328 PoCA to enter into an arrangement which a person knows or suspects facilitates (by whatever means) the acquisition, retention, use or control of criminal property by or on behalf of another person.

2. An arrangement offence under s.328 PoCA can be committed even if no money passes through the solicitor's client account.

3. It does not matter how small the financial benefit gained from the criminal conduct may be; nor when or where the criminal conduct took place, as long as it would be a criminal offence if committed in this country.

4. All criminal offences amount to 'criminal conduct' from which criminal property can arise, including tax evasion and social security fraud.

5. When a solicitor acts in ancillary relief proceedings (or proposed proceedings), from the moment they know or suspects that assets which include the proceeds of criminal conduct (criminal property) are involved they risk committing the arrangement offence.

Withdrawing

6. If the solicitor does not wish to continue to act, they may at that stage withdraw.

7. It is necessary and appropriate for the solicitor, in giving legal advice to the client or in acting in connection with the legal proceedings, to advise their client that, in the light of their knowledge or suspicion, if they continue to act for the client, both they and their client will commit a money laundering offence unless an authorised disclosure is made to NCIS and the appropriate consent is received from NCIS to continue (see below at paragraph 15). In so doing however solicitors must be careful to avoid committing the offences of tipping off or prejudicing an investigation and should carefully consider the advice given below at paragraphs 19 onwards. In the event the client does not consent to the solicitor making an authorised disclosure, the solicitor should withdraw.

8. Once the solicitor has withdrawn, whether or not they should report his knowledge or suspicion to NCIS will depend upon the circumstances in which they came by that knowledge or suspicion.

9. If the solicitor's knowledge or suspicion arises from a confidential communication received by the solicitor for the sole or dominant purpose of the proceedings, it is likely that such a communication takes place in privileged circumstances. This of course will not be the case if the purpose of the communication is a criminal one – whether on the part of the client or another.

10. Solicitors in the *regulated* sector, commit an offence if they fail to make the required disclosure when in the course of business they acquire knowledge, suspicion or reasonable grounds for knowledge or suspicion that another person is engaged in money laundering unless the information came to them in privileged circumstances. Therefore solicitors in the regulated sector must carefully consider upon withdrawal whether their knowledge or suspicion arises in privileged circumstances. If it does, they commit no offence under s.330 by failing to report; if it does not, then they commit an offence under s.330.

11. It is crucial that solicitors should realise that legal professional privilege (as opposed to without prejudice privilege) does not attach to communications between opposing parties in litigation. Therefore if the solicitor's knowledge or suspicion arises from a communication from their opponent in the proceedings, it will not have come to them in privileged circumstances.

12. One of the effects of the Money Laundering Regulations 2003 is that from 1 March 2004, those involved in providing 'legal services . . . which involve participation in a financial or real property transaction' will be in the regulated sector. It is likely that this will include solicitors who provide ancillary relief advice.

13. If the solicitor is in the *non-regulated* sector then upon withdrawal they commit no offence of failure to report under s.330 whether or not their knowledge or suspicion arose in privileged circumstances. The solicitor may of course make a protected disclosure, under PoCA 2002, s.337. This is clearly of limited application and is likely to cease to be relevant to those providing ancillary relief services after 1 March 2004.

14. It seems unlikely that by failing to make a disclosure in such circumstances the solicitor commits an offence of concealment under s.327 PoCA. If this were so, then the protection from prosecution given to a solicitor in the regulated sector who fails to disclose knowledge or suspicion gained in privileged circumstances would be made redundant, for they could still be liable to prosecution for concealment under s.327.

Continuing to act

15. Solicitors wishing to continue to act, to avoid prosecution for an arrangement offence, should make a report to NCIS and obtain appropriate consent before any substantive steps in the case are taken, that is to say further negotiations take place or the proceedings are progressed in any other way (although taking instructions, or seeking clarification from the other side as to issues, especially those that may affect whether a report needs to be made, may be acceptable).

16. Once the disclosure has been made to NCIS, it can give or withhold consent within seven working days; if no response is received in this period, consent to proceed is deemed to have been given. If NCIS refuses consent, a solicitor risks committing a money laundering offence if they take any step within the proceedings in the 31 day period following the date of refusal.

17. The arrangement offence, and reporting defence, apply regardless of whether it is the solicitor's own client who is the suspected party, or the other side.

18. As has been indicated above from 1 March 2004 most solicitors will be in the regulated sector which will impose criminal penalties for non disclosure. Solicitors should also bear in mind the specific offences which apply to nominated officers (MLROs) both in the regulated sector (s.331) and outside the regulated sector (s.332). In the event that an MLRO receives a report as nominated officer which is based upon information which has been received by a 'professional legal adviser' in his firm in privileged circumstances, it is the Law Society's view that the MLRO has a 'reasonable excuse' for not reporting that privileged information to NCIS.

Tipping off and prejudicing an investigation

Informing the client

19. Can the solicitor tell his client that they intend to make, or have made, a report to NCIS? The answer will depend upon the circumstances.

20. It is an offence of 'tipping off' (s.333) to make a disclosure which is likely to prejudice any investigation that might be conducted, following a report that the solicitor knows, (or suspects) has been made.

21. It is also an offence of prejudicing an investigation (s.342). If the solicitor knows that an appropriate officer is acting or proposing to act in connection with a confiscation, money laundering or civil recovery investigation which is being or about to be conducted, and he makes a disclosure which is likely to prejudice that investigation.

22.   There is a defence to both of these offences for the professional legal adviser who makes a disclosure (most probably, to his client) in privileged circumstances, that is, 'in connection with the giving by the adviser of legal advice to the client, or to any person in connection with legal proceedings or contemplated legal proceedings' (ss.333(3) and 342(4)). The President held that a central element of advising and representing a client 'must be, in my view, the duty to keep one's client informed and not to withhold information from them'.

23.   However, if the solicitor's purpose in informing his client falls outside this strict exception he may commit either or both offences; this is the position whether or not the solicitor's intention is criminal.

24.   In circumstances when the exception does apply, there is no absolute duty upon solicitors to tell their clients that they have, or intend to, make a report to NCIS. An important factor which solicitors should bear in mind when deciding whether to discuss reporting with a client is whether either they or their staff may be put in danger as a result, perhaps because the underlying crime is serious, e.g. drugs trafficking.

25.   Once the PoCA provisions are explained to them, clients may wish to make their own report, or to make a joint report with their legal representatives. Doing so may, by obtaining consent, also give the client protection from commission of the s.328 arrangement offence, even if the report is made by, or on behalf of, the suspected party themselves.

26.   If a solicitor discusses reporting with his client, but the client does not agree with an NCIS report being made, the solicitor should withdraw from the case. The solicitor should consider carefully in accordance with the guidelines set out above, whether he should himself make a report to NCIS after withdrawing.

Informing the other side

27.   The President recognised in *P* v. *P* that in family proceedings (and particularly in ancillary relief) there is an enhanced duty upon lawyers of full and frank disclosure, to enable a court to have the true facts and to enable the parties to negotiate a genuine settlement. She concluded these enhanced duties in family proceedings appeared to attract protection under ss.333(3) and 343(4), which permitted a legal adviser to communicate such information to his client or opponent 'as is necessary and appropriate in connection with the giving of legal advice or acting in connection with actual or contemplated legal proceedings'.

Timing – when to tell the client/opponent

28.   If it is 'necessary and appropriate' to inform the client/opponent, neither s.333 nor s.342 impose a time limit in which a solicitor may inform their client of a disclosure to NCIS.

29.   The court in *P* v. *P* suggested guidelines for good practice (rather than statutory obligation):

   • In most cases a seven day delay before telling the client would not cause particular difficulty to the solicitor's obligation to their client and opponent.

- In the event that consent was refused by NCIS and a 31 day moratorium imposed, the solicitor and NCIS should seek to agree the degree of information to be disclosed.
- In the absence of agreement or in urgent cases where delay in disclosure to the client would be unacceptable, the court's guidance may be sought.

NCIS guidance

30. In the light of the *P* v. *P* judgment, NCIS have published guidance about disclosures by the legal profession, which can be found at **www.ncis.co.uk**. This has recently been changed to incorporate a number of important amendments to its previous version:

    (i) There is no requirement for Counsel to make separate reports if their solicitors have made report relating all relevant facts known to Counsel. There will usually not be a danger of tipping off in solicitors and Counsel discussing reports as there will be little likelihood of prejudice being caused to an investigation for the purposes of the tipping off offences.
    (ii) On the other hand legal advisers must not presume that the other side in any matter has reported.
    (iii) Where the client or legal adviser have made a joint report the client may be protected from commission of any of the offences under ss.327–329.

Application of the *P* v. *P* judgment in other areas of law

This judgment arose in an ancillary relief case, and is particularly relevant to family proceedings. Solicitors must be extremely cautious however in seeking to extend its findings to general areas of practice.

The Law Society considers that whilst it does give the following general guidance on the interpretation of the statutory provisions dealing with tipping off (s.333) and prejudicing an investigation (s.342), solicitors must exercise the greatest caution when advising in such circumstances:

- A solicitor commits neither offence in properly advising their client that they have made, or will make, an authorised report to NCIS when it is necessary and appropriate to do so in connection with the giving of legal advice or acting in connection with actual or contemplated legal proceedings.
- No such protection is available to the solicitor if their intention in making such a disclosure to their client is the furtherance of a criminal purpose.

NCIS guidance in relation to disclosures by the legal profession

PART 7 PROCEEDS OF CRIME ACT 2002

1. In the view of the NCIS the following constitutes good practice on the part of a legal advisor who is advising a client in relation to a matter that might involve a suspicious financial arrangement.

2. There is no need to seek the consent of the NCIS to act – that is to take instructions and learn what a case is about. The NCIS will not accept such requests for consent.

3. Should a concern arise in relation to a prospective financial arrangement then the legal advisor should learn sufficient about the client and the source (or final destination) of any funds involved in the arrangement, including as necessary seeking information from the legal advisors, if any, on the other side.

4. Should the legal advisor then have a suspicion at the stage that there is a step to be taken in the case that would involve the legal advisor or their client becoming involved in an arrangement which he knows or suspects facilitates by whatever means the acquisition, retention, use or control of criminal property by or on behalf of another person or there is the possibility of offences under section 327 or section 329 of Proceeds of Crime Act 2002, a written report (a template is available at **www.ncis.gov.uk/disclosure.asp**) setting out all relevant details including the grounds for any suspicion should be submitted to the NCIS.

5. In the event that a solicitor makes a disclosure before instructing counsel there would be no requirement for counsel to make a further disclosure if the facts upon which he would otherwise have disclosed remain as they were when the solicitor made the original disclosure.

6. Legal advisors must not assume that 'the other side' in any matter has reported a suspicion to the NCIS and such enquiries should not be made of the NCIS.

7. Where the client of the legal advisor has joined in the disclosure that has been made the client would, from the point in time when a disclosure is made to the NCIS, not be regarded as having committed an offence under sections 327–329. Where a legal advisor makes a disclosure without the knowledge of their client then plainly and necessarily such protection for the client would not apply.

8.   Where consent is sought to enter into or be concerned in an arrangement that is time sensitive this fact should be explicitly stated and highlighted in the written report faxed to the NCIS Consent Desk (formerly the Duty Desk).

9.   For there to be a disclosure there is no necessity at all for any funds to be contemplated as having to pass through the legal advisor's client account or actually to pass through such an account. The test for the legal advisor would simply be whether he had become concerned in an arrangement.

10. Following a disclosure the NCIS will follow the procedure in accordance with section 335 either giving or withholding consent as the case may be. That is that they will give or refuse consent within 7 days; if after 7 days there has been no response from the NCIS consent to proceed on the basis of the information disclosed will be deemed to have occurred. If the NCIS refuse to give consent then there would follow a 31 day period from the date of the refusal during which the legal advisor could not proceed with the arrangement, without risking the commission of a money laundering offence.

11. Once a disclosure has been made to the NCIS then the solicitor is free to continue with the arrangement (as reported to NCIS) if consent is given, or at the end of the moratorium period if consent is withheld.

12. The NCIS would wish the legal profession to note that subject to section 333(4), under section 333(3) POCA there is no restriction on the legal advisor informing any person of the fact that they have made a report to the NCIS if such a disclosure is to a client or his representative in connection with the giving of legal advice to the client or the disclosure is made in connection with legal proceedings or contemplated legal proceedings.

PART 8 PROCEEDS OF CRIME ACT 2002

13. However, if a legal advisor takes the view that he should inform his client (or any other person) of a disclosure to the NCIS, then he must also have regard to section 342. The section provides that if a person including a legal advisor at least suspecting that a person responsible for investigation under the Act is acting or proposing to act in connection with a confiscation, money laundering or civil recovery investigation which is being or is about to be conducted the offence of prejudicing an investigation is made out if a disclosure is made which is likely to prejudice such an investigation, whether or not there has been a disclosure to the NCIS. The legal advisor will note the defence contained in s.342(3) which permits disclosures to a client or to any person in connection with legal proceedings or the giving of legal advice. This would have to be borne in mind when considering whether or not it was necessary to inform a client or another person of a disclosure whether actual or contemplated.

THE NCIS PREFERRED APPROACH POST-DISCLOSURE

14. Where the legal advisor has made a disclosure to the NCIS, the NCIS would prefer as a matter of practise the legal advisor not to make any reference to that fact during the seven days following the disclosure or during the period of 31 days following a refusal to consent to an arrangement, unless not to do so would be in breach of a disclosure obligation imposed by the particular proceedings.

15. In the event that the legal advisor considers that a requirement of the legal proceedings is to require disclosure of the fact of the disclosure to the NCIS, but there has been no consent from NCIS within seven days or the moratorium period is applicable, then the legal advisor should firstly inform the NCIS and try to seek agreement on the way ahead. In the absence of such agreement the legal advisor should consider making a without notice application to the Court for directions giving the NCIS an opportunity to make representations. (See *C* v. *S and others* (*Money Laundering: Discovery of Documents*) [1999] 1 WLR 1551 and *Bank of Scotland* v. *A Limited* [2001] 1 WLR 752.)

(NCIS October 2003)

C1

Client identification form

Client Name

Date of Birth

Address

Postcode

[Client No.]

I certify that I have carried out the appropriate client verification procedures as follows:

<u>**Individuals (including partnerships and unincorporated businesses)**</u>   **Tick** ☐

I have obtained the client's/clients':

(a)   full name
(b)   current permanent address
(c)   date of birth

by reference to at least one document from each of the following lists:

List A (evidence of name and date of birth)

(a)   current valid full passport
(b)   national identity card or resident's permit
(c)   current photocard driving licence
(d)   firearms certificate
(e)   state pension or benefit book
(f)   inland revenue tax notification

List B (evidence of address)

(a) home visit
(b) electoral roll check
(c) recent utility or local authority council tax bill
(d) recent bank/building society statement
(e) recent mortgage statement
(f) current driving licence (not if used in List A)
(g) local council rent card or tenancy agreement.

I confirm having seen the original documents and that any photograph of the client bore a good likeness to the client. A copy of each document is attached to this form.

<u>Corporate</u>   Tick ☐

I confirm that I have carried out a company search and attach a copy to this form. I also confirm that the identity of a director/shareholder instructing the firm has been obtained in accordance with the procedures for individuals and a copy of each document is attached to this form.

<u>Trusts, nominees and fiduciaries</u>   Tick ☐

I confirm that I have received a certified copy of the trust (and the grant of probate or copy of the will creating the trust in the case of a deceased settlor). The trustees have been identified in accordance with the procedures for individuals or companies noted above.

I also confirm that as far as I am aware the client(s) is/are acting in his/her/their own name(s) and not as agent for any other person.*

(*delete if necessary. If a client is acting as agent for another person, a separate identification record is required for the other person/principal)

Signed .... **Date** ....

[Note: this form provides a basic precedent for a client identification form. It should be developed to suit the needs of individual firms. Reference should be made to **Appendix B1**, the Law Society **Money Laundering Guidance** on 'How can identity be established'.]

Precedent for a basic money laundering manual

1. WHAT IS MONEY LAUNDERING?

Money laundering is the process by which the identity of 'dirty money' is changed so that the proceeds of crime appear to originate from a legitimate source. It is important that solicitors and their employees take steps to ensure that their services are not used by those seeking to legitimise the proceeds of crime. Solicitors must be aware that they may be involved in the money laundering process.

It is the policy of *[Firm name]* that we will take no avoidable risks and will co-operate fully with the authorities where necessary. No matter how much you want to help your client, you must not be a party to any form of dishonesty. You must be alert to the possibility that transactions on which we are instructed may involve money laundering. You must therefore follow the firm's policy in order to reduce the risk of:

(a) our clients suffering loss as a result of innocent involvement in money laundering transactions;
(b) our reputation being harmed if we are a party to a money laundering transaction; and
(c) a possible civil claim against the firm by the true owner of any property involved in a money laundering transaction.

2. THE FIRM'S POLICY

Recent legislation (in particular the Proceeds of Crime Act 2002 and the Money Laundering Regulations 2003) has made significant changes to our responsibilities relating to money laundering. These changes are reflected in this manual.

3. THE CRIMINAL OFFENCES

The law relating to money laundering changed in February 2003 as a result of the Proceeds of Crime Act 2002. The Money Laundering Regulations 2003 came into force on 1 March 2004.

There are a number of criminal offences relevant to a solicitor's practice. The offences divide into three categories:

A. *Offences where the firm is involved in a client matter or transaction*

It is an offence:

(a) to acquire, use or possess criminal property;

(b) to conceal, disguise, convert, transfer or remove from the UK criminal property; or

(c) to enter into or become concerned in an arrangement which facilitates the acquisition, retention, use or control of another person's criminal property,

in all cases where we know or suspect that this is the case.

Criminal property is defined as constituting or representing a person's benefit from criminal conduct. Criminal conduct for these purposes means any conduct which constitutes a crime in the UK or if undertaken abroad, would have constituted a crime if committed in the UK. The very wide definition will include, for example, tax evasion. The offence of 'facilitating the acquisition, retention, use or control' (noted in (c) above) does not require the firm to be in possession of any money or other asset which constitutes a person's criminal property. Advising a client on the structure of a transaction to evade tax (as opposed to avoid tax lawfully) is an offence.

Examples of what might amount to suspicion for these purposes are to be found below in the next section of this manual.

A defence is available where you disclose your knowledge or suspicion to a nominated officer (i.e. a person nominated by the firm to receive internal disclosures). The firm's nominated officer is *[name]*. In his/her absence disclosure should be made to the firm's deputy nominated officer, *[deputy's name]*.

If you have any knowledge or suspicion which requires reporting, you may initially discuss your concerns with your *[group partner]*. If after such discussion you still have concerns a formal disclosure report should be made to the nominated officer using the Internal Reporting Form (a copy of which is attached to this document as Appendix 1).

Note that any disclosure you make must be made before the prohibited act (i.e. the act of facilitation or otherwise). If the disclosure is made after you have committed the prohibited act you will only have a defence **if you can show that there was a good reason for your failure to make the disclosure before the act.** (A similar offence relating to the laundering of 'terrorist property' appears in the Terrorism Act 2000.)

B. *Offences following a disclosure report made to the firm's nominated officer*

It is an offence to disclose to any person (including your client) that a report has been made to the firm's nominated officer in circumstances where this is likely to prejudice an investigation. (Further, even if no disclosure report has been made, an offence is committed if you know or suspect that a money laundering investigation is or is likely to be conducted and you disclose any information which is likely to prejudice the investigation.)

Once a report has been made to the nominated officer it may be an offence to continue to act for the client without the consent of the nominated officer. The nominated officer can only give consent if (s)he has disclosed details to the National Criminal Intelligence Service (NCIS) and NCIS have, in turn, given consent for the firm to continue to act.

Consequently, once a disclosure has been made to the nominated officer, (s)he must be involved in every decision relating to that client matter and you must not communicate any information concerning the subject matter of the disclosure to the client or to any other person (including your work colleagues) without the express consent of the nominated officer. **Failure to comply with this procedure could lead to a criminal offence being committed.**

C. *Offences involving a failure to disclose knowledge or suspicion of money laundering*

It is an offence for a person who knows or suspects or who has reasonable grounds for knowing or suspecting that another is engaged in money laundering not to disclose that information where the information came to him in the course of business in the regulated sector.

The disclosure should be made to the firm's nominated officer using the same procedures as noted above.

This offence does not require the firm to be acting for a particular client, nor for the firm to be in possession, etc. of criminal property, nor involved in an arrangement which facilitates the acquisition, retention, use or control of criminal property. Further, the offence is not limited to knowledge or suspicion of our client – it applies to any knowledge or suspicion of money laundering offences committed by any person.

The obligation to report arises simply if the information comes into your possession in the course of our business in the regulated sector. The definition of the regulated sector has been extended significantly. The sector now covers the bulk of our work for clients. Consequently it is the policy of the firm to assume that all client work falls within the regulated sector and that accordingly all knowledge or suspicion of money laundering must be reported to the nominated officer where the information arises in the course of our business.

The definition of money laundering for these purposes includes the three crimes noted above in category (A). In particular it should be appreciated that the crimes involving 'acquisition, use and possession' and 'concealing etc'. can be committed by the perpetrator of the crime. A person guilty of theft or tax evasion will also have committed a money laundering offence if he is in possession of criminal property.

There is a similar obligation to report knowledge or suspicion (or reasonable grounds for knowledge or suspicion) that another is engaged in certain terrorist offences where that information comes into your possession in the course of business in the regulated sector (Terrorism Act 2000).

4. THE DANGER SIGNS TO WATCH FOR

Unusual settlement requests: Settlement by cash of any large transaction involving the purchase of property or other investment should give rise to caution.

Payment by way of a third party cheque or money transfer where there is a variation between the account holder, the signatory and a prospective investor should give rise to additional enquiries.

Fictitious buyer: Especially if the buyer is introduced to the Firm by a third party (e.g. a broker or an estate agent) who is not well known to you. Beware of clients you never meet – they may be fictitious. Wherever a meeting with the client is not possible, special care is needed.

Unusual instructions: Care should always be taken when dealing with a client who has no discernible reason for using the Firm's services, e.g. clients with distant addresses who could find the same service nearer their home base; or clients whose requirements do not fit into the normal pattern of the Firm's business and could be more easily serviced elsewhere. Similarly care should be taken if you are instructed to remit the net proceeds of sale to the estate agent who was instructed.

Misrepresentation of the purchase price: Make sure that the true cash price for a property which is to be actually paid is the price shown in the contract and the transfer, and is identical to the price shown in the mortgage instructions.

A deposit paid direct: A deposit, perhaps exceeding the normal 10 per cent, paid direct, or said to be direct, to the seller should give rise to concern.

Incomplete contract documentation: Contract documents not fully completed by the seller's representative, e.g. dates missing or the identity of the parties not fully described.

Changes in the purchase price: Adjustments to the purchase price, particularly in high percentage mortgage cases, or allowances off the purchase price for, e.g. works to be carried out.

Unusual transactions: Those which do not follow their normal course or the usual pattern of events.

Large sums of cash: Always be cautious when requested to hold large sums of cash in client account, either pending further instructions from the client or for no other purpose than for onward transmission to a third party. It is the firm's policy not to accept sums of cash in excess of [£500] unless prior approval of the firm's nominated officer has been obtained.

The secretive client: A personal client who is reluctant to provide details of his or her identity. Be particularly cautious about the client you do not meet in person.

Suspect territory: Caution should be exercised whenever a client is introduced by an overseas bank, other investor or third party based in countries where production of drugs or drug trafficking may be prevalent.

Mortgage fraud: It is possible that a member of staff may unwittingly assist in a mortgage fraud. This is especially true of staff who deal with any form of conveyancing, whether domestic or commercial. We must therefore be very vigilant to protect our mortgagee clients and ourselves. If you turn a blind eye to any form of dishonesty over mortgages, no matter how small, you could be personally implicated in the fraud. It is important to stress that the penalties are criminal as well as civil.

5. IDENTIFICATION: GENERAL POINTS

5.1.   In the light of the changes contained in the Money Laundering Regulations 2003 it is the firm's policy to verify the identity of all new clients and all existing clients at the start of a new matter unless they have been identified already.

5.2.   Documentary evidence must be obtained in accordance with the procedure set out below. It is important that the original of any document is examined and copied. The fee earner should endorse the copy with the words 'original seen' followed by the fee earner's signature.

5.3.   Particular care must be taken when acting on the instructions of someone on behalf of the true client or where our client is clearly an agent for a third party. In those circumstances our procedures must ensure that reasonable measures are taken to establish the identity of both parties.

5.4.   The identification procedures must be carried out as soon as reasonably practicable after first contact is made between the firm and client. It is not necessary for the firm to wait until the verification process is complete before commencing work for the client. However, if it proves impossible to satisfactorily complete the process **we must cease to act for the client.**

5.5.   No client money should be accepted from the client for payment into client account until the verification process has been satisfactorily completed.

5.6.   A Client Identification form should be completed and *[kept with the file/submitted to   ]* (see Appendix 2).

5.7.   The copy of evidence taken to confirm a client's identity *[must be kept with the file/submitted to   ]* (the Firm's policy is to keep all client files for a minimum of *[6]* years).

6. IDENTIFICATION: PROCEDURES

The method for identifying clients will depend upon the type of client. The procedure below and the documentary evidence referred to are not to be taken as an exhaustive list of requirements. A judgement must be made by fee earners as to whether alternative or additional information should be sought. If in doubt you should seek advice from the nominated officer.

A. *Companies*

In the case of a corporate client we need to be satisfied that the company exists and that we are dealing with that company. The existence of the company can be determined by making a company search which reveals the following information:

(a)   name and registered address
(b)   registered number
(c)   list of directors
(d)   members or shareholders
(e)   nature of the company's business
(f)   certificate of incorporation
(g)   if a subsidiary, the name of the holding company.

If the company is listed or traded on a recognised investment exchange or is a wholly-owned subsidiary of such a company, there is no need to obtain a list of directors or shareholders.

If the company is not listed, and does not have directors or shareholders whose identities have already been verified, you should seek identification of those individuals instructing the firm in accordance with the procedures noted for individuals below.

B. Individuals

The following information should be obtained for individuals:

(a) full name
(b) current permanent address (including postcode)
(c) date of birth.

At least one document from each of the following lists should be produced:

List A (evidence of name and date of birth)

(i) current valid full passport
(ii) national identity card or resident's permit
(iii) current photocard driving licence
(iv) firearms certificate
(v) state pension or benefit book
(vi) inland revenue tax notification

List B (evidence of address)

(i) home visit
(ii) electoral roll check
(iii) recent utility or local authority council tax bill
(iv) recent bank/building society statement
(v) recent mortgage statement
(vi) current driving licence (not if used in List A)
(vii) local council rent card or tenancy agreement.

*[Additional documents are listed in the Law Society's Guidance – see **Appendix B1**. This list may be added to depending upon the firm's typical client profile]*

Where joint instructions are received, identification procedures should be applied to each client. If joint clients have the same name and address (e.g. spouses) the verification of the address for one client only is sufficient.

C. Partnerships and other unincorporated businesses

If the business is regulated by an independent public body, the evidence of the name, address and existence of the business should be obtained from that body.

In other cases, evidence of identification should be obtained from the individuals or partners by reference to the procedure for individuals as noted above.

D. Trusts, nominees and fiduciaries

Where the trust is regulated by an independent public body (e.g. the Charities Commission) the evidence of the existence of the trust and the identity of the trustees should be sought from that body.

In other cases a certified copy of the trust (and the grant of probate or copy of the will creating the trust in the case of a deceased settlor) must be obtained. The trustees must also be identified in accordance with the procedures for individuals or companies noted above.

Particular care must be taken where the trust is offshore since these trusts present a high risk of money laundering.

E. Non-UK Clients

Non-UK individual clients should produce passports or national identity cards together with separate evidence of the client's permanent address obtained from the best source available. PO Box numbers are not sufficient evidence of an address.

Non-UK corporate clients should produce equivalent information to that obtained by making a UK company search. The results of company searches made abroad will depend upon the filing requirements in the local jurisdiction.

F. Clients where there is no face-to-face contact

Where contact with the client is not face-to face but by post or telephone, it is still necessary to obtain evidence of identity in accordance with the above procedures. Such evidence can be produced by way of an original document or by way of a certified copy provided that the copy is certified by a reputable institution, such as a bank or firm of lawyers, who should verify the name used, the current permanent address and the client's signature. The name and address of the institution providing the certification should be noted and checked by reference to a professional directory. This procedure may be appropriate where the client is a foreign national resident abroad.

If you are unable to obtain satisfactory evidence of identity in accordance with the above procedures you must contact the firm's nominated officer who will advise on any alternative steps which may be taken or consider whether instructions must be terminated.

7. DEPARTMENTAL INSTRUCTIONS

[If appropriate include under this heading typical circumstances where different departments of the firm might find themselves at risk. Details can be found in **Chapter 12** *in the main text of this book]*

8. HELP

Money laundering is real and it will affect us. **If you have any concerns regarding the firm's policy and/or your responsibilities contact *[name of nominated officer]* or in his/her absence *[name of deputy]*.**

9. CONCLUSION

To minimise the risks of liability:

Verify the identity and bona fides of your client: Meet the client or clients where possible and get to know them.

Question unusual instructions: Make sure that you discuss them fully with your client, and note all such discussions carefully on the file.

Discuss any aspects of the transaction which worry you with your client: For example, if you suspect that your client may have submitted a false mortgage application or references, or if you know or suspect the Lender's valuation exceeds the actual price paid, discuss this with your client and, if you believe they intend to proceed with a fraudulent application, you must refuse to continue to act for the buyer and the mortgagee.

Check that the true price is shown in all documentation: Check that the actual price paid is stated in the contract, transfer and mortgage instructions. Ensure that your client understands that, where you are also acting for the Lender, you will have to report all allowances and incentives to the Mortgagee.

Do not witness pre-signed documentation: No deed should be witnessed by a solicitor or staff unless the person signing does so in the presence of a witness. If a deed is pre-signed, ensure that it is re-signed in the presence of a witness.

Verify signatures: Consider whether signatures on all documents connected with a transaction should be examined and compared with signatures on any other documentation.

Make a Company Search: Where a private company is the seller or the seller has purchased from a private company in the recent past and you suspect that there may be a connection between the company and the seller or the buyer which is being used for improper purposes, then consideration would be given to ascertain the names and addresses of the officers and shareholders which can then be compared with the names of those connected with the transaction and the seller and buyer.

APPENDIX 1

MONEY LAUNDERING INTERNAL REPORTING FORM
*[For a precedent, see **Appendix C3** to this book]*

APPENDIX 2

CLIENT IDENTIFICATION FORM
*[For a precedent, see **Appendix C1** to this book]*

C3

Internal reporting form

1. Name of client/s:

   Aliases/Trading names:

2. Address (including postcode,
   telephone, fax, e-mail and contact name):

3. Date of Birth:

4. Summary of instructions:

5. If not acting as principal:

   (a) Name of Principal:

   (b) Address of Principal (including postcode,
   telephone, fax, e-mail and contact name):

6.   Evidence of identity (please attach):

7.   Value of transaction:

8.   Name and address of introducer (if any):

9.   Source and destination of funds:

        (a)   source of cash/bank/other securities

        (b)   destination

10.   Reason for suspicion:

11.   Does Professional Privilege apply? YES/NO

Signed ....   Date...

To be completed by nominated officer only:

Report to NCIS?   YES/NO

If No, give reasons:

Date Business completed ....

Record destruction date ....

(If a report has been made to NCIS this record must not be destroyed at the 'date of destruction' without first referring to NCIS)

C4

NCIS reporting forms and guidance notes

PROCEEDS OF CRIME ACT 2002 AND TERRORISM ACT 2000 – STANDARD REPORT

Scope and Purpose

This document provides guidance for the completion of protected and authorised disclosures, under sections 337 and 338 of the Proceeds of Crime Act (2002). This guidance should be read alongside the preferred Standard forms (the Forms) which have been issued by NCIS for the completion of disclosures. Both the Forms and Guidance have been prepared by NCIS following consultation with a number of organisations representing the Regulated Sector.

The Form has not been prescribed by the Secretary of State under section 339 of the Proceeds of Crime Act 2002 and, therefore, use of the form as a method for reporting money laundering is not mandatory. However, these Forms are the preferred format by NCIS as they have been designed to:–

- accommodate the needs of different Regulated Sector businesses and
- facilitate the efficient and effective handling of disclosures by NCIS

Although none of the fields in the form is mandatory, since the format is not prescribed, those submitting disclosures should take account of regulatory and sector approved guidance. NCIS' feedback to reporting institutions will assess the quality of reporting against relevant guidance.

How to obtain the new Forms and Guidance

Those organisations which currently use the Money.web system or Bulk File submission should continue to submit reports electronically, using the existing input screens or reporting format.

Organisations **not** using the money.web system or Bulk File Submission, are advised to obtain a copy of the preferred Forms. Those reporters who wish to complete reports on their own computer should download the Form(s) from the NCIS website. Alternatively, please send a request for the Form(s) and Guidance to **ECBDutyDesk@ncis.co.uk**.

If you wish **to complete a report by hand** you will need to request a special version of the Form by telephoning 020 7238 8282. **Please do not complete the version of the Form downloaded from the Internet by hand.**

Sending your report to NCIS

Those organisations which currently use the money.web system or Bulk File submission method, should continue to submit reports in the normal way. Please do not email completed disclosures to NCIS without encryption.

Other organisations will need to submit reports by fax to 020 7238 8286 or by post to PO Box 8000, London SE11 5EN. Note, if you complete a Form on your computer, you will need to print it off and submit it by fax or post.

Types of Report

Specific forms have been designed to support the submission of both 'Standard Reports' and 'Limited Intelligence Value Reports'. Further details of what constitutes a Limited Intelligence Value Report and the format of such a report can be found within the **Guidance Notes for the NCIS Regulated Sector Disclosure Report – Proceeds of Crime Act 2002 – Limited Intelligence Value Report**. Please refer to the NCIS' Internet site (**www.NCIS.gov.uk**).

Structure of the Standard Form

The Standard Report is the default version which reporting institutions should complete unless the disclosure fits the criteria for a Limited Intelligence Value report. (Please see **Guidance Notes for the NCIS Regulated Sector Disclosure Report – Proceeds of Crime Act 2002 – Limited Intelligence Value Report** for further information concerning this method of disclosure).

The Standard Form comprises five separate sheets, or modules, (Modules/*Appendices 2–6*). In addition, the Source Registration Document (Module/*Appendix 1*) should be completed when an organisation makes its first disclosure to NCIS or when its contact details change.

The five modules which comprise the Form may be submitted in different combinations depending on the amount and type of information the author of the report has available to disclose. Multiple copies of a particular sheet may be required and in some circumstances it may be appropriate for particular sheets to be omitted. It is essential that the Summary Section of Module/*Appendix 2* is clearly completed thereby enabling NCIS to check whether it has received the correct number of sheets and in the correct order.

The Form has been designed to be read by Image Character Recognition (ICR) technology. Therefore any amendments or additions outside the structure of the Form will significantly hamper NCIS' capability to process the disclosure efficiently.

A document entitled 'Field Values List' is available through the NCIS website under the heading 'additional information'. It contains various options for completing particular fields in the Form. The relevant fields are highlighted throughout the 'Completion Instructions' which follow.

Completion Instructions

Source Registration Document (Module/Appendix 1)

In order to record disclosures and correspond accurately in a timely manner with the regulated sector, NCIS needs accurate contact details of each reporting organisation. A **Source Registration Document** has been constructed to capture this information as concisely as possible. NCIS already holds such details for organisations which have previously disclosed, therefore **this form should only be used by organisations that have never previously reported and then only when making their first report**. It will not be required for each subsequent disclosure. **However, all organisations should use the source registration document to update NCIS about any changes to their contact details in order that NCIS' records can be accurately maintained**.

Institution Name   Please provide details of the Registered and/or Trading name of the company or individual making the report.

Institution Type   Please provide details of the type of company or individual making the report, e.g. Money Transmission agent, Bank, Bureau de Change, Estate Agent etc.

Regulator   Please provide details of your regulator, where applicable, (e.g. FSA, Gaming Board of Great Britain etc).

Regulator ID   Please provide details of your regulator's Identity Number, where known to you (e.g. FSA's register number).

Contact Details (1)   This will be NCIS' primary point of contact with you.

Forename   Please provide full details of your Forename/s.

Surname   Please provide full details of your Surname.

Position   Please provide details as to the position you hold within your employing organisation where applicable.

Address   Please provide your full postal address details (inc Post Code).

Telephone Details   Please provide details of your principal contact number.

Facsimile Details   Please provide details of your principal contact number.

E-mail Address   Please provide details where applicable. The use of this medium will speed up the delivery of correspondence to you.

Contact Details (2)   This will be NCIS' point of contact with you in the absence of (where applicable) the above detailed individual, if applicable.

Forename   As above.

Surname   As above.

Position   As above.

Address   As above.

Telephone Details   As above.

Facsimile Details   Please provide details of your principal contact number.

E-mail Address   As above.

Disclosure Reports Details Sheet (Module/Appendix 2)

Reporting Institution   Please provide details of the company or individual **making** the report. If a Money Laundering Reporting Officer (MLRO) is completing the form it is not essential at any point to mention by name the person making the initial disclosure.

Your Reference   Please provide details of your own reference number relevant to the disclosure in question. **This is an important field as the information supplied will be quoted by NCIS in any correspondence with you relating to this disclosure**. We are shortly to explore a system change so that our automated response letters will quote **only** your reference number (alongside our own Intelligence Reference Number).

Branch/Office   This information will enable NCIS to ascertain which of your outlets is reporting the activity, assisting NCIS to decide which law enforcement agency to allocate the disclosure to.

Disclosure Date   The date upon which you submit your report to NCIS. The format DD/MMM/YYYY has been used to prevent any transposition of Day and Month. Please insert two digits in the DD field to state the day, three letters in the MMM field (for example, JAN for January) and four digits to show the year in the YYYY field.

Disclosure Reason   Confirmation of under which piece of Legislation your report is being made. **Only one piece of legislation should be indicated**. **Consent Required** If you require Consent to undertake a prohibited act, under s336 of the **Proceeds of Crime Act 2002**, please ensure that this field is clearly indicated. This will help NCIS to respond to you as speedily as possible.

Type   Please indicate into which category your report falls.

A **New** disclosure concerns a person, legal entity or criminal property upon whom/which you have never previously disclosed. Alternatively you may have previously submitted a disclosure, in respect of the person or legal entity, but have now received information causing you to formulate a new suspicion or acquire new knowledge of money laundering.

An **Update** is classified as revised or additional information that has come to light about a subject or legal entity whom/which you have already reported in a disclosure, e.g. Identification details or a change to an address. **New transactions which you regard as suspicious should be reported in a new disclosure**.

Existing Disclosure Ids   When you submit a **new** disclosure about an entity or individual whom you have previously reported, please state the original Intelligence Reference Number(s) supplied by NCIS here.

Report Summary Sheet (Module/Appendix 2 continued)

This part of the form should be used to summarise the number of sheets used by you in the completion of your report and should be filled out once your report has been completed. This summary will ensure that all the sheets are correctly ordered and accounted for by NCIS.

Number of Subject Details' sheets appended relating to a Main Subject:

This is the person who the report is about. Normally, there will be such a person, although in some circumstances this is not the case, for example you may be reporting a fraud where the perpetrator is unknown.

Number of 'Additional Details' sheets appended relating to Main Subject:

Multiple sheets are acceptable. *However they must be ordered to ensure the correct details are connected to the correct subject (especially important if there is more than one subject).*

Number of 'Subject Details' sheets appended relating to Associated Subject/s:

This is anyone linked to the Main Subject through the reported activity. There may be any number of Associated Subjects. Please complete a separate sheet for each Associated Subject.

Number of 'Additional Details' sheets appended relating to Associated Subject/s:

Please complete, if applicable, as many sheets as is necessary for each Associated Subject. These sheets should be placed immediately behind the Associated Subject to which they refer and numbered accordingly.

Number of 'Transaction Detail' sheets appended:

This sheet will not be relevant for every disclosure since it is largely designed to capture information relating to financial transactions. However, reporters outside the banking sector may be able to complete some of the fields on this sheet, in particular the date that a business relationship commenced and finished.

Number of 'Reason for Disclosure' sheets appended:

Please provide details of the reason(s) why you have knowledge or suspicion or reasonable grounds for knowing or suspecting that another person is engaged in money laundering. This is essential to enable law enforcement to decide whether to commence a money laundering investigation.

Total Number of Pages Submitted:

This field should summarise the total amount of all sheet types being submitted. The information will be used by NCIS to ensure that all the information you consider you provided was received.

Subject Details Sheet (Module/Appendix 3)

Subject Type This indicates the category of the subject about whom you are reporting. This sheet has dual purpose and can be completed when referring to either a 'Main Subject' or an 'Associated Subject' (an individual linked to the Main Subject). However do not provide the details of a 'Main Subject' and 'Associated Subject' on the same sheet.

(Please note that normally, there will be either a Main Subject or an Associated Subject although in some circumstances this is not the case. For example, you may be reporting a fraud where the perpetrator is unknown).

If you have more than one subject you should consider which one you feel to be the Main Subject or the focus of your report, completing his/her details accordingly. All other subjects should be noted as 'Associated Subjects' on separate 'Subject Details Sheets'. If your disclosure refers only to one subject then they should be notified to NCIS as the Main Subject.

If you are providing details of more than one Associated Subject then please use additional copies of this sheet but remember to number them accordingly (e.g. 1 of 3, 2 of 3 etc). This becomes particularly important if you are providing 'Additional Details', enabling you and NCIS to cross-refer any 'Additional Details' forms to the appropriate 'Associated Subject'.

IMPORTANT NOTICE – For any one Subject, only one, of either the 'Individual's Details' Section (top half of sheet) or the 'Legal Entity Details Section' (lower half of sheet), should be completed irrespective of whether the sheet is being used to report a 'Main Subject' or an 'Associated Subject'. Please do not complete both sections.

Subject Status Please indicate **only one** box from 'Suspect' or 'Victim'

<u>Suspect</u> should be ticked if you know or suspect or have reasonable grounds for knowing or suspecting that this individual is engaged in money laundering.

<u>Victim</u> is the person or entity who/which is harmed by or loses as a result of the criminal activity which you are reporting. To ensure that any intrusion against a victim's privacy is minimised, the victim's details should not, ideally, be included in subject fields. The personal details of victims should only be included if, in the judgement of the nominated officer, the details are essential to understanding the activity being reported.

Surname Please provide details as appropriate

Forename 1   Please provide details as appropriate of primary forename

Forename 2   Please provide details as appropriate of secondary forename.

Occupation   Please provide details as appropriate. If this information is not known to you please quote 'Unknown'.

Date of birth (DoB)   This is an important field. Date of birth information helps law enforcement to positively identify individuals when cross-matching personal data. The format DD/MMM/YYYY has been used to prevent any transposition of Day and Month. Please insert two digits in the DD field to state the day, three letters in the MMM field (for example, JAN for January) and four digits to show the year in the YYYY field.

Title   Please provide details as appropriate. Common options are provided as tick boxes. If the correct title is not shown, please specify the relevant title in the 'Other' field. Existing options are available from the Field Values List.

Gender   Please select from 'Male' or 'Female' options. If your records do not provide such details please leave both blank

Reason for Association   **This field should only be completed if using the sheet to report 'Associated Subject' details**. The information required would be the reason that links the Associated Subject to the Main Subject. *Appropriate options are provided in the Field Values List.*

Subject Status   Please indicate **only one** box from 'Suspect' or 'Victim'.

Suspect should be ticked if this entity is central to any known or suspected money laundering which your report outlines.

Victim is the person or entity who/which is harmed by or loses as a result of the criminal activity which you are reporting. To ensure that any intrusion against a victim's privacy is minimised, the victim's details should not, ideally, be included in subject fields. The personal details of victims should only be included if, in the judgement of the nominated officer, the details are essential to understanding the activity being reported.

Legal Entity Name Please provide details as appropriate, e.g. a Company Name or Charity.

Legal Entity Number Please provide details as appropriate, e.g. a Company Number.

VAT no Please complete as appropriate.

Country of Registration Please provide details as appropriate, e.g. the country where the legal entity is registered. *Appropriate options are provided in the Field Values List.*

Type of Business Please provide details as appropriate.

Reason for Association This field should only be completed if you are using the sheet to provide 'Associated Subject' details. The information required is the reason that links the Associated Subject to the Main Subject. *Appropriate options are provided in the Field Values List.*

Additional Details Sheet (Module/Appendix 4)

This sheet should be used to provide Address/es, Identification or any other appropriate details as known to you relating to either the Main or Associated Subject/s. When completed, each of these sheets should be placed immediately behind the relevant Main or Associated Subject sheet to which it refers.

'Details refer to' Please select either Main Subject **or** Associated Subject. **Important** When providing Additional Details in which you report more than one Associated Subject, please number each Associate concurrently (e.g. 1 of 2; 2 of 2). This will enable you to cross-refer any additional details to the appropriate Associate Subject.

Subject Name	Please provide details as appropriate
Premise No/Name	Please provide details as appropriate
Current	Please indicate with a tick if this is known to be the subject's present address.
Street	Please provide details as appropriate
City/Town	Please provide details as appropriate
County	Please provide details as appropriate
Country	Please provide details as appropriate
Post Code	Please provide details as appropriate
Type	Please state the type of address (i.e. home, previous, registered). *Appropriate options are provided in the Field Values List.*

Note

Up to three addresses can be provided on each sheet. If you wish to provide additional addresses please use another copy of the 'Additional Details' sheet. For each Main or Associated Subject, please match the numbering that you state within the **'Details refer to'** box of the 'Subject Details' sheet to the relevant Additional Details sheet; (e.g. the additional details for the Associate who was numbered '3 of 5' should also be numbered '3 of 5').

Information Type
This field is intended to assist law enforcement identify a main or associated subject reported in your disclosure. The field may comprise details of Identification taken for the Subject (e.g. National Insurance Number, Passport or Drivers Licence, MSB Number, Company Number etc) or any other details you may hold such as telephone numbers or Car registration details which you feel will assist any investigation. *Appropriate options are provided in the Field Values List.*

Unique Information Identifier
This field refers to the unique information relevant to the Information Type field (e.g. a Passport Number, National Insurance Number or Drivers Licence Number)

Extra information / Description
This field refers to additional relevant details (e.g. British Passport or Full/Provisional Licence)

Note

Up to two pieces of identification can be recorded on one sheet. If you wish to provide additional identification details, please use another copy of the 'Additional Details' sheet. For each Main or Associated Subject about whom you provide additional identification details, please match the number that you state within the **'Details refer to'** box of the 'Subject Details' sheet to the relevant Additional Details sheet; (e.g. the additional details for the Associate who was numbered '3 of 5' should also be numbered '3 of 5').

Transaction Details Sheet (Module/Appendix 5)

The completion of this sheet depends on the nature of the activity that you are reporting and your sector. For some sectors this sheet may not be applicable, although reporters should note that they may be able to complete the date that a business relationship commenced and finished, even if most or all of the transaction fields are irrelevant. A separate sheet should be completed for each different account which is relevant to the disclosure. Note, there is no general requirement to provide a lengthy list of transactions. Only provide detail if you think it will add to law enforcement's understanding of the criminality that you are knowledgeable or suspicious about.

Main Subject Account Summary

Institution Name
Please provide details as appropriate of the asset holding institution.

Account Name
Please provide details as appropriate

Sort Code
Please provide details as appropriate

Account Number/Identifier
Please provide details as appropriate

Business Relationship Commenced/Account Opened

Please provide details as appropriate. Note that this field is more widely applicable than the banking sector alone.

Business Relationship Finished/Account Closed

Please provide details as appropriate. Note that this field is more widely applicable than the banking sector alone.

Account Balance Please provide details as appropriate.

Balance Date Please provide details as appropriate.

Turnover Period Please provide details, as appropriate
Appropriate options are provided with the Field Values List.

Credit Turnover Please provide details as appropriate.

Debit Turnover Please provide details as appropriate.

Transaction/s

Activity Type Please provide details, as appropriate.
Appropriate options are provided in the Field Values List.

Activity Date Please provide details as appropriate

Amount Please provide details as appropriate.

Currency Please provide details as appropriate.
Appropriate options are provided in the Field Values List.

Credit or Debit Please provide details as appropriate

Other Party Name Please provide details, as appropriate, of the counterparty to the transaction/activity reported.

Institution Name or Sort Code

Please provide details as appropriate of the counterparty institution to the transaction/activity reported.

Account No / Identifier

Please provide details as appropriate of the counterparty institution to the transaction/activity reported.

Note

Up to four separate transactions can be provided on this sheet. If you need to provide additional transactions please use additional copies of the 'Transaction Details' sheet as appropriate.

Version 1 Febuary 23rd 2004 Appendix 1

PO Box 8000
London
SE11 5EN
Tel: 020 7238 8282
Fax: 020 7238 8286

SOURCE REGISTRATION DOCUMENT

IMPORTANT - THE DETAILS IN THIS FORM MUST BE PROVIDED WITH YOUR FIRST DISCLOSURE TO NCIS OR FOLLOWING ANY SUBSEQUENT CHANGE TO THOSE DETAILS.

Institution Name:

Institution Type:

Regulator:

Regulator ID:

Contact Details (1): Forename:

Surname:

Position:

Address:

Telephone Details:

Facsimile Details:

E-mail Address:

Contact Details (2): Forename:
(where applicable)

Surname:

Position:

Address:

Telephone Details:

Facsimile Details:

E-mail Address:

Version 1 Febuary 23rd 2004 Appendix 2

PO Box 8000
London
SE11 5EN
Tel: 020 7238 8282
Fax: 020 7238 8286/3441

DISCLOSURE REPORT DETAILS: STANDARD REPORT:

Reporting Institution:

Your Ref:

Disclosure Reason:

PoCA 2002: ○   Terrorism Act 2000: ○

Branch/ Office:

Consent Required: ☐

Disclosure Date: ☐ - ☐ - ☐   **Type:** New ○   OR Update ○

D D   M M M   Y Y Y Y

Existing Disclosure ID/s: (where applicable)

Please use whichever sheets you feel are necessary and indicate below how many of each you are submitting.

REPORT SUMMARY:

Number of 'Subject Details' sheet appended relating to a Main Subject: ☐

Number of 'Additional Details' sheets appended relating to Main Subject: ☐

Number of 'Subjects Details' sheets appended relating to Associated Subject/s: ☐

Number of 'Additional Details' sheets' appended relating to Associated Subject/s: ☐

Number of 'Transaction Detail' sheet/s appended: ☐

Number of 'Reason For Disclosure Sheets' appended: ☐

Once completed please collate your sheets in the above mentioned order and then sequentially number your sheets at the bottom of each page. This will ensure that the information is processed in the correct sequence.

Total number of pages submitted including this Header: ☐

Page 1 of ☐

SUBJECT DETAILS: Version 1 Febuary 23rd 2004 Appendix 3

Subject Type: Main Subject: ○   **OR**   Associated Subject: ○   (number ☐ of ☐)

Individual's Details:

Subject Status: Suspect : ○   **OR**   Victim: ○

Surname: _____

Forename 1: _____

Forename 2: _____

Occupation: _____

DoB: ☐ - ☐ - ☐   Gender: Male ○   Female ○
     D D   M M M   Y Y Y Y

Title: Mr ○   Mrs ○   Miss ○   Ms ○   Other _____

Reason for Association of this subject to the Main Subject (for use only with Associated Subject details)

_____

OR

Legal Entity's Details

Subject Status: Suspect : ○   **OR**   Victim: ○

Legal Entity Name: _____

Legal Entity No: _____   VAT No: _____

Country of Reg: _____

Type of Business: _____

Reason for Association of this subject to the Main Subject (for use only with Associated Subject details)

_____

Page ☐ of ☐

ADDITIONAL DETAILS: Version 1 Febuary 23rd 2004 Appendix 4

Do these details refer to the Main Subject: ○ OR to an Associated Subject ○

(Please indicate the Associate's number where applicable)

Subject Name:

Premise No/Name: Current: ☐ Type:

Street:

City/Town:

County: Post Code:

Country:

Premise No/Name: Current: ☐ Type:

Street:

City/Town:

County: Post Code:

Country:

Premise No/Name: Current: ☐ Type:

Street:

City/Town:

County: Post Code:

Country:

Information Type: Unique Information Identifier:

Extra Information / Description

Information Type: Unique Information Identifier:

Extra Information / Description

Page ☐ of ☐

251

■   **TRANSACTION DETAILS: (Complete if applicable)**   ■

MAIN SUBJECT ACCOUNT SUMMARY   Version 1 Febuary 23rd 2004 Appendix 5

Institution Name:

Account Name:

Sort Code: Account No /Identifier:

Business Relationship Commenced: (DD-MMM-YYYY)   [ ] - [ ] - [ ]   Acct Bal:

Business Relationship Finished: (DD-MMM-YYYY)   [ ] - [ ] - [ ]   Bal Date: (DD-MMM-YYYY)   [ ] - [ ] - [ ]

Turnover Period: Credit Turnover:

                                          Debit Turnover:

TRANSACTION/S

Activity Type: Activity Date: (DD-MMM-YYYY)   [ ] - [ ] - [ ]

Amount: Currency: Credit: ○ or Debit: ○

Other party name: Account No/ Identifier:

Institution Name or Sort Code:

Activity Type: Activity Date: (DD-MMM-YYYY)   [ ] - [ ] - [ ]

Amount: Currency: Credit: ○ or Debit: ○

Other party name: Account No/ Identifier:

Institution Name or Sort Code:

Activity Type: Activity Date: (DD-MMM-YYYY)   [ ] - [ ] - [ ]

Amount: Currency: Credit: ○ or Debit: ○

Other party name: Account No/ Identifier:

Institution Name or Sort Code:

Activity Type: Activity Date: (DD-MMM-YYYY)   [ ] - [ ] - [ ]

Amount: Currency: Credit: ○ or Debit: ○

Other party name: Account No/ Identifier:

Institution Name or Sort Code:

Page [   ] of [   ]

REASON FOR DISCLOSURE: Version 1 Febuary 23rd 2004 Appendix 6

Main Subject Name: (cross reference purposes)	

Report Activity Assessment
(Please use only where you know or suspect what the offence behind the reported activity may be)

Drugs: ☐   Missing Trader, Inter Community (VAT) Fraud ☐   Immigration: ☐   Tobacco/Alcohol Excise Fraud: ☐

Personal Tax Fraud: ☐   Corporate Tax Fraud: ☐   Other Offences:

Reason for Disclosure:

Page ☐ of ☐

PROCEEDS OF CRIME ACT 2002 – LIMITED INTELLIGENCE VALUE REPORTS

Scope and Purpose

This document provides guidance for the completion of authorised and protected disclosures, under sections 337 and 338 of the Proceeds of Crime Act (2002), categorised as 'Limited Intelligence Value Reports'. This guidance should be read alongside the Limited Intelligence Value Report (Appendix 7) which has been issued by NCIS. Both the Form and Guidance have been completed following consultation with organisations representing the Regulated Sector. **Please note that Limited Intelligence Value Reports should only be made under the Proceeds of Crime Act (PoCA). Any reports being made under the Terrorism Act (2000) should be Standard Reports.**

The Form has not been prescribed by the Secretary of State and therefore is not mandatory. However the Form has been agreed by NCIS and organisations representing the Regulated Sector as the preferred format for all reports. The Form has been designed to reflect the different needs of the sectors as well as NCIS' requirement to handle the disclosures as efficiently and effectively as possible.

Although none of the fields in the form is mandatory, since the format is not prescribed, those submitting disclosures should take account of regulatory and sectoral approved guidance. NCIS' feedback to reporting institutions will assess the quality of reporting against relevant guidance.

How to obtain the new Forms and Guidance

Those organisations which currently use the Money.web system or Bulk File submission should continue to submit reports electronically, using the existing input screens or reporting format.

Organisations **not** using the money.web system or Bulk File Submission, are advised to obtain a copy of the preferred Forms. Those reporters who wish to complete reports on their own computer should download the Form(s) from the NCIS website. Alternatively, please send a request for the Form(s) and Guidance to **ECBDutyDesk@ncis.co.uk**.

If you wish **to complete a report by hand** you will need to request a special version of the Form by telephoning 020 7238 8282. **Please do not complete the version of the Form downloaded from the Internet by hand**.

Sending your report to NCIS

Those organisations which currently use the money.web system or Bulk File submission method, should continue to submit reports in the normal way. Please do not email completed disclosures to NCIS without encryption.

Other organisations will need to submit reports by fax to 0207 238 8286 or by post to PO Box 8000, London SE11 5EN. Note, if you complete a Form on your computer, you will need to print it off and submit it by fax or post.

Report Structure

These Guidance Notes are provided to explain the various fields within the Report and assist you in its completion and should be read alongside the Report Forms themselves.

The Form has been designed to be read by Image Character Recognition (ICR) technology. Therefore any amendments or additions outside the structure of the Form will significantly hamper NCIS's capability to process the disclosure efficiently.

Limited Intelligence Value Reports

NCIS recognises that POCA results in reports being required in some circumstances where, individually, there is likely to be limited intelligence value to law enforcement, although wider analysis of such reports may provide useful data. The table below provides guidance on the types of circumstance that are appropriate for abbreviated information to be provided in the form of a Limited Intelligence Value report. NCIS reserves the right, in all cases, to ask for the Standard Report format to be used and will monitor disclosures submitted to ensure that Limited Intelligence Value reporting is not exploited as a 'short cut' where its use is not justified.

Type	Detail	Comments
1 Certain classes of crimes committed overseas	This is intended to apply where the suspicious activity takes place outside the UK and:- • Is not a criminal offence in the jurisdiction where committed, and • Relates either to local differences in regulation or social and cultural practices.	A Limited Intelligence Value Report is not appropriate to report money laundering relating to serious tax evasion or occasions where the underlying offence is a serious crime such as terrorism, offences relating to drugs, paedophilia etc. In these circumstances, a full report is appropriate.
2 Minor irregularities where there is nothing to suggest that these are the result of dishonest behaviour.	Balance discrepancies and minor credit balances not returned because of the administrative costs involved, or other small discrepancies which are judged to have resulted from a mistake rather than dishonest behaviour.	If reporting institutions are satisfied that no criminal property is involved (as defined by s340 (3) of the Proceeds of Crime Act, 2002), they may conclude that a report is not required. However where reporting institutions feel obliged to make a disclosure, a Limited Intelligence Value report is appropriate.

Type	Detail	Comments
3 The subject of the report cannot be deduced from the information to hand and the proceeds have disappeared without trace.	This would include bank raids, driving away from a petrol station without paying, shoplifting, retail shrinkage and various cheque and credit card frauds.	None.
4 Accountants, auditors and tax advisers. Multiple instances of suspicion arising during one audit: 'Aggregation of incidents to form one report'	Multiple incidents may be aggregated within a single Limited Intelligence Value Report provided that:- <ul><li>One or more of the other categories in this table for limited intelligence value reporting is met, for example number three (above): bank raids, driving away from a petrol station without paying, shoplifting, retail shrinkage and various cheque and credit card frauds;</li><li>The reason for the aggregate report is summarised;</li><li>Aggregate reports relate to a single audit only.</li></ul>	The Act refers to reports being made 'as soon as practicable'. NCIS accepts that this will not always mean 'immediately' and is content to receive aggregate Limited Intelligence Value Reports within one month of the completion of an audit, provided that during the assignment no time sensitive information is discovered (that may, for example, allow the recovery of proceeds of crime if communicated immediately). Reporters should note that a Standard Report is appropriate should the issue of a Hansard (CoP9) Letter by the Inland Revenue, taken with such other information as may be available, cause (or provide reasonable grounds for) knowledge or suspicion of money laundering.
5 Duplicate reports to NCIS, or a prosecuting authority (including regulators with powers of prosecution)	Where the institution considering whether to disclose knows (as opposed to assumes) that a report has been made to NCIS, another prosecuting authority or	Provided the caveat of 'no additional information' is adhered to, a Limited Intelligence Value report is appropriate.

Type	Detail	Comments
	to another person authorised by NCIS to receive reports, and a further report would provide no additional information. An example is where a client in the regulated sector has filed a report and an auditor or accountant knows this.	Note that the Inland Revenue is not authorised to receive disclosures direct from the regulated sector under POCA.
6 Law enforcement prosecutor, regulator or other Government agency already aware of an offence that also happens to be an instance of suspected money laundering	This category is intended to capture a range of regulatory/procedural offences. Examples include health and safety offences, environmental offences, and failure to file annual returns with the Companies Registrar.	Provided the caveat of 'no additional information' is adhered to, a Limited Intelligence Value report is appropriate. However, any knowledge or suspicion of money laundering relating to serious tax evasion, including cases covered by the Hansard procedure, should be reported in a Standard Report.
7 Section 167 (3) Customs and Excise Management Act 1979	This makes the submission of an incorrect VAT or Customs return, however innocent, a criminal offence.	It is the position of NCIS that a disclosure is not required for innocent error in these circumstances. Where the person knows of the omission and does not rectify the situation there will be a duty to report. Where reporting institutions feel obliged to make a disclosure, a Limited Intelligence Value report is appropriate.
8 Reporting institution served with a Court Order, which prompts suspicion		A Limited Intelligence Value report is appropriate except where the suspicion and report relate to matters

Type	Detail	Comments
		not covered by the Court Order letter, in which case a report on the Standard Form should be submitted.
9 Where the benefit from criminal conduct is in the form of cost savings, such as breaches of employment law and the illegal copying or distribution of software licences within a company.		

Completion Instructions

Source Registration Document (Module 1)

In order to record disclosures and correspond accurately and in a timely manner with the regulated sector, NCIS needs accurate contact details of each reporting organisation. **A Source Registration Document** has been constructed to capture this information as concisely as possible. NCIS already holds such details for organisations which have previously disclosed, therefore **this sheet should only be used by organisations that have never previously reported and then only when making their first report**. It will not be required for each subsequent disclosure. **However, all organisations should use the source registration document to update NCIS about any changes to their contact details in order that NCIS' records can be accurately maintained**.

Institution Name   Please provide details of the Registered and/or Trading name of the company or individual making the report.

Institution Type   Please provide details of the type of company or individual making the report, e.g. Money Transmission Agent, Bank, Estate Agent etc.

Regulator   Please provide details of your regulator, where applicable, (e.g. FSA, Gaming Board of Great Britain, etc.).

Regulator ID   Please provide details of your regulator's Identity Number, where known to you.

Contact Details (1)   This will be NCIS' primary point of contact with you.

Forename   Please provide full details of your Forename/s.

Surname   Please provide full details of your Surname.

Position Please provide details as to the position you hold within your employer, where applicable.

Address Please provide your full postal address details (inc Post Code).

Telephone Details Please provide details of your principal contact number.

E-mail Address Please provide details where applicable. The ability to use this medium will enhance the speed of delivery of our correspondence with you.

Contact Details (2) This will be NCIS' point of contact with you in the absence
(where applicable) of the above detailed individual, if applicable.

Name As above.

Position As above.

Address As above.

Telephone Details As above.

E-mail Address As above.

Limited intelligence Value Report

Reporting Institution Please provide details of the company or individual **making** the report. If a Money Laundering Reporting Officer (MLRO) is completing the form it is not essential at any point to mention by name the person making the initial disclosure.

Your Reference Please provide details of your own reference number relevant to the disclosure in question. **This is an important field as the information supplied will be quoted by NCIS in any correspondence with you relating to this disclosure**. We are shortly to explore a system change so that our automated response letters will quote **only** your reference number (alongside our own Intelligence Reference Number).

Branch/Office This information will enable NCIS to ascertain which of your outlets is reporting the activity, assisting NCIS decide which law enforcement agency to allocate the disclosure to.

Disclosure Date The date upon which you submit your report to NCIS. The format DD/MMM/YYYY has been used to prevent any transposition of Day and Month. Please insert two digits in the DD field to state the day, three letters in the MMM field (for example, JAN for January) and four digits to show the year in the YYYY field.

Subject Details

This is the Person/Legal Entity about whom/which the report is being made. Normally, reporters will be in a position to complete one of these fields, although in some circumstances this is not the case. For example you may be reporting a fraud where the perpetrator is unknown

This section of the sheet can be used to refer to an Individual or a Legal Entity. **However only one of these sections should be completed**. This sheet should not be used for both an individual and a Legal Entity at the same time.

Subject Status   Please indicate **only one** box from 'Suspect' or 'Victim'.

Suspect should be ticked if you know or suspect or have reasonable grounds for knowing or suspecting that this person is engaged in money laundering.

Victim is the person or entity who/which is harmed by or loses as a result of the criminal activity which you are reporting. To ensure that any intrusion against a victim's privacy is minimised, the victim's details should not, ideally, be included in subject fields. The personal details of victims should only be included if, in the judgement of the nominated officer, the details are essential to understanding the activity being reported.

PLEASE COMPLETE EITHER THE INDIVIDUAL'S DETAILS SECTION OF THE SHEET OR THE LEGAL ENTITY SECTION. PLEASE DO NOT COMPLETE BOTH.

Surname   Please provide details, as appropriate.

Forename 1   Please provide details, as appropriate.

Date of Birth   This is an important field. Date of birth information helps law enforcement to positively identify individuals when cross-matching personal data. The format DD/MMM/YYYY has been used to prevent any transposition of Day and Month. Please insert two digits in the DD field to state the day, three letters in the MMM field (for example, JAN for January) and four digits to show the year in the YYYY field.

Gender   Please select from options provided.

Title   Please select from options provided. If the correct title is not shown, please specify the relevant title within the 'Other' field. *Appropriate options are provided with the Field Values List.*

OR

Legal Entity Name   Please provide details as appropriate, e.g. a Company or Charity Name.

260

Legal Entity Number Please provide details as appropriate, e.g. a Company or Charity Number.

VAT Number Please provide details as appropriate.

Reason for Disclosure

This area is free text and should include any information not already provided which you feel is relevant to your Report. It should provide details of the reason(s) why you have knowledge or suspicion or reasonable grounds for knowledge or suspicion that another person is engaged in money laundering and why you feel that a Limited Value Report is suitable.

Version 1 Febuary 23rd 2004 Appendix 7

PO Box 8000
London
SE11 5EN
Tel: 020 7238 8282
Fax: 020 7238 8286/3441

PROCEEDS OF CRIME ACT 2002 - LIMITED INTELLIGENCE VALUE REPORT

Reporting Institution

Your Ref:

Branch/ Office:

Disclosure Date:

[ ] - [ ] - [ ]

D D - M M M - Y Y Y Y

SUBJECT DETAILS:

Individual's Details: **Main Subject Status:** Suspect : ○ **OR** V ictim: ○

Surname:

Forename:

DoB: [ ] - [ ] - [ ]
D D   M M M   Y Y Y Y

Gender: Male ○ Female ○

Title: Mr ○ Mrs ○ Miss ○ Ms ○ **Other** [ ]

Legal Entity Details:

Legal Entity Name:

Legal entity No: **VAT No:**

REASON FOR DISCLOSURE:

Index

Practice Management Handbook

General Editor: *Peter Scott*

Practice Management
Handbook

This book demonstrates how to develop and implement strategic plans for every aspect of a firm. Managers can delve into the relevant chapter and find practical ideas which will help them tackle fundamental issues, such as:

- how the firm should be organised
- its people and how they should be valued and rewarded
- building strong relationships with clients
- winning new business
- managing knowledge and risk
- managing the finances of the firm
- IT management.

Adapting to change is a theme that runs through the whole of the book, clearly demonstrating how firms can survive and prosper by adapting to the regulatory, technological and client-driven changes going on around them.

Available from Marston Book Services:
Tel. 01235 465 656.

1 85328 915 9
288 pages
£49.95
June 2004

The Law Society

Solicitors' Accounts Manual

9th edition

The Law Society

The *Solicitors' Accounts Manual*
contains all the information that
solicitors' staff and reporting
accountants require to ensure that
firms comply with the Law Society's
Solicitors' Accounts Rules.

The 9th edition has been fully updated to take account of all
the latest changes to the rules, including:

• the treatment of standard monthly payments and other regular
  payments from the Legal Services Commission
• the retention of digital images of paid cheques
• the Solicitors Disciplinary Tribunal finding against the use of
  client accounts to provide banking facilities, helping to reduce
  the risk of money laundering.

This user-friendly manual has been prepared by the Law Society
of England and Wales. It will prove invaluable to all legal practice
management and accounting staff.

Available from Marston Book Services:
Tel. 01235 465 656.

1 85328 907 8
132 pages
£24.95
July 2004

The Law Society